The Bedside
Guardian 2016

The Bedside Guardian 2016

EDITED BY CLAIRE ARMITSTEAD

guardianbooks

Published by Guardian Books 2016

2 4 6 8 10 9 7 5 3 1

Copyright © Guardian News and Media Ltd 2016

Claire Armitstead has asserted her right under the Copyright, Designs
and Patents Act 1988 to be identified as the editor of this work.

First published in Great Britain in 2016 by
Guardian Books
Kings Place, 90 York Way
London N1 9GU

www.guardianbooks.co.uk

A CIP catalogue record for this book is available from the British Library

ISBN 978-1783-56124-7

Cover design by Two Associates
Typeset by seagulls.net

Printed and bound in Great Britain by
CPI Group (UK) Ltd, Croydon CR0 4YY

Contents

SUMMER

Foreword

DAVID HARE

There are very few cultural organisations about which people care enough to dispute with any vigour. In my youth, the dismissive puritanism of the Royal Court Theatre in London raised temperatures whenever its name came up. The same was true of William Shawn's *New Yorker* in the 1970s, when a lone magazine seemed to define both the strengths and limits of American dissent. More recently, you couldn't pass time with painters and sculptors without them laying into the junkyard academicism of Tate Britain. And, of course, the BBC's drama output is always guaranteed to throw sparks on dry grass. You might say that the ability to provoke passionate antagonism is backhanded proof of vitality.

If that's the test, then the *Guardian* has no rival as Britain's most vital daily newspaper. It's certainly been through some tough times, during which it hasn't lacked for critics. In the first years of the century, as the *Guardian* pioneered the move from print to digital, it developed a tiresome obsession with itself. As grandiose articles about the future of journalism multiplied beyond number in its pages, so some of its staff became nakedly competitive with actors and television presenters, as though the new platforms offered journalists the chance to pretend to be stars – and, what's worse, stars who had a snarky opinion of stars in rival media. The perceived flaws in Angelina Jolie's character were receiving more coverage than the flaws in the coalition's policies. The impression of narcissism was inadvertently reinforced by the decline of paid advertising. Suddenly all the ads in the *Guardian* seemed to be for the *Guardian*.

It has taken a succession of significant upheavals in the world for the paper to rediscover its purpose and its confidence. The *Guardian* is looking outwards again. Both the ascent of Jeremy Corbyn to the Labour party leadership and the prospect of Scottish secession split editorial as sharply as they split the readership, and sometimes the coverage gave a scrappy, bewildered impression, running to keep up with a public that was some way ahead. But the collapse of the Greek economy, the spread of a terrifying civil war in Syria, the uncertain handling of the immigration crisis throughout Europe, the abuse of surveillance powers by western security agencies, the westward expansion of Russia, the revival of fascist demagoguery in both Europe and the United States, and the brutality of successive massacres in France all presented challenges to which reporters and experts rose triumphantly. As the problems of the world grew more urgent, so too did the paper. The ability to disentangle fact from official propaganda had never been more valuable, or more valued.

No event in 2016 did more for the *Guardian*'s standing than the 52–48 victory for leavers in the EU referendum. In my lifetime, Britain had engineered three versions of itself in the hope of recapturing the confidence it had radiated when governing an empire. First, from 1945 on, Britain prospered as a half-socialist democracy, defined by a compassionate welfare state and an expanding National Health Service. In the 1980s Britain was reimagined as an entrepreneurial, share-holding capitalist paradise in which private enterprise was given status and advantages way above public service. And in recent years, some synthesis was attempted between the two, with the notion of a European state that was socially progressive but operating an invasive foreign policy. All three provisional identities came crashing down on 23 June, when the electorate, more in hope than expectation, voted to leave the EU. A gamey-smelling band of rightwing politicians had convinced their grumbling countrymen and women not into an alternative vision of their homeland, but into something more like a gaping void. It was a void for which the advocates, by their own admission, had made no preparation.

One of the obvious side-effects of the vote was to deepen the Labour party's continuing crisis. Things could only get worse. Labour's parliamentary and its popular representation had come disastrously adrift, with neither side showing many signs of wanting to do too much about it. But meanwhile, if you listened more carefully, you could also hear ominous creaking below deck in the engine rooms of the Conservative project. In the always-thoughtful *Guardian* Review, Terry Eagleton's demolition of Steve Hilton's book *More Human* – 'Perhaps he lived through the 2008 financial crash with a paper bag over his head' – was not just a joyous piece of polemic against the prime minister's most influential adviser. It was a complete intellectual rout of the Notting Hill nonsense that free-market conservatism could ever align itself with humane values. After the EU vote, brought about by a government's feebleness and insincerity, friends who had previously thought me – and critics like me – overly harsh in our judgments on David Cameron's character approached us to apologise. Only a shallow chancer could have delivered the country into such a cul-de-sac.

I am told that during those weeks in June and July the *Guardian*'s circulation spiked as never before. I am not surprised. We were all living without handholds. At such times you may want to turn to your friends. You may also find that you value your newspaper as much for the things you're not interested in as the things you are. I could hardly care less about trendy restaurants, but Marina O'Loughlin is the best prose stylist on the *Guardian* since Nancy Banks-Smith, so she can write about watering cans or weevils and I'll still want to read her. The regular run of old operas doesn't do much for me either, but Martin Kettle, knowing about a whole lot more things than music, will always write more interestingly than those who know about music alone. Catherine Shoard is another critic who profits from being as interested in the effect of her chosen art form on the world as she is in the films themselves, while Judith Mackrell writes beautifully about ballets I will never see. Sometimes the people Decca Aitkenhead interviews seem familiar, but after just three paragraphs of her fresh and funny reports you realise you never knew them at all. All *Guardian* readers miss Simon Hoggart – perhaps Simon alone could have done justice to a justice secretary, strangely resembling Kenneth Williams, who in his bungling attempts to assassinate others assassinated only himself – but we have John Crace. And Steve Bell. And Rafael Behr. And recent events have had the effect of turning the commanding Jonathan Freedland back into a radical. Some silver lining! Some cloud!

Certain things on the *Guardian* never change, and perhaps never will. I have written 32 plays since 1970 and almost every one of them has been reviewed by Michael Billington. When I fled to Adelaide in 1982 to premiere a new play as far away from England as possible, there he was in the foyer of the Opera Theatre in South Australia, waiting to write about it. We've become like two old prizefighters who've boxed so often we can anticipate each other's every move. But for the majority of us who need there to be a mainstream national newspaper that combines the best instincts of liberals and the left, it's great to have the *Guardian* back and so clearly refreshed. It may be unfortunate that it has taken successive disasters at home and abroad to restore its edge, but let's be grateful.

The murder of the wonderful Jo Cox – for me, the most affecting domestic event of the year, and inevitably the least influential – reinforced the characteristic feeling of the period. We are all powerless. Brexiteers who promised us that we would take back control knew they were dangling the most potent fantasy available. Citizens are witnessing crazy events and we are driven more crazy by the certainty that we cannot affect them. But we can describe them, and then, having described them, seek to interpret them. In a country lately overrun by the crooked and the third-rate, at least we can do that.

September 2016

Introduction

CLAIRE ARMITSTEAD

'It's easy enough these days to wake troubled even before you remember the cause. Then you do. Everything is changed utterly.' So wrote Ian McEwan in an elegant meditation on the nightmare of Brexit for those of us who regard ourselves as European. But as the result of the EU referendum so clearly showed, many of us don't think of ourselves that way. The vote to leave the EU revealed a fault line running through British society which fractured in a way that few, even among those Brexiteers who had been so determinedly chiselling away at it, quite expected.

So intense was the minute-by-minute drama of referendum night that it seems right to make a centrepiece of the liveblog, written through the night by two dozen reporters from many specialisms, in the UK and abroad, and ably anchored by Andrew Sparrow. At 10.06pm, YouGov predicted a 52 per cent victory for Remain; at 3.09am it changed its mind. At 4.59am, Japan's Nikkei stock market index fell by 7 per cent – 'the worst one-day fall since March 2011, when Fukushima was hit by a devastating earthquake that triggered a tsunami and a nuclear disaster'. At 8.25am, David Cameron announced he would resign as prime minister. This is the sort of journalism that rarely wins plaudits for the individuals involved, but it's a brilliant example of the collaborative, white-knuckle reporting that is so central to any major international story in the age of internet journalism.

The before and after of the Brexit vote could have filled a whole book on its own with some of the finest writing of the year – from the blazing satirical insights of Marina Hyde to the grief, rage and disbelief of many more political commentators than can be accommodated in these pages. Jonathan Freedland, writing on the 100th anniversary of the Battle of the Somme on 1 July, spoke for many when he proclaimed, 'On this day when we mourn what horror the Europe before the European Union was capable of, we should say loud and clear of those that did this: we won't forget them.'

But Brexit was one shock among many in a year when rigorous reporting, informed reflection and wide-ranging opinion have never been more urgently needed. McEwan's ringing phrase – 'everything is changed utterly' – could as easily apply to terrorist-stricken Paris, Brussels and Nice, to besieged Aleppo or to earthquake-ravaged Amatrice. On several occasions photographs spoke more powerfully than words, not least the image of five-year-old Syrian Omran Daqneesh, bleeding and dazed after being pulled from a bombed building. But as volunteer physician Dr Zaher Sahloul pointed out, 'doctors in Aleppo see dozens of desperate children like him every week, often with worse injuries, many entirely beyond help'.

As this book goes to press, American voters have yet to decide whether to throw their lot in with Hillary Clinton or Donald Trump, and the UK's new prime minister Theresa May has yet to trigger the Brexit process, so more shocks may yet be in store. But on one issue we have a queasy sort of closure. The *Bedside* year began back in September 2015 with a local revolution, as Jeremy Corbyn was swept into the leadership of the Labour party on the shoulders of a new generation of supporters chanting

'Jez We Can'. 'This opportunity mustn't be squandered,' warned a *Guardian* leader at the end of Corbyn's first seven days, predicting a power struggle that has unfolded pretty much on script. A year of infighting and breast-beating has been neatly bookended by the result of the new election.

But the Westminster soap opera, however horribly compelling, is only one small part of the political picture. In April we unleashed the Panama Papers – an investigation of offshore tax holdings which spanned the globe, and which involved an international collaboration between 110 media outlets. Juliette Garside tells the inside story of an operation that led to the resignation of one premier – Iceland's – and the embarrassment of many others. 'In 70 countries around the world,' she wrote, 'the reverberations are still being felt.'

Other investigations have taken us into the heart of the NHS, where we spent a month reporting from the frontline of an increasingly stretched service (to see how stretched, check out the humbling account of a day in the life of a GP), and out into cyberspace, where editor-in-chief Katharine Viner commissioned a survey of bullying behaviour on the web as a first step towards formulating a new ethics. She followed it up with a benchmark essay that laid bare the huge moral and ethical challenges facing journalism in an age in which, as she wrote, technology has 'disrupted the truth'.

2016 has also been a year marked by the death of heroes, so many that it sometimes feels as if they too could fill a book on their own: Prince, Zaha Hadid, Alan Rickman, Victoria Wood, Caroline Aherne, to name a few. David Bowie was the first to go, early in the new year, and by the time Muhammad Ali followed him, in June, we were punch-drunk. As Kevin Mitchell wrote: 'He lived in an era of mass communication that led John Lennon to claim the Beatles were more popular than Jesus Christ; Ali made a compelling case to push them into second and third place.' Some humbler deaths are commemorated here too: Leonard Cohen said so long to Marianne; Tim Dowling lost his dog.

But just as it felt as if happiness had been cancelled for a year, along came the Olympics with its sometimes curious sports (anyone for keirin?) and its fabulous success stories. Spoiled for choice, I picked Barney Ronay's summary of Super Saturday, the rerun – when Mo Farah struck gold in the men's 10,000m, while Jessica Ennis-Hill was throwing javelin for silver and Greg Rutherford was long-jumping to bronze. This year of sporting marvels began much earlier, when little Leicester City topped the Premier League, causing jubilation among fans who had placed early bets and forcing Julian Barnes to honour a long-standing pledge to write it up if they ever were to win. At Wimbledon, as Owen Gibson astutely blogged, Andy Murray achieved the feat of making victory look almost ordinary, while in Paris, the final of Euro 2016 offered the surreal spectacle of Cristiano Ronaldo being upstaged by a moth.

How to pack so much into so few pages? With difficulty, as every editor of this volume habitually complains. Fortunately, Roger Tooth was on hand once more to curate a pictorial record to complement the written one. I'm grateful to all my colleagues who offered advice, and apologetic to those whose precious work was left out in the final cut. I'm also immensely grateful to those *Guardian* Members who responded to a plea for their favourite pieces of the year with a trenchant and witty range of recommendations ranging from 'anything by Polly Toynbee or Owen Jones' to Victoria Coren on bras. I might not have been able to accommodate every suggestion, but each played a part in helping to steer this anthology towards its final shape.

Acknowledgements

I'd like to thank editor-in-chief Katharine Viner for trusting me to edit this year's *Bedside Guardian*; Lindsay Davies from Guardian Books for spotting all the pieces I missed and giving me confidence that it was possible to keep track of this crazy year; *Guardian* head of photography Roger Tooth for his wise picture selection, and copy-editor Gemma Wain for her careful attention to the text. The referendum night liveblog was produced by so many dedicated and professional *Guardian* reporters who are the lifeblood of our journalism – you know who you are; I'm sorry I couldn't name you all. Thanks also to the following *Guardian* Members whose enthusiasms have made this a better book:

Maya Anaokar

Diana Chambers

Rebecca Dowman

Sarah P Garcia Jones

Hilary Graham

Richard Harvey

Ted Honderich

Henry Lubienski

Ben Myers

Simon Parten

Jenny Perkins

John Perkins

David Roffey

Margaret Sheather

Pulina Whitaker

Ruth Whitehead

Autumn

On a new era of politics

STEVE BELL

18 September

The *Guardian* view on Jeremy Corbyn: seven days that shook the Labour party

GUARDIAN LEADER

Rarely has a week been a longer time in politics. Seven days ago Jeremy Corbyn remained on the backbenches, where he had sat snugly for 32 years. The myriad thousands – some young, some idealistic, some angry, some all three – who had been drawn into the unfashionable business of party politics over the summer, waited to see whether or not they had pulled off their aim of shaking things up. And the Labour party was still controlled by cautious MPs who believed that the cause of progress can only ever be advanced through careful compromise.

Mr Corbyn's revolution was not made for television, but it has been televised. Each of the first few days brought a new and very public misstep: the clumsy unveiling of the big male appointments to the shadow cabinet before the numerous female names; one storm about the new leader's two-tone poppy policy; another about his lips staying still during the national anthem. But there have been some notable successes too – the construction of a broad frontbench, and a novel, courteous and quietly serious turn at prime minister's questions. Through the highs and lows, the single biggest danger for both the party and its new leader remains what it was always going to be: the gulf between a movement in the country that chants 'Jez We Can' and a parliamentary party that is privately thinking 'Jeezus, no'.

Regardless of party rules on the election of a leader, in a parliamentary democracy their influence and authority depend upon the acquiescence of their colleagues in the legislature, which is where the day-to-day work of opposition also has to be done. The world has seen serious parties – such as the Australian Democrats, deregistered by the Australian electoral commission this year – cease to function because of parliamentary and voluntary wings pulling apart.

The implications for Mr Corbyn, whom nine in 10 Labour MPs opposed, are stark: he must pick his fights carefully, and give ground elsewhere. Compromise has hardly featured in his long career, but last week provided him with a crash course, not least in his clarification that Labour would not be campaigning to pull Britain out of the EU in the referendum, a wise concession to the reality that most Labour MPs wouldn't countenance anything else. MPs fear their voters, making them a valuable check on the dead-end politics that brooks no compromise with the electorate.

The gulf between the parliamentary party and the members outside creates stark problems for most Labour MPs. The wiser among them are keen to engage with the great Corbyn influx of members and supporters. For as long as most of them can remember, activists' ranks have been thinning, and so this opportunity mustn't be squandered. Shrewd MPs will make calls, write letters and welcome newbies into the arcane world of branch meetings. Stalwart sticklers for subcommittee procedures and minute-keeping should be told to lighten up.

Above all, the new members must be approached with open ears, as people who might have something to say. The party, even among long-standing Labour members, has conveyed a demand for change that MPs need to heed, particularly when it comes to economics. While sketchy Corbynite schemes such as 'people's quantitative easing' must be approached with a measure of scepticism, the deficiencies of the orthodoxy also need to be faced. With the Bank of England's chief economist floating such emergency measures as negative interest rates, the macroeconomic argument is plainly one that Labour needs to have with an open mind.

But if the movement politics that carried Mr Corbyn to power poses challenges for Labour MPs, it also raises questions of the man himself. Arriving in an empty office devoid of any levers of power, Mr Corbyn has been hiring fixers who learned their craft in Ken Livingstone's mayoral office and the big trade unions. This is understandable enough, but it is only too easy to imagine the idealistic new activism giving way to the old political machine. The opposition should be tapping into community networks such as Citizens UK, and maybe even the agitprop activists of UK Uncut. Those few MPs, such as Stella Creasy, who have shown they can organise to campaign in their own communities ought to be encouraged to come up with ideas for doing the same thing on a wider stage. Mr Corbyn may have benefited from a novel wave of activism; the next step must be to prove that he actually understands it.

24 SEPTEMBER

Morrissey: what we learned about him from *List of the Lost*

MICHAEL HANN

It's commonplace in this kind of article to tell you we're reading the book so you don't have to. It's a tease, usually. In the case of *List of the Lost*, however, it's absolutely true. Do not read this book; do not sully yourself with it, no matter how temptingly brief it seems. All those who shepherded it to print should hang their heads in shame, for it's hard to imagine anything this bad has been put between covers by anyone other than a vanity publisher. It is an unpolished turd of a book, the stale excrement of Morrissey's imagination.

The singer himself has described it thus: 'The theme is demonology ... the left-handed path of black magic. It is about a sports relay team in 1970s America who accidentally kill a wretch who, in esoteric language, might be known as a Fetch ... a discarnate entity in physical form. He appears, though, as an omen of the immediate deaths of each member of the relay team. He is a life force of a devil incarnate, yet in his astral shell he is one phase removed from life. The wretch begins a banishing ritual of the four main characters, and therefore his own death at the beginning of the book is illusory.'

Not that you need to know that, really. All you need to know is not to buy it. Please don't encourage Morrissey to write any more novels. While *Autobiography* was fascinating, at times beautiful, and with enough charm to balance out the bitterness, *List of the Lost* offers nothing but the astonishing feat, in a book so brief, of being boring.

But what can we learn from it?

Morrissey's ego remains untrammelled

That, surely, is the only reason for the publication of *List of the Lost* in this form. It appears to be unedited, the curse of the writer whose commercial clout is stronger than their publisher's will-power. It's not just the typos and grammatical errors – of which there are plenty – but the endless digressions, the inability to come to any sort of a point. There might be a tolerable 20-page short story nestling in here somewhere (there probably isn't, but let's be generous for a moment), but no editor has been allowed to search for it. The ego that demanded *Autobiography* be published as an instant Penguin Classic has this one published in a jacket redolent of the great Penguin editions of the 1960s. This book is not fit to share a bookshop with them, let alone a bookshelf.

Morrissey is still hugely hung up about sex

We learned in *Autobiography* that Morrissey has had partners. We learn from *List of the Lost* that his attitude towards sex remains odd: it is associated with death, for one thing. It seems to be predatory: older men feed upon the young. Morrissey writes about his track team in such a fetishising way: 'Imperishable, they train insatiably, companions in pleasure and passionate in sentiments, they are the living picture of the desired physique.' (Ask yourself if a 56-year-old man writing in that manner about women in their teens or early 20s would be considered anything other than a bit creepy.) When he comes to describe sex itself, it's even worse: 'Eliza and Ezra rolled together into the one giggling snowball of full-figured copulation, screaming and shouting as they playfully bit and pulled at each other in a dangerous and clamorous rollercoaster coil of sexually violent rotation with Eliza's breasts barrel-rolled across Ezra's howling mouth and the pained frenzy of his bulbous salutation extenuating his excitement as it whacked and smacked its way into every muscle of Eliza's body except for the otherwise central zone.'

Morrissey can't write dialogue

Every character in *List of the Lost* speaks like a parody of Morrissey at his most florid and self-indulgent: bad puns, hopeless 'quickfire' dialogue, and desperate self-pity. 'I suffer greatly in painful silence and I speak to you, now, with servitude whilst also pleading for your understanding. I am alone and I agonise in an exasperated state.' That, one strongly suspects, was not a common pattern of speech in Boston in 1975. One might defend the line by saying it comes from what might very well be an apparition, yet the apparition speaks much as the flesh-and-blood characters do – you could not tell the characters apart from their speech – and in the next paragraph goes into a remarkable, matter-of-fact description of where to find the body of her murdered child, 'all neatly blanketed by a durable covering of weather-soaked layers of sheet metal'. Durable covering, you say? Hmm. What sealant did the murderer use? Not something weather-resistant, evidently ...

Morrissey still has scores to settle (part one)

Character upon character reminds us that justice and law are different things, and that the legal system is not to be trusted. That judge who branded Morrissey 'devious, truculent and unreliable', and who failed to find in his favour when the Smiths' rhythm section sought more money, has not been forgiven. Even the 'Fetch' Morrissey has referred to – a homeless man the four relay runners encounter in some woods – manages to get in his dig at judges before being unceremoniously killed. 'Judges don't live in the ghetto ... they are exclusively verbal beings. What can they understand about the way life moves? ... Would judges even recognize dog shit if they saw it? ... Judges have to live in secrecy, don't they, because they've done so much harm to society.' One half expects the character, with his dying breath, to sigh: 'And Joyce and Rourke never deserved a penny!' Bafflingly, this American demon, in an American wood, speaking to American people, also wants to let them know that royalty is a meaningless concept. It's possible, living in a republic, that they already knew that.

Morrissey still has scores to settle (part two)

Remember those belligerent ghouls who ran Manchester schools? Turns out they're running Boston colleges as well. Only this time they're doing worse than grabbing and devouring, and kicking while you're showering. In fact, this one prefers to sodomise with 'hatred and bloodlust and bigotry'. But let's not ruin it for the poor souls who plan to read *List of the Lost*.

Morrissey still has scores to settle (part three)

Damn you, meat eaters. You might think there would be no particular reason for a lecture about the slaughter of animals in a book about athletes being stalked by a malevolent force. You would, of course, be wrong. 'At the human hand the animals are whacked and hacked into chopped meat whilst gazing up at their protector with disbelief and pleading for a mercy not familiar to the human spirit, ground and round into hash or stew for the Big Mac pleasure of fat-podge children.'

Morrissey still has scores to settle (part four)

His greatest grievance is with Britain itself. A whole section, inexplicably, is devoted to Morrissey's disgust at the conduct of the British establishment during the second world war (along with a contemptuous repetition of the rumour that Winston Churchill and Ivor Novello were lovers, which is odd, given that he also complains that Churchill being credited with winning the war stole the credit from Alan Turing, denied glory because he was gay). Rare is the writer who is willing to complain that the big problem with Churchill during the war was that he was, frankly, a bit of a coward and unwilling to try to identify with the people he governed, but Morrissey is that writer. 'Churchill himself would experience World War 2 safely and in a suite of rooms at Claridge's most luxurious Mayfair hotel, with not a complicated twitch or pang to trouble his elaborate evening meal.' We'll leave aside the fact that he makes it sound like Claridge's is a chain, with the Mayfair branch simply its most upscale outpost – 'Yeah, I was going to go stop at the Travelodge, but I got a deal on the Claridge's at Peterborough services' – and instead note that the entire passage reads like a polemic written by a particularly single-minded street-corner pamphleteer (see also Morrissey's writing about the pernicious power of, wait for it, local television news. Damn you, *Look North*, with your hegemony!).

Morrissey does not favour the light touch

The most prominent character in *List of the Lost* is Ezra. He is the one who loves and is loved, the one who seeks justice for the wronged, the unofficial leader of the gang. Yet he's also the one who commits the crime that sets the tragedies in motion. Ezra's surname is Pound. Ezra Pound, of course, was the poet and defender of his contemporaries who went on to become a fascist, and who broadcast propaganda against his native United States from Italy during the second world war. Think about it, yeah?

Morrissey may not be the world's leading expert on sport

One of the more surprising revelations of *Autobiography* was that Morrissey had been a talented runner, so it's perhaps not surprising that a relay team is at the centre of the narrative. What's more surprising is that they are a half-mile relay team. Now, I am willing to be corrected on this, but I've looked around and can see no evidence of such an event existing. There are two rarely contested relays that might fit the bill – the 4x200m and the 4x800m – but they appear to be *so* rarely contested that it seems hugely unlikely a college would have a specialist team in either, or that such an event would be part of a televised college athletics meeting. Frankly, though, that's the least of *List of the Lost*'s problems.

6 October

The genius of *The Great British Bake Off* (extract)

CHARLOTTE HIGGINS

The season finale of *The Great British Bake Off* was the third most popular programme on television last year – outflanked only by two World Cup football matches. The final episode of this season, airing tomorrow, will in all likelihood be the most-watched show of 2015. Over the last five years, in fact, *Bake Off* has so thoroughly entangled itself with the consciousness of the nation that it has become easy to forget how very, very strange it is that 10 million Britons switch on their TV sets each Wednesday evening to watch a baking contest filmed in a tent in the countryside.

No one predicted the scale of its success. Richard McKerrow and Anna Beattie, who founded Love Productions, which makes the show, tried to sell the idea for four years before BBC2 finally picked it up. Their original inspiration, they told me, was the rural baking competition at a village fete; they liked the idea that bakers were naturally generous – making delicious things for others. And they felt that baking said much about Britain and its regional quiddities, from Dundee cakes to bara brith to Bakewell tarts. But their pitch was repeatedly passed over, for the perfectly understandable reason that TV commissioners felt that watching people make cakes would be unutterably dull. Imagine that someone had told you in 2009 that by 2015 the great television success would be a baking competition presented by two decidedly unglitzy middle-aged women, one of them gay, and judged by an octogenarian cookbook writer and a Liverpudlian professional baker of whom you had never heard. You might have cheered for the sisterhood, but you probably wouldn't have believed it.

Much of the tone of the show – as light and sweet as a sponge – is carried by its presenters, the impish Sue Perkins and Mel Giedroyc, and their end-of-pier, *Carry On*-style humour. 'I've never eaten a nun before,' Sue remarked solemnly after the contestants were set the task of making a French choux pastry called a religieuse. If Mel and Sue give *Bake Off* its wit, the judges – the grandmotherly, somewhat patrician Mary Berry and the flinty-but-twinkly master baker Paul Hollywood – are its twin deities. 'Alvin has really got to pull up his socks' is a typically nannyish remark from Mary, who reacts to baking disasters more in sorrow than in anger; 'Queen Victoria would be proud' represents the zenith of her lexicon of praise.

Paul and Mary treat each other with an indulgent respect, across a gaping class divide. Squarely built, Paul has a particular way of standing: legs apart, shirt cuffs tucked once over his sleeves, hands on hips. He employs a Paddington stare through narrowed, Arctic-blue eyes to impart scepticism when bakers head off on the wrong track – daring to introduce gritty pomegranates to a silky bavarois, for instance.

The rules of the show are simple. At the beginning of the series, 12 amateur bakers are introduced to viewers. Each week is designated a broad theme: bread, say, or pastry, or desserts. Within the hour-long show (compressed from a weekend of filming), bakers compete in three rounds, after which the weakest is dispatched and the strongest accorded the title 'star baker'. This continues until three bakers are left, when the grand final unfolds. For the viewer, an hour in the *Bake Off* tent is like peeping through the window into a charmed land of plenty: a fairytale landscape of tottering choux towers, charlotte russes filled with trembling expanses of bavarois, gingerbread houses and cheesecake tiers and lady fingers and sponges and macarons and frangipanes. But the competition throbs with drama. Will the sponge sink? Will the custard split? Will the ice cream melt? Has the doe-eyed, bashful junior doctor Tamal Ray, one of this year's finalists, used the strong flour necessary (it turns out!) to make eclairs that are sturdy enough to hold the weight of a further tier of iced eclairs? Will prison governor Paul Jagger underbake his eclairs, causing them to be soft and bend – 'which would be ghastly', in Mary's words?

In the moment of watching, I find myself punching the air, or gasping in excitement, or clutching at my head in despair. The characters might be attempting to scale a mountain or swim an ocean, so badly does one begin to care about their fates. As the series progresses, one begins to recognise their particularities. A nation's eyes rolled when Ian Cumming, another of this season's finalists, declared that he was baking with eggs laid by his own guinea fowl: *of course* he fashioned his own device to cut lady fingers to precisely 9cm long; *of course* it was he who constructed a well from tempered chocolate with a bucket that drew a lemon-flavoured, white chocolate drink from its depths.

It was the moment when Tamal affixed crescent moons and delicate pastry roses – inspired by the *Arabian Nights* and Persian gardens – to his raised game pie that I really fell for him. When Nadiya Hussain, lip trembling with trepidation, presented her sculpted chocolate peacock to the judges (and secured her own route to the final), I cried.

Bake Off is rapturous, it is agonising, it is hilarious. And yet, how minuscule and how utterly ridiculous, after all. This is an economy of minor anxieties and insignificant dangers: the emotional range of a comfortable life, fretted by quotidian storms – a parking ticket, a stressful day at work, a forgotten lunch date. *Bake Off* validates the small quiet dramas of the trifling everyday.

None of this has come about by chance. The *Bake Off* formula has developed and matured since its debut in 2010. In season one, the mix was a little stodgy. The tent travelled around the country, sometimes pitched (implausibly, it now seems) in car parks, with passers-by peeking in. Mel and Sue were not quite funny, yet, and much of their job consisted of interviewing food experts (six alone in the first episode) for lengthy exegeses of baking history. Mary, limp-haired, had not yet been given the casual-chic wardrobe of bright, tailored jackets and jeans. In season two, the format began to firm up: the star baker idea was introduced, and Mel and Sue began to chant 'Ready, get set, bake' before each challenge. It was in season two that *Bake Off* really took off on Twitter, when the camera lingered for a second on a squirrel displaying a pair of enormous testicles, a cause of enormous hilarity among the commentariat.

In season four there was an all-female final with a memorable cast: the designer Frances Quinn, who was always having 'ideas'; the confident, self-assured Kimberley Wilson, who, to no one's surprise, knew a word in Japanese for the notion of always being able to push yourself beyond your apparent limits; and the coltishly beautiful Ruby Tandoh, who flavoured her bakes with a brooding melancholy. (Sue: 'You're studying Wittgenstein!' Ruby: 'That's nothing compared to this.')

The programme-makers only gradually learned to set tasks pleasing to the eye: in the first season, one challenge consisted of making three puddings – one with bread, one with suet, and a crumble – brown blobs in Pyrex dishes. Over time, challenges became more perilously architectural – a croquembouche (chouxpuff tower) in season two, and in season three a gingerbread building (the eventual winner, John, recreated the Roman Colosseum). Season five's final saw the construction of a cake-and-sugar coal mine, complete with winding gear. That series also contained a full-on tabloid scandal when one contender, Diana Beard, was widely accused of sabotage after she removed an alaska, not hers, from a freezer. (It belonged to Iain Watters, and he presented his ruined pudding to the judges from the murky depths of a flip-top bin, whither he had cast it in a fury; this event was even more scandalous than the custard theft of 2013 – don't ask.)

Bake Off is, in fact, as much about a secondary discourse played out in the press and social media as it is about the show itself. This conversation has been harnessed by the BBC itself, with its cheery spinoff show *An Extra Slice*, presented by comedian Jo Brand, in which 'celebrity fans' gather to discuss the preceding week's events in a studio carefully styled to resemble the *Bake Off* tent. At the time of writing, the *Daily Telegraph* has published 73 articles about the programme since 1 August; supermarket aisles groan with muffin tins and piping bags and cake stands come *Bake Off* season. The show has shrugged off the bonds of mere TV, and garnered a cultural presence rarely seen since the shows of the 1970s – the so-called 'golden age' of television.

The Great British Bake Off is a fully fledged cultural phenomenon – and it may be the perfect show for Britain, now. We exist in a world where the difficult words 'Great' and 'British' cannot safely be applied to much. But they can be applied to a baking contest.

In the summer of 2009, the year before *Bake Off* first aired, Britain was reeling from the financial crisis. One sunny Manchester morning, Jeremy Deller – an artist who put flower arrangements made by members of the Women's Institute in the Tate – staged a procession, complete with embroidered banners and lovingly decorated floats, that he had created with members of the local community. The following day, the artist Antony Gormley began a project in which members of the public occupied the normally empty fourth plinth in the north-west corner of Trafalgar Square,

London: for an hour at a time they sang, or danced, or simply enjoyed their time in the sun (or rain). The project had been conceived long before the crash, and in more prosperous times might have stood as a monument to vainglorious individuality. As it was, it had a kind of unforced charm; it became a celebration of ordinariness.

There was a new spirit in the land, one that had been quietly gathering strength in the boom years and found new resonance in a post-crash Britain. Knitting circles became chic. New branches of the Women's Institute, hitherto firmly associated in the national imagination with the dowdy, jam-making elders of rural communities, began to be founded by 30-somethings in fashionable urban neighbourhoods. (A branch calling itself the Shoreditch Sisters, set up in 2007, has concerned itself with crocheting protest signs and campaigning against female genital mutilation.)

To the cynical, such activities represented self-deception and false consciousness: people used to knit clothes because they couldn't afford to buy them, not as some kind of folksy hobby. The knitters, by and large, seemed to recognise that. The activity was simultaneously a knowing re-creation of something that might never have quite existed, and a sincerely enjoyed, personally enriching, everyday act of creativity. This is the spirit that Love Productions has so successfully mined – the way in which these small daily acts, if you only looked at them afresh, might become extraordinary. They have followed the success of *Bake Off* with *The Great British Sewing Bee* and, coming this autumn to BBC2, *The Great British Pottery Throw Down*.

Bake Off may have appealed to a nation that, in economically bleak times, cleaved to domestic comforts, but it has also tapped into a plangent sense of Britishness – one that recalls some unspecified and ungraspable past. The tent is calculated to recall the marquees of the rural flower and produce show. The set dressing, in each series more skilfully achieved, waxes nostalgic, in the carefully manufactured way of Cath Kidston, the designer of floral tea towels and spotty cushion covers. The contestants work at their own mini kitchen islands, wooden-topped units painted in pale ice-cream colours. Electric mixers are similarly pastel-coloured, as are the retro fridge-freezers. The walls are set about with union jack bunting, and at the front of the tent are tables with gingham cloths, little assemblages of wicker baskets to evoke a picnic outing from the 1950s, and eggshell-blue-painted dressers and chests adorned with china, enamel jugs and vintage bread bins.

The whole aesthetic evokes the notion of the cheerful farmhouse kitchen, despite bearing no resemblance to the dark, scruffy farm kitchens I remember from growing up in the country – cats perched on dog-eared piles of *Farmers Weekly*, shelves lined with ancient, grimy newspaper. It is important that *Bake Off* is not set in the antiseptic surroundings of an urban studio, but rather in a carefully chosen and people-free landscape, which can be glimpsed through the windows of the marquee. (This year and last it has been pitched in the gardens of Welford Park near Newbury in Berkshire.) This is the English countryside in all its May-time loveliness – which the viewer actually watches months later, as they contemplate damp September – to be admired through lovingly filmed heads of cow parsley nodding under the weight of spring raindrops, or via long shots of fields of buttercups.

Bake Off is pure English pastoral: it is Delius, Vaughan Williams and Blake. It is Miss Marple. It is the National Trust. It is the first tableau in Danny Boyle's opening ceremony for the 2012 London Olympics: a village cricket match played out in a green and pleasant land. It is the England that former prime minister

John Major vowed would never vanish in a famous 1993 speech: 'Long shadows on county grounds, warm beer, invincible green suburbs, dog lovers and pools fillers and – as George Orwell said – "old maids bicycling to holy communion through the morning mist".' Major was mining Orwell's wartime essay 'The Lion and the Unicorn', whose tone was one of reassurance – that the national culture will survive, despite everything: 'The gentleness, the hypocrisy, the thoughtlessness, the reverence for law and the hatred of uniforms will remain, along with the suet puddings and the misty skies.'

Orwell and Major were both asserting the strength of a national culture at times when Britishness – for both men, basically Englishness – was felt to be under threat from outside dangers (war; integration into Europe). The *Bake Off* tent operates similarly. There it sits, in inviolable splendour, a blessed plot, an island amid a sea of green. Into this demi-paradise the dangerous clamour of less happy lands cannot intrude. The tent stands in for a utopian little Britain in which all – the firefighter, the student, the grandmother, the doctor, the nurse, the prison governor, the full-time mother, the musician – exist in harmony. This little world is rather middle class (some people in the real world are too posh to bake, some too impoverished, and they are not in the tent). It is a world in which any number of distinctions have been erased, and many pressing and anxious-making things are left outside. In the real world, Tamal may tweet about the iniquities of the government's contracts for junior doctors, but this side of him is never expressed in the tent, just as it is unthinkable that Paul-the-prison-governor might so much as mention the criminal justice system. It is, of course, a wish-fulfilment, this equalising Albion of common purpose, meritocratic effort and vanished difference. But how delightful and seductive it is, this little world, where all that matters is the rise of your sponge.

Which is not to say that the multiculturalism of the tent is unimportant: Nadiya is the first British woman who wears a hijab to have occupied such a positive, joyous role in British mass culture. On Monday, prime minister David Cameron was reported as backing her to win, praising her 'coolness under pressure'. Merely by making meringues, she may have done wonders for interfaith harmony.

The brilliance of the ideology of the *Bake Off* tent is that it works whatever one's political persuasion. The *Mail* may have complained about 'politically correct' multiracial casting, but there's enough of old England (leave alone the patriotic title) to please the conservative and the Conservatives.

When we spoke, Anna Beattie downplayed the matter of casting, as if it came about quite naturally. (Simon Evans, the show's editor, on the other hand, paid tribute to the excellence of the casting team.) From thousands of applicants this year, around 150 were invited 'to bake to camera, in front of us', she explained. Not that many people are good at baking both bread and cakes, she said, and there is an even smaller number who can bake and talk simultaneously. Those who came across as 'wannabes' – keener on celebrity than baking – were also discarded. Having winnowed the applicants down to those who baked best on the screen test, 'then it was about trying to get a representative mix'.

'Representative of what?' I asked. 'I don't know,' she replied. 'Britain?'

29 OCTOBER

Of course I believe in ghosts – my sanity depends on it

GILES FRASER

I believe in ghosts. I live with them all the time. But it wasn't always the case. Foolishly, I used to pretend they didn't exist, that the dead stayed dead, that they had no purchase on my life. But now I speak to them all the time, and they speak to me. I have photographs of them on my study wall. And I have even come to love them, in a strange kind of way. But I don't call them ghosts. I call them memories, many half buried, many faintly conceived. For one of the surprising things unearthed for me by the extraordinary chemistry of psychoanalysis was the continuing presence of my ancestors. Ghosts are psychological unfinished business, often associated with unprocessed pain.

It is exactly a hundred years since Sigmund Freud set pen to paper to write his groundbreaking paper 'Mourning and Melancholia'. Published in 1917, Freud distinguished between two responses to loss: mourning, when the object of loss is clear and obvious, and thus can be emotionally processed; and melancholia, a state of being in which one is affected by a loss that one is unable to name. Melancholia is, as it were, a loss that one doesn't realise has been lost. And because one cannot properly name this loss, because it exists in the psychic shadows, one cannot go through the process of mourning it properly. The pain goes unburied. So it hangs around and continually haunts you. This state is often associated with depression.

It was four years ago last Monday that I resigned from St Paul's Cathedral. Dealing with the emotional fallout led me back to therapy. Initially, I thought the subsequent depression was to do with something obvious, like a loss of ego-status or a life crisis that had yet to be properly worked through. But as the lens widened, something unexpected came into view. My ancestors arrived on these shores escaping persecution. Many were central European refugees fleeing tsarist pogroms. As Jews were being gassed in Nazi Germany, my family were desperately seeking to rebuild their lives, searching for normality and acceptance. And for some, the best way to do this was to forget the past and to blend in. My dad became a Christian. I became a priest. Unconsciously, it was the ultimate way not to talk about what had happened. But theologically, it was the ultimate betrayal.

And yet, for me, the dead refused to stay dead. The Jewish talking cure, also invented by a man running away from his religion, returned to me these buried presences and invited me to walk among them again: my great-grandfather Louis, working for the Jewish Board of Guardians looking after 'swarms' (cf David Cameron) of desperate refugees in the East End; his brother Samuel, who wore an Anglican-looking dog collar but led the Princes Road synagogue in Liverpool. They both changed their names from Friedeberg. And, interestingly, they were both of Freud's generation. For me, only by remembering the dead would melancholia be converted into plain old mourning. My healing was to be found among the ghosts.

The year before Freud was writing 'Mourning and Melancholia', the fascinating ethnographer Shlomo Ansky was writing his own Jewish ghost story, called *The Dybbuk* and subtitled 'Between Two Worlds'. In Jewish mythology, the dybbuk is a dark lost soul, suspended in some intermediate state between life and death. For a secular socialist like Ansky, his story was an expression of mourning for a religious culture that was collapsing both around him and inside him. The Jewish faith was something he rejected and yet needed at the same time. 'My life was broken, split, torn,' as he put it. Freud invented psychoanalysis and Ansky wrote about ghosts. But they were doing a similar thing: resurrecting the half-dead, so as to give them a proper burial. Freud's melancholia is the psychological condition of the dybbuk, the lost soul. And psychoanalysis is a form of exorcism. So, yes, I believe in ghosts. My sanity depends upon it. Happy Halloween.

5 NOVEMBER

England's brown and pleasant land needs protection too

CATHERINE SHOARD

The Ebbsfleet elephant died about 420,000 years ago, killed by early humans with bits of flint. His substantial remains – he weighed the same as four Hondas – were uncovered in 2003, during the construction of the HS1 high-speed rail link from St Pancras to the Channel tunnel. To pay a trip to his penultimate resting place (Southampton is now home to the bones), you need to exit Ebbsfleet International, walk down Station Road and head for the junction with the B259.

It's unmarked. The cars roar by, past a pristine verge. Not even the place for a picnic, let alone a quiet prayer. For maximum atmosphere you'd be better off taking a look at the painting that accompanies an academic report on the find. In this, our doomed elephant cheerfully waves its trunk at some deer across the swamp. Other animals wander around (also uncovered was evidence of rhinos, lions, aurochs and monkeys). All are unaware of the butt-naked hunter watching from the shore.

Little of this landscape still exists. The swamp became shells, and the chalk was then bulldozed into muddy plains, awaiting redevelopment. Artists' impressions of the area now show gleaming executive culs-de-sac with an abundance of parking. Families enjoying the prestige lifestyle opportunities that accompany buying a house in Britain's youngest garden city.

But there is trouble in paradise. Although Ebbsfleet was earmarked for major development back in 2003, and permission has been granted for 15,000 housing units, only 350 have so far been built. This is credited to a reluctance on the part of private firms to fork out for infrastructure, rather than a lack of demand. And so, accordingly, £200m of public money is being used to jumpstart the process.

Small wonder. The government cannot allow Ebbsfleet to fail. The investment already committed is enormous. HS1, too, didn't come cheap, and public feeling about HS2, its Midlands sister, depends to some extent on its success. Plus, Ebbsfleet isn't just any old new garden city, it's the first of three proposed. Whither Bicester (earmarked as number two) if this one shrivels?

There is another reason, too. The project is a de facto poster child for a significant piece of policy brought in shortly after the 2015 election. This policy loosens planning controls and all but guarantees consent to develop any suitable brownfield sites for housing – including, where necessary, compulsory purchase orders.

Reaction at the time was positive. We need more houses, after all. But the easy ride is also a matter of rhetoric: endlessly invoked, rarely queried. Better brownfield than green, right? Obviously it's preferable to raze wasteland than ravage undefiled countryside.

No. Not so obviously. Supposedly Arcadian greenfield Britain includes intensively farmed prairies, fields of polytunnels and industrial forestry hospitable neither to walkers nor wildlife. Indeed, it's the destruction of much of our countryside that has made brownfield so invaluable. The lack of human and chemical intervention in these disused quarries and rubbish dumps, railway sidings and former factories, gives nature a fighting chance of survival.

Yet even before this summer, such territory was vulnerable. In 2013, research found that over 50 per cent of wildlife-rich brownfield in the Thames Gateway has been lost, damaged or is under threat. The fallout from the new ruling will push that figure far higher.

Caveats do still exist, if lobbying is strong enough. Just last month, the dingy skipper – our most moth-like butterfly – blocked a housing development on a former heliport in Newcastle. A similar story in Plymouth involved the horrid ground-weaver spider, a type thought dead for decades. Meanwhile, near Linlithgow, the residency of the hobo spider in a scrapyard has meant it's to be turned into a wildflower meadow. Would-be litter-pickers have been invited to the site, with instructions to bring wellies and approach 'from Pier Road off the A904', next to the funeral parlour.

Directions like these make my heart lift. I was lucky enough to be raised by an intrepid explorer of the brownfield, and to own an audiobook of *Stig of the Dump*. But others, too, must know it's the unsung wilderness that usually proves the most romantic – and the most accessible. Cars can transport you to country parks with tarmac paths and to honeypot mountains, but for many, mysterious pockets of brownfield are the natural space closest to home.

Just how close may come as a surprise, however. In a set of recommendations published in March, Lord Adonis re-emphasised the status of the land on which council estates sit, as brownfield. Technically this is correct: if it isn't green (gardens are exempt), it is brown. Whether you are a local authority tenant or not, if you live and work in an urban area then you likely do so, in theory at least, on brownfield.

What we need is a much more sophisticated approach to categorisation. The same scepticism should be extended to official use of the words 'green' and 'brown' as 'black' and 'white'. We like to think we're savvy enough to spot attempts to persuade us to pay more for a yoghurt by billing it as luxury or natural. So why can't we recognise spin here?

Half a million years ago, our ancestors brought down a really big elephant with a few bits of rock. We ought to be able to manage this too.

28 NOVEMBER

He gave his unforgettable work for nothing. Shouldn't the designer of the peace symbol be commemorated?

IAN JACK

In the early evening of 21 February 1958, a middle-aged man travelled right across London, from his home in suburban Twickenham to a shabby Victorian building in Finsbury Park. Among the press of commuters, Gerald Holtom stood out as someone slightly different – 'arty-looking', as they used to say – with a portfolio under his arm and disorderly hair that hadn't been smoothed with Brylcreem or trapped by a hat. Eventually, after a journey by green suburban train and then a change of tube, he reached the top of Blackstock Road and a dark doorway next to a familiar landmark: Fish & Cook, printers and stationers. Holtom walked up the stairs to an office where several people who would soon be of interest to special branch had already gathered. 'So, Gerry, let's see what you have for us,' one of them said. Holtom untied his portfolio and took out some sheets. 'I've tried a simple approach,' he began ...

The film script at this point would call for puzzlement and a gathering sense of outrage among Holtom's small audience. 'But we wanted a dove,' somebody says. 'Or an olive branch,' says another. 'Or a cheek in the act of turning,' says a third. 'This business of the three lines inside a circle won't do at all.' These sunflowers will never sell, Monsieur van Gogh. Conventional narrative calls for rejection and dejection before the artist gathers his strength, tries again, and this time triumphs.

In fact, the meeting of the Direct Action Committee Against Nuclear War (DAC) seems to have liked Holtom's design without any equivocation. According to *Peace News*'s honorary archivist, Bill Hetherington, it was 'immediately accepted' as the symbol for the demonstration that the committee had planned for Easter. On Good Friday, which that year fell on 4 April, the peace symbol made its first public appearance when it was carried aloft on the 52-mile march from Trafalgar Square to the Atomic Weapons Research Establishment at Aldermaston in Berkshire.

This was the first of the big Aldermaston marches, and the last one to have Aldermaston as its finishing point. All future marches went the other way, reflecting the difference between the DAC and the Campaign for Nuclear Disarmament (CND), the DAC's successor as the march's loudest voice. The DAC wanted to draw attention to the unobtrusive manufacture of nuclear bombs in the home counties: to protest at the thing itself. CND favoured the more traditional pattern of British dissent – a march on London – and the publicity that came with a climactic moment only a few hundred yards from Fleet Street and Westminster, the twin centres of media and political power. But whatever the sectarian differences that existed inside the anti-nuclear movement, Holtom's symbol remained common to all. Nobody had rights to it. Holtom himself had never claimed copyright; he wanted the design to be freely available to any group who fought the same cause.

Its success was almost immediate. By 1964, the writer Christopher Driver (a pacifist, later to edit the *Good Food Guide*) could justifiably describe it as 'probably the most powerful, memorable and adaptable image ever designed for a secular cause'. The rest of the world adopted it for other movements – in the US, it stood for feminism and civil rights as well as opposition to the Vietnam war – so that it slowly lost its strict association with the phrase 'ban the bomb' and came instead to represent peace and justice more generally, especially when those ideas conflicted with the establishment view. It has had several enemies – in 1973, South Africa's apartheid government tried to ban it – but rather more adaptors. The encircled 'A' of anarchism may have its roots in the 19th century – the 'A' may stand for anarchism and the 'O' for the order that 'A' is the mother of (Proudhon said that, apparently) – but it's hard not to suspect that its popular form as a punk monogram took Holtom's design as its inspiration.

Earlier this month, French graphic designer Jean Jullien turned the internal lines into an instantly recognisable Eiffel Tower by adding three short brushstrokes – a couple of horizontals at the base and an extension of the vertical so that it broke the circle. It may be the most memorable adaptation in the symbol's 60-year history, and according to Jullien it sprang from 'an instinctive, human reaction [rather than] an illustrator's reaction'. Within 24 hours of the terrorist attacks on Paris on 13 November, it had been printed on T-shirts, posters and flags. An unwatched child might have drawn it, but (or and) it managed to convey both sorrow and hope. Jullien said that in his opinion 'the strongest images are the ones that don't require any deep background in culture or art history to decipher ... It needs to be something that people from different backgrounds can recognise automatically ... You understand before you decipher the image, and I think with words, sometimes, the barrier is higher.'

But Jullien had the Eiffel Tower. Why Holtom drew what he did is harder to explain. According to one school of thought, the lines inside the circle form a composite of the semaphore for the letters 'N' and 'D', standing for Nuclear and Disarmament. Holtom himself, writing in 1973, believed his design to be a kind of self-portrait: 'I was in ... deep despair. I drew myself ... with hands palm outstretched outwards and downwards in the manner of Goya's peasant before the firing squad. I formalised the drawing into a line and put a circle round it.'

Both explanations seem after the fact and too literal. Drawings, like sentences, can come out of an unknowable elsewhere. And who in any case needs an explanation? I remember my first sight of what I then thought of as a CND badge: how taken I was with the elegance of its white-on-black design, how pure it looked and yet how rebellious and mysterious. It was 1961. I travelled by train to collect more badges, and literature too, from a friendly doctor's wife in the next to nearest town. I was a sincere unilateralist, not simply a badge-lover, but I noticed that among the one or two of my school friends who agreed to take a badge there was an aesthetic appreciation of the tin button itself. Logos are commonplace now – rarer then. There was the circle and straight line of London Transport, of course, and the RAF roundel, but otherwise the tendency still ran towards heraldry, and initial letters made illegible through compression or entanglement. What Holtom's badge was, above all, was new.

He died aged 71 in 1985. He was a graduate of the Royal College of Art, a conscientious objector in the second world war, and an early anti-nuclear activist. So far as I can tell, he never made a penny from his design or wanted to. Should he not have a memorial or plaque? This week I discovered that in the 1960s an office block replaced his house at 2 Holly Road, Twickenham; there seems little point in remembering him somewhere so changed. On the other hand, the Finsbury Park building that he visited with his portfolio in February 1958 still exists. The meeting that adopted his design was held in a room then occupied by *Peace News*, which long ago left for King's Cross. Today the offices belong to a solicitor. Down below, miraculously, Fish & Cook is still selling stationery, though via a Mr Raj rather than a Fish or a Cook. The shop sits among Algerian cake shops, halal butchers, Ethiopian delicatessens and Chinese noodle bars. Here, surely, is a fitting place to remember the man who drew for peace.

30 NOVEMBER

Country diary: a wild creature loose in Wharfedale

CAREY DAVIES

The river Wharfe has broken out of its enclosure. Normally lovely, languorous and impeccably well-behaved, it has mutated in the heavy rain and now runs rampant through fields, climbs high up leaf-littered banks of ivy and alder, and carries huge tree trunks away with it like twigs in a game of Poohsticks.

Scores of people have come out to watch the spectacle, milling around on roads cleared of traffic; friends and strangers alike chatting together. There is nothing like a bit of threatened calamity to get tongues wagging. Usually as translucent as clear beer, the water has turned a monsoon brown, boiling with the force of countless tons and churning white as it surges under the seven arches of Otley's bridge, leaving only a tight gap of air. Some houses are already swamped and the water is lapping at the Victorian terraces of Farnley Lane, but its residents seem impressively philosophical – or simply well-insured.

Although realistically it represents little threat to life and limb, the flood gives a glimpse of something fierce and powerful. I imagine the river could easily fold me away if I fell in, particularly the deafening maelstroms under the bridge. But perhaps more significant is the origin of the water: whereas previous floods have often involved snowmelt from the moors and mountains of the Yorkshire Dales upstream, this one is caused by rain alone. One consequence of the world's changing climate is predicted to be wetter winters for Britain, and every flood now feels portentous.

I walk out of town and up the wooded ridge of the Chevin, where beech trees are losing their last shreds of leaf in the high winds. The top gives a bird's-eye view of roads submerged, traffic halted and pastures turned into paddy fields all the way up and down the valley. Like me, people have walked or driven their cars up here to stand on the gritstone boulders of Surprise View and take in the extent of it. They are oddly quiet as they survey the scene. A wild creature is loose in Wharfedale, and it is compelling.

Winter

Star Wars: The Force Awakens review – a spectacular homecoming

PETER BRADSHAW

It's here – the real Episode IV! From the first few minutes, or even the first few frames, JJ Abrams's exciting, spectacular and seductively innocent *Star Wars: The Force Awakens* shows itself a movie in the spirit of the original trilogy, which ended with *Return of the Jedi* in 1983. (This one takes up the story 30 years later.)

Technically, of course, that was reconfigured as Episode VI, but *The Force Awakens* makes you forget about the redundancy and pedantry of the prequel trilogy that came 15 years later. It restores the comedy that *The Phantom Menace* abandoned. *The Force Awakens* is in touch with the force of action-adventure and fun. My only minor reservation, which I will get out of the way now, is with a tiny new droid who has a bit of a Scrappy-Doo vibe about him.

The Force Awakens reawakened my love of the first movie and turned my inner fanboy into my outer fanboy. There are very few films that leave me facially exhausted after grinning for 135 minutes, but this is one. And when Han Solo and Chewie came on, I had a feeling in the cinema I haven't had since I was 16: not knowing whether to burst into tears or into applause.

Abrams and veteran co-writer Lawrence Kasdan have created a film that is both a narrative progression from the earlier three films and a shrewdly affectionate next-gen reboot of the original 1977 *Star Wars* – rather in the style of Abrams's tremendous reimagining of the Kirk/Spock *Star Trek*. Familiar personae, situations and weapons will appear like covers or remixes, and mesh in with new storylines. This notice will be a safe space, incidentally, with a trigger warning only for basic plot points and material already in the public domain.

The original movies were always based on the most extraordinary nexus of personal and family dysfunction: a motor of guilt, shame and conflict. Luke was driven by an increasingly complex Freudian animus against Darth Vader; Han Solo referred to the *Millennium Falcon* as 'she'; male audiences were encouraged both to identify with Luke and to lech over Princess Leia in her outrageous gold slave bikini – and then, with exquisite narrative sadism, we were told they were brother and sister. All this agony is reborn in *The Force Awakens*: new contortions of fear and black-comic absurdity amidst the romance and excitement.

Luke has been famously absent from the poster for this film, which led me to fear at first that over the past 30 years, like Atticus Finch in Harper Lee's *Go Set a Watchman*, he had gone over to the dark side. Suffice it to say that Luke, played by a now grizzled Mark Hamill, is a potent but unwontedly enigmatic presence.

Princess Leia is now a general and still the warrior queen of the resistance – a tougher and more grandmotherly figure. The dark force is resurgent in the form of the First Order, intent on re-establishing a more candidly fascist control, with quasi-Nuremberg rallies. Ranged against them are new fighters for good. There is Rey, a resourceful survivor on the remote planet of Jakku, who feels destiny within her: she is played by newcomer Daisy Ridley with the brittle determination of a young Keira Knightley. British actor John Boyega plays Finn, a former stormtrooper who seeks redemption through betraying his evil masters.

This brings me to the terrific performance from Adam Driver as Kylo Ren, the new dark lord with a terrible secret. He is gorgeously cruel, spiteful and capricious – and unlike the Vader of old, he is given to petulant temper tantrums, with his lightsaber drawn, when uniformed subordinates have the unwelcome task of telling him of some new, temporary victory for the resistance. Driver's almost unreadably droll facial expression is very suited to Kylo Ren's fastidious and amused contempt for his enemies' weakness and compassion. There is a brilliant moment when he uses the telekinetic power of the Force against a laser shot.

The lightsaber contests themselves are of course more athletic than in the 1970s and 80s but also somehow more humanly interesting: Rey herself needs no condescending advice from men on either unarmed combat or flying the *Millennium Falcon*.

JJ Abrams has an instinctive sympathy for the classic *Star Wars* landscapes and lays them out with elan: the switch from galaxies to shadowy forests and vast rippling deserts. In almost her first appearance, Rey is seen tobogganing down a huge dune on a sled made of rope. For me it's a reminder that though the first *Star Wars* was avowedly inspired by Kurosawa's *The Hidden Fortress*, I think it originally derived its look from David Lean's *Lawrence of Arabia* or even the dreamscapes of Dalí.

But of course this film is part of an entertainment world so huge it need refer only to itself. *The Force Awakens* does not, in the way of other franchises, feel the need to be 'dark' – having repudiated the dark side. It basically powers along on a great surging riptide of idealism and optimism, that family-movie ethic which some have derided for killing off the dystopian tradition of sci-fi. In fact, *Star Wars* has now gone beyond the sci-fi genre to its own kind of intergalactic quasi-Arthurian romance – that and a return to the world of Saturday-morning pictures. *The Force Awakens* is ridiculous and melodramatic and sentimental, of course, but exciting and brimming with energy and its own kind of generosity.

18 DECEMBER

Strictly Come Dancing is a success story that could only work at the BBC

JONATHAN FREEDLAND

Saturday night is the *Strictly* final and all I can think of is Jeremy Vine in his pants. That image might be disturbing enough by itself. Except in the scene now lodged in my mind, the Radio 2 presenter and *Strictly Come Dancing* contestant is not alone. He is standing in his underwear confronted with culture secretary John Whittingdale, three civil servants, and an equal number of top BBC executives. This all happened moments before Vine dressed up in a cowboy outfit and rode a giant plastic horse.

We shall return to that little tableau later. For it makes sense only once you contemplate the phenomenon that is *Strictly*, which competes with *The Great British Bake Off* and *Britain's Got Talent* to be the highest-rated show on British television.

And this interest is not merely passive. When I went to see the show as it was televised a few weeks back – the week Vine mounted the plastic horse, as it happens – I was one of 500 sitting in a warehouse-sized studio on a backlot in Elstree. But those 500 had been picked from the 5.2 million people who had applied for tickets. Five point two million! To give you a sense of how far ahead of any normal TV programme that is, consider that the BBC's next hottest studio audience ticket was for *Strictly*'s nightly spin-off show, *It Takes Two*: 435,000 applied to see that in person. In third place was Jools Holland's *Later*, which had

357,000 would-be audience members. *Strictly* is in a league of its own, versions proliferating across the globe, already anointed the world's most successful TV show of its kind by the *Guinness Book of Records*.

Which is odd, because ballroom dancing was not exactly a mass pursuit before 2004, when the show debuted. And my childhood memory tells me *Come Dancing* was always a bit naff: stiff, upright and on the margins of the schedules. Yet *Strictly* has become an embedded part of the British autumn, beginning when the evenings are still long in September and culminating just before Christmas. As the Saturday nights darken, multiple generations gather round to see the glitter and spangle, the heel leads and unwanted 'gapping', the rumbas and American Smooths that have become as sure a sign of the calendar as falling leaves.

What explains the appeal? Part of it is glamour: the casting formula always allows a decent quotient of eye candy, both male and female. It helps that the competition is not between individuals but couples. Heidi Stephens, who writes the *Guardian*'s *Strictly* liveblog, reckons the 'chemistry' of the pairings matters – she's tipping Jay and Aliona to win for that reason – which, she says, gives the show its 'soap opera quality'. The papers always like an off-dancefloor romance between partners, whether real or imagined.

Some identify the show's strength as its niceness and civility – such a contrast to the *Hunger Games*-style cruelties of *The X Factor*: no one is ever intentionally humiliated on *Strictly*, no dance halted by a klaxon. Even the show's resident villain, Craig Revel Horwood, is picky rather than sadistic. The overall vibe is cosiness and continuity: three of the four judges have been there from the start. For Stephens, it's as unthreatening as a 'favourite jumper'.

The show's advocates would have you believe that *Strictly* reveals a collective love of dance as an art form, a passion we didn't know we had. I'm not so sure. I suspect the heart of its appeal is that *Strictly* delivers on that most basic promise of entertainment: escape. Tellingly, the contestants are allowed no brand names, or even proper nouns, on the clothes they wear when filmed training. On the pre-recorded results show, if they refer to any public event – say, in news or sport – it will be cut. The outside world must never intrude. The day after the Paris attacks, *Strictly* cha-cha-cha'd as if nothing had happened. For 90 minutes, the viewer is invited into a gaudy, sparkling bubble where there is no recession, no migration crisis, no Isis. The gravest concern is Len's need for a reverse fleckerl.

Which brings us back to Jeremy Vine in his pants, rudely interrupted during a costume change as the culture secretary made a discreet inspection last month of the BBC's flagship Saturday-night show. Whittingdale was there because, before taking the job, he had questioned whether the BBC should be making *Strictly* at all, especially if it meant going into a head-to-head ratings battle against ITV.

It's a familiar argument. It says that a public service broadcaster should confine itself to filling the gaps left by the market. Given that commercial networks are already providing Saturday-night light entertainment, why use the licence fee to provide more of it? Better to use that public cash to plug the holes: documentaries in Welsh, say, or rolling coverage of parliament.

I hope seeing *Strictly* up close that night cured Whittingdale of such thinking. It should be obvious that if the BBC is funded by the entire public, then it has to be used and valued by the entire public. A universal service has to provide something for everyone: Radio 3 and the *Today* programme, of course, but also *EastEnders* and *Strictly*.

And the two are linked. When they barged in on Vine, one BBC executive told the cabinet minister that if they'd come to Elstree in May, they'd have seen the broadcaster preparing not to dance a tango dressed as a cowboy but to cover the general election: 'And that range is what the BBC is all about.' As Vine himself puts it, programmes such as *Strictly* are a 'portal': 'You might come through the portal of *Strictly* and end up watching David Attenborough or listening to Melvyn Bragg.' Lord Reith wanted the BBC to inform, educate and entertain – but he surely understood that you earn the chance to do the first two only if you also do the third.

And yet if Whittingdale was won over, that might not be what clinched it. He might have been impressed by the conspicuous lack of extravagance: costumes in bin bags, corridors whose aroma suggests broken toilets, dressing rooms that are modest and cramped. The BBC – not some Simon Cowell-like TV impresario – has made piles of cash through the global success of the *Strictly* format, but it is not spraying that cash around.

Or the cabinet minister may have been blown away, as I was, by something else about *Strictly*. When you watch at home you see, in between dances, a short film of the next couple, showing their previous week in training. What you don't see is that, at that very moment, an army of stagehands, lighting engineers, set-builders and carpenters enters with military precision. Within a couple of minutes, they dismantle the lavish, complicated set used in the previous number and build, from scratch, a new one – with seconds to spare.

The sheer professionalism, the craft skill on display, is something to behold. The same is true of the live band and the singers, able to perform Puccini one moment, Christina Aguilera the next. The costume team make bespoke, unrepeated outfits week after week, thinking nothing of gluing 2,500 sequins on to a single dress by hand.

The entire operation – delivering a long, flawless show and doing it live – is a weekly advertisement for the BBC and for the peculiarly British model of public service broadcasting. You know that if commercial TV did *Strictly*, it wouldn't be the same: that the silly, rather innocent bubble would be filled instead with brands, sponsors and hard-selling. Or, at the other end of the broadcasting spectrum, just look across the Atlantic, to PBS and NPR, to see the absence of anything like it.

I hope Whittingdale realised that – in the BBC – Britain has been blessed with something that, for all its anomalies and illogicalities, really works. Maybe it doesn't fit into a neat, ideological rubric of where the market ends and the state should begin, but it is one of this country's few truly world-class assets. Whatever else Whittingdale does, I hope he allows the BBC to keep dancing.

31 DECEMBER

The gift I'll never forget: lessons I learned about life from my mother's early death

GARY YOUNGE

As gifts go, I would have done anything to return it. To turn the clock back and not receive it. To live my life without it. But fate would have it otherwise. So on a balmy day in Edinburgh in late May 1988, as I shuttled between the university library and anti-apartheid meetings, came the news that my mother, who had raised me on her own, had died. At 44, her death was both sudden and unexpected. She was supposed to be coming up to see me the next day. At 19, I was bereft and bereaved. Naturally, the 'gift' in this loss was not immediately apparent. I spent the next few years going through the motions, turning days into weeks and weeks into terms. Time may be a great healer, but those palliative qualities are rarely evident in real time. However, as I emerged from the numbing sense of isolation, I realised that my mother's life had taught me three valuable lessons I would probably never have learned without her untimely death.

The first is that life is short and precarious. By my early 20s I had been cruelly disabused of the notion that the young live for ever. I was left with a sense that my time on this planet was finite. That made me driven in a way that had precious little to do with conventional ambition. I just felt very keenly that I could die at any time. To some this is scary; I found it liberating. It freed me from relationships that were toxic, 'opportunities' I had no interest in and myriad journeys, both literal and metaphorical, that I did not want to take. At a relatively early age, I felt the urgency to be a protagonist, rather than a passive recipient, in my own life.

The second is that you only get one life, and while it might be short, it's long enough to make a difference. My mum crammed a lot into those 44 years. She'd raised three kids, fostered two more, migrated to a different continent, trained as a nurse, retrained as a teacher and was a community activist. She taught numeracy and literacy at night school and tutored Asian women English on Saturday mornings. She was a strident, working-class black lady in a world that has never valued those qualities in the same person. I saw her face down policemen, racist neighbours and negligent union officials. These challenges did not provide her with the easiest path in life. But it was her path, and when she'd completed it she could rest easy.

The way in which her death was mourned in my home town, including by some of the very people she'd had cross words with, made me realise why it was important to own your own life. To say what you had to say and do what you had to do in the knowledge that the clock was always ticking and no one else would say or do it for you. That the praise and criticism of others could only define you if you allowed them to. That I had to be myself because nobody else could do that for me.

The third lesson was that you take nothing with you. My mother was raised by her mother, who cut cane in Barbados. She came into the world with little and left with not a whole lot more. For most of our lives, we were broke. Like most who grew up broke, I didn't want to be broke again. But like many who suffer bereavement, death had tainted my view of material wealth. It just seemed silly to be chasing wealth when you could be chasing experiences.

Later in life all three would become cliches – chocolate-box desiderata for casual conversation. Of course, some people come to these realisations in other ways, while some abide by their own, perfectly decent adages. What was different for me was that they came to me from a raw and honest place at such a young age. They did not dawn on me in middle age as the result of a child's birth, a divorce, financial calamity or a health scare. They came early enough to enable me to live my life more aware of its limitations and my potential, rather than to have to apply that knowledge retrospectively to make sense of what happened to me.

They have been the lens through which I have made big decisions (work, family, migration) and small (arguments to engage in or avoid, meals to splash out on or forgo, friendships to fight for or let atrophy). My mother's death has been the most devastating event in my life thus far. But since her mortality was never in my gift, and I could not return it, I took the lessons of her death and used them to live my life.

11 January

David Bowie: the man who thrilled the world

ALEXIS PETRIDIS

When David Bowie's final album, *Blackstar*, was released on 8 January, a great deal of energy was expended trying to unpick the lyrics. As on its predecessor, 2013's *The Next Day*, or any number of classic Bowie albums, from *Hunky Dory* to *Station to Station*, they were frequently dense and allusive: much attention was focused on the title track, which one of *Blackstar*'s backing musicians, saxophonist Donny McCaslin, claimed was about the rise of Isis, a suggestion Bowie's spokesperson subsequently denied. Now, with the knowledge that Bowie was terminally ill during its making, the most striking thing about the album is how elegiac it frequently sounds. 'If I never see the English evergreens I'm running to, it's nothing to me,' he sings on 'Dollar Days'. 'Saying no, but meaning yes, this is all I ever meant, that's the message that I sent,' runs the closing 'I Can't Give Everything Away'. Most arresting of all is 'Lazarus': 'Look up here, I'm in heaven. I've got scars that can't be seen, I've got drama can't be stolen; everybody knows me now.'

Most people assumed that 'Lazarus' was written from the viewpoint of Thomas Jerome Newton, the alien Bowie portrayed in Nicolas Roeg's *The Man Who Fell to Earth*; it was the title track of an off-Broadway musical based on the 1976 film. Now it feels suspiciously like Bowie was writing his own epitaph, asserting his own fame, vast artistic importance and inimitability, while wryly pointing out that, after nearly 50 years in the spotlight, he'd somehow managed to retain a sense of mystery.

Dozens of books have been written about him, some hugely illuminating, but something unknowable lurked at the centre. Almost from the start, Bowie's career raised questions to which a definitive answer seemed elusive. If he was, as he loudly claimed in 1971, gay, then what was the deal with the very visible wife and the son he'd just written a touching little song about? If he was, as he dramatically announced from the stage of the Hammer-smith Odeon in July 1973, retiring – either from music, or from live performance, or from the character of Ziggy Stardust – then what was he doing back onstage in London three months later, belting out 'The Jean Genie' in full Ziggy drag? How does anyone in the state Bowie was, by all accounts, in by 1975 – ravaged by cocaine to the point where he seemed to have genuinely gone insane; paranoid and hallucinating – make an album like *Station to Station*: not a messily compelling document of a mind unravel-ling, like the solo albums of his great idol Syd Barrett, but a work of precision and focus and exquisitely controlled power that's arguably his best? In a world of cameraphones and social media, how could anyone as famous as Bowie disappear from public view as completely as he seemed to between 2008 and 2013; moreover, how could anyone as famous as Bowie record a comeback album in the middle of Manhattan without anyone noticing or leaking details to the media? How does anyone stage-manage their own death as dramatically as Bowie appears to have done: releasing their most acclaimed album in decades, filled with strange, enig-matic songs whose meaning suddenly becomes apparent when their author dies two days later?

It was a dramatic end to a career that began inauspiciously. Bowie spent the 1960s trying to fit in with prevalent trends, a task to which he was uniquely ill-suited: he didn't make for a terribly convincing blues-influenced rock'n'roller, or hippy troubadour, or MOR singer-songwriter, just as two decades later he wouldn't make for a terribly convincing mainstream stadium-rock star, trapped in what he subsequently called the 'netherworld of commercial acceptance'.

Tellingly, the first truly great song he wrote focused on the outsider: recorded at the height of Swinging London, 1966's 'The London Boys' offered up the era's gloomy flipside, a monochrome drama of poverty, amphetamine psychosis, grimy bedsits and cafes. Even when he finally had a hit, with 1969's 'Space Oddity', his success seemed far from assured. For all the song's eerie brilliance, the public clearly thought of it as a novelty record, capitalising on the moon landings: they declined to buy its follow-up, 'The Prettiest Star', or the accompanying eponymous album. All along, however, Bowie was picking up ideas he would subsequently pull into focus. His then manager Ken Pitt introduced him to the Velvet Underground, whose distortion, avant-garde inclinations and transgressive subject matter would reverberate throughout Bowie's career: you can hear echoes of their tumultuous sound in the feedback-laden glam rock of 1973's 'Aladdin Sane', the wilfully synthetic racket he conjured up on 1977's 'Heroes', and the sonic commotion of *Blackstar*'s ''Tis a Pity She Was a Whore'. He tried to incorporate what he'd learned studying mime under Lindsay Kemp into his stage act, which kicked off a fruitful obsession with drawing ideas from other areas of the arts – films, theatre, literature, fashion – into rock music.

As the 1970s dawned, he found the perfect musical foil in guitarist Mick Ronson and his songwriting got better and better – 1971's *Hunky Dory* was as rich and brilliant a collection of songs as he ever wrote – but almost no one noticed. The closest *Hunky Dory* came to commercial success was when 'Oh! You Pretty Things' made No. 12, courtesy of a jaunty, prim cover version by Peter Noone – toothsome former frontman of the 1960s' least threatening superstars, Herman's Hermits – which was clearly some distance from the seismic rupture Bowie had predicted on the album's opening track 'Changes': 'Look out, you rock'n'rollers!'

How he made them notice was via one of the most audacious gambles in rock history. Infatuated with the Velvet Underground's world of drag queens and sneering, bitchy put-downs, Bowie seemed to realise that, for all the generation-gap-rendering shocks that British rock music had delivered over the preceding decade, it had never really dared touch on the subject of homosexuality. Beyond the thanks-but-no-thanks saga of the Kinks' 'Lola', there were only glancing references, so oblique as to be the stuff of rumour rather than fact: 'See My Friends', also by the Kinks; the Beatles' 'You've Got to Hide Your Love Away'; Donovan's 'To Try for the Sun'. Tellingly, the *Melody Maker* journalist to whom Bowie came out as bisexual, Michael Watts, doesn't seem to have been terribly convinced: 'Mmmmmm,' he responded doubtfully, despite the fact that Bowie had already posed on the cover of 1970's 'The Man Who Sold the World' wearing 'a man's dress' and larded the lyrics of 'The Width of a Circle' and 'Queen Bitch' with intimations of homosexual encounters.

It didn't matter. The interview drew enough attention to make the launch of his next album and its accompanying character, Ziggy Stardust – who debuted a fortnight later in the unpromising environs of the Toby Jug pub in Tolworth – feel like an event. The momentum was electrified further by his appearance on *Top of the Pops* in July 1972, arguably the most celebrated three minutes of music television ever broadcast in the UK. Listen to a bootleg of Bowie live in Aylesbury the preceding year and he sounds nervous and uncertain; performing 'Starman' on *Top of the Pops*, he seems imperious. There's a touch of Lord Kitchener about the moment Bowie points down the camera as he sings the line 'I had to phone someone so I picked on you'. He looks like a man recruiting an army of teenage misfits. No matter how weird and alien you felt, you couldn't be as weird and alien as Bowie and his bandmates looked: 'You're not alone, give me your hands 'cause you're wonderful,' he sang on the accompanying album.

It helped that *Ziggy Stardust* was the right record for the moment. The standard line is that glam rock represented a diversion from the misery of early-70s life, a glittery, space-age dreamworld in which you could hide from rising unemployment, industrial unrest and terrorism. But *The Rise and Fall of Ziggy Stardust and the Spiders from Mars* is riven with dread and horror, mired in what the journalist Francis Wheen later called the 'collective nervous breakdown' of the decade. Even at its most escapist, it underlined what you might be escaping from: 'Tony went to fight in Belfast, Rudi stayed at home to starve,' opened the rock'n'roll fantasy of 'Star'. As time wore on and Bowie became an ever more influential and commanding figure – capable of reactivating others' careers at a stroke – his music became more dense and apocalyptic. By the time of 1974's *Diamond Dogs*, it sounded so decadent and diseased and sensational that it was hard to work out where he could possibly go next.

As it turned out, he was just getting started on a series of musical shifts so brilliantly executed they seemed to drag the rest of pop music along in their wake. If his early-70s albums informed punk – a genre heavily staffed by kids who'd been galvanised by his 1972 *Top of the Pops* appearance – then the 'plastic soul' and electronic experiments of his late-70s albums presaged a vast quantity of what happened after punk. Quite apart from his willingness to reinvent himself so dramatically, it seems a miracle his fans kept up – 'it might as well have been a completely different artist', said one fan who witnessed both the glammy, theatrical early dates and the funk-inspired later shows of the 1974 tour that finally made Bowie a star in America.

What was remarkable was how thoroughly Bowie could impose himself on different genres, how he could take other people's ideas and twist them until they seemed entirely his own. 1975's *Young Americans* was recorded at Sigma Sound, home of the luscious string-laden soul released on Philadelphia International, but it didn't sound like a Philly soul record. Recorded with Brian Eno, 1977's *Low* and *Heroes* were clearly in thrall to the music of German experimentalists Kraftwerk and Neu!, but they didn't sound much like Kraftwerk or Neu!. They sounded like David Bowie, even though they sounded nothing like anything David Bowie had recorded before.

There was a lovely circularity about the release of 1980's *Scary Monsters (And Super Creeps)* and its accompanying No. 1 single, 'Ashes to Ashes', at the height of the New Romantic movement he'd almost single-handedly inspired: public confirmation that Bowie was the most important and influential artist since the Beatles. But the 1980s were to prove a more problematic decade than that suggested. His career in the 1970s had been scarred by bad business deals, and once he was out of a contract with Tony Defries that entitled his former manager to 16 per cent of his earnings until 1982, Bowie seemed determined to make money. He succeeded – 1983's Serious Moonlight tour sold 2.6 million tickets – but, as he later admitted, his artistry suffered. *Let's Dance* – released in 1983, and his biggest hit album with 7 million sales – had its moments. The following year's *Tonight*, however, did not.

By the decade's end, Bowie seemed aware that something had gone awry. He tried to kick-start his muse: by forming a heavy rock band, Tin Machine; by announcing that he would no longer play old material in concert; by reconnecting with collaborators who'd spurred him on in the past, including Brian Eno and Mick Ronson; by dabbling in the voguish dance genre of drum'n'bass. He occasionally made brilliant records – not least 1995's impenetrable but rewarding *Outside* – but nothing matched what he'd achieved in the 1970s. Indeed, by the mid-90s, his real innovations seemed to be happening away from the recording studio: he released a download-only single in 1996, nine years before iTunes. He made himself available to fans on the messageboard of his website, foreshadowing the 360-degree connectivity that artists are expected to maintain in the age of Twitter and Facebook, and which he himself shunned completely in the years before his death.

By the early noughties, he seemed to be settling into the life of a heritage rock star: making well-received albums that knowingly referenced his past; playing classic albums in their entirety; seeming to acknowledge tacitly both the extent of his influence and that his greatest achievements were behind him. It's a pragmatic approach that has served everyone from Paul McCartney to Iggy Pop well, but it sat uneasily with Bowie. His music had never wallowed in nostalgia. It had been iconoclastic and antagonistic towards the past ('my brother's back at home with his Beatles and his Stones ... what a drag', he wrote on 1972's 'All the Young Dudes'): it was about the present, or better still, the future. Although his withdrawal into semi-retirement after 2003's *Reality* was precipitated by emergency surgery on a blocked artery, it made a strange kind of sense.

Most observers assumed it was permanent. Instead, he suddenly reappeared in 2013 with 'Where Are We Now?' The song appeared on the internet on his 66th birthday, without advance promotion or fanfare, its author declining to give interviews: in its own way, as audacious a move as the interview he gave the *Melody Maker* in 1972. The subsequent album, *The Next Day*, wasn't a million miles removed from the albums he'd been making before his sabbatical – solid songwriting, lots of references to his past – but its follow-up was something else entirely. On release, *Blackstar* sounded remarkably like the kind of confident, decisive departure Bowie kept making at the height of his powers: the thrillingly exploratory, jazz-influenced sound had as little to do with the music on *The Next Day* as the soul of *Young Americans* had with the glam albums that preceded it. It sounded like a new beginning, but it was the exact opposite: it was a farewell, a puzzle, filled with clues no one picked up on, that would suddenly be solved by his death. David Bowie went out the way he spent most of his career: unknowable, one step ahead of everyone else.

12 January

Gentrification X: how an academic argument became the people's protest

DAN HANCOX

When Amal had stopped crying, she apologised. 'I wake up so sick, you know? I have to go to study but I feel so sick.' A victim of domestic violence and now a single mother, she was living with her three young children in grimy temporary accommodation in Tooting, south London. She told me that Wandsworth council, which has a legal obligation to house the family, had tried sending them to a rented flat on the outskirts of Newcastle, then suggested West Bromwich. She'd never heard of either place. 'I said to them, "I already told you, I have a job interview in London, I am studying in London, my children are at school in London, my ex-husband visits every week to help with the children."'

West Bromwich, the council insisted, was her last chance. Otherwise she would be declared 'intentionally homeless', and be put out on the street with her young children. 'They said, "Just one option: West Bromwich." If I said no, they wouldn't give me another chance.'

This was one London council's response to the housing crisis – to spend £5m on properties for their poorer families, hundreds of miles away, while across the borough, the Meccano scaffolds rose up for the £15bn development of Nine Elms, where most flats will cost more than £1m.

In the year that I met Amal, 2014, the now notorious Focus E15 Mums were stepping up their campaign to remain in the city where they'd been born. 'Nine billion pounds on the Olympics and they're telling us and our babies we have to go live in Hastings,' lamented 19-year-old Adora Chilaisha during their occupation of East Thames housing association offices, as the hokey cokey played out in the background. 'There's no way I'm going anywhere,' she said. 'My boy Desean is one, and I don't want him to grow up away from his family, from his home. I don't know anyone in Hastings.'

Two years later, both Amal and Adora and their children are still in London after a long and exhausting struggle against the authorities simply to stay where they are. Meanwhile, those same authorities prostrate themselves before luxury property developers, Chinese business conglomerates and buy-to-let rentiers.

Gentrification is an intensely emotive issue, which speaks to fundamental questions of home, identity and community, how those places define us, and how we define them. The displacement of society's poorest members is, of course, not new. You can trace it back centuries, to a time when there was a literal gentry responsible for social cleansing; when the bailiffs were on horseback and 'artisanal' was a descriptor of a pre-industrial social class, rather than voguish hipster branding.

Nonetheless, there is something of the zeitgeist about it. Until a few years ago, only academic geographers and housing campaigners used the term. Now, the subject has entered the mainstream, and the word has become increasingly ubiquitous in cities around the world. But it is not only the debate that has intensified: opposition to gentrification is rapidly becoming less marginal, and more organised.

The tipping point in the UK came last autumn, when members of Class War's so-called Fuck Parade, flaming torches in hand, daubed 'SCUM' on the windows of east London's quintessential hipster cafe, Cereal Killer. The restaurant had already been castigated by Channel 4 News for serving £4 bowls of cereal in a borough where poor families can't afford to feed their children. Although the bearded cereal entrepreneurs were hardly gentrification's true villains, the news was reported around the world as the expression of a rising tide of anger. The issue had leaped into the mainstream.

Last month, the pre-Christmas episode of *This American Life* featured an astonishing segment about a San Francisco dad going to see his six-year-old daughter in her school play, and discovering that the entire show was a fierce polemic against the malign influence of tech companies making the city 'a sterile playground for the rich'. The play culminates in a huge demonstration outside city hall, with the young children holding placards reading 'resistance = love of community' and singing that the city is not for sale.

So why now? The short answer is demand and supply: demand for well-positioned urban space is higher than ever, while the supply of housing options for the urban poor, and the strength and willingness of the state to provide them, is weaker than in decades. In urban policy, we are witnessing the triumph of the market and the capitulation of the state. If an area becomes desirable to those with money – regardless of whether it was hitherto undesirable or dominated by public housing – then sooner or later, the wealthy will get what they want. 'The problem,' said Yolande Barthes from Savills estate agents at a *Guardian* Live debate, 'is the area of London that people want to live in hasn't expanded at the same rate as the population.'

As London's affordable housing crisis deepens – spurred by the collapse of new social housing construction and the sale of hundreds of thousands more social flats under right to buy – the galvanisation of local communities has been astonishing. A customised Google Map, created by Action East End, drops pins on the map for each hyper-local campaign. From 'Save Chrisp Street Market' in the east to 'Save Portobello Road Market' in the west, the campaigns range from demands to protect existing social housing to protests against new luxury-flat developments or against the destruction of community assets such as much-loved markets, nurseries, pubs and small businesses. At the time of writing, there are 53 different campaigns.

One is Reclaim Brixton, which formed in March 2015 in opposition to the rapidly accelerating gentrification of the south London area. Co-founder Cyndi Anafo's mother used to run a Ghanaian grocery in the covered market that has recently been rebranded Brixton Village, a target destination for food tourists and wealthy Londoners. Via social media, Anafo and friends arranged meetings, leading to a carnival-cum-demonstration in Brixton town centre that drew thousands and attracted widespread media attention.

While the transformation of Brixton is visible in the proliferation of more expensive shops, bars and restaurants, Anafo is clear that the cultural and commercial changes are not the main event. 'It all comes down to housing,' she says. 'Being a kind of "accidental activist", and getting to know all the existing housing groups, made me realise the severity of the situation on the ground in Brixton, meeting people who are on eviction lists. People moan about particular types of businesses or shops, or estate agents like Foxtons, but my feeling is that rent stabilisation is something that could help everyone.'

Last June, Berlin made headlines when it began enforcing rent controls for all, limiting landlords to charging new tenants no more than 10 per cent above the local average. The previous year, rents had gone up by more than 9 per cent. 'We don't want a situation like in London or Paris,' said Reiner Wild of the Berlin Tenants' Association. Such strident legislation to protect poorer citizens does not just drop out of the sky, of course. It emerges from a history of equally robust civic campaigning on housing, gentrification and the right to the city.

University of Nottingham geographer Alex Vasudevan, author of a recent book on the subject, *Metropolitan Preoccupations*, says Berlin is in a sense diametrically different from London – it's a very poor city, where wages are one-third lower than its western German neighbours. 'In the wake of unification Berlin has seen waves of gentrification, while remaining very poor by German standards,' says Vasudevan. 'Before the fall of the wall, there were subsidies given to squatters to renovate buildings, and they would be legalised as a result – a kind of compromise. But that programme ended in 2002, and since the wall came down Berlin has become this laboratory of neoliberal urban governance.'

As in London, Vasudevan says, funding for social housing collapsed, and simultaneously thousands of what used to be social housing properties were privatised. 'Berlin tried to become a financial centre. It failed. So then they went with the whole "creative city" agenda, or at least a version of it, connected with touristification and this kind of "Airbnb urbanism". There's a great Airbnb map of Kreuzberg: until recently there was only one property on it that was available on the normal rental market – everything else was Airbnb.'

Grassroots resistance in Berlin has revolved mostly around 'very local geographies', such as saving one particular building, park, housing project, or even fighting the eviction of a much-loved Turkish grocery store. Nonetheless, Vasudevan explains that each victory has galvanised the city as a whole, and made gentrification even more of a common talking point than it is in London. The challenge has been scaling up, making connections, and sharing information between neighbourhoods – and even internationally.

'They've managed to get the rent cap by just being incredibly well organised, and absolutely dogged – and they are also good at talking to each other. You have local working-class Germans, who remained in Kreuzberg, and Turkish migrants collaborating; so everything is written in both German and Turkish, they're all networked.'

They're also talking to the Plataforma de Afectados por la Hipoteca (PAH) in Spain, the grassroots group whose phenomenal success in blocking thousands of evictions propelled its spokeswoman, Ada Colau, to become mayor of Barcelona. Spain's housing crisis has been so destructive that the PAH's use of community self-organisation and support, and direct action to block evictions, has been copied across the world. I've seen *Sí Se Puede*, the PAH documentary, screened to housing activists in London. The international sharing of both tactics and inspiration highlights globalisation's double-edged sword: property developers and investors may be operating simultaneously in Berlin, London and Barcelona, but the people resisting gentrification in these cities are beginning to network themselves, too.

What remains to be seen is whether campaigning against gentrification will grow into any citywide protests. Certainly, the 'G' word has been tapped as the new culprit for a lot of urban tensions emerging from the influx of younger, whiter, wealthier people into city cores. After a 'yarn-bombing' artist, with the support of the hipster Bushwick Flea market, put up a 15-foot crochet homage to Wes Anderson on the exterior wall of his family home in Bushwick without asking for permission, New Yorker Will Giron wrote: 'Gentrification has gotten to the point where every time I see a group of young white millennials in the hood my heart starts racing and a sense of anxiety starts falling over me.'

Inevitably, the rise of anti-gentrification sentiment has provoked a counterattack, either to defend the process or deny it exists. Critics of gentrification romanticise working-class poverty, goes the main line of argument. They hate change, and fetishise urban decrepitude. Don't you want the area to look nice? Don't you want poor people to have better lives? Giles Coren characterised anti-gentrifiers last year as 'middle-aged, middle-class dinosaurs who are determined to keep London shitty'. Why? A mixture, he said, of aesthetics, nostalgia and condescension: 'Snob[s who] like the thought of people less well off than themselves scoffing ... rubbish [food], so they can keep on looking down at them for it.'

Another argument used against anti-gentrification campaigns is that they are fighting a force of nature. There is a tendency for older, more experienced commentators to take a puff on their pipe and remark, 'Oh you hotheads, do you think any of this is new?' This kind of response, while containing some truth, is often used to stifle action. 'This has all happened before' carries with it an unstated corollary: '... and is thus an organic, inevitable and inexorable process.'

It is true that the feared mass exodus of poorer residents from inner London since the Conservatives introduced the bedroom tax and benefit caps has not occurred. Anecdotal evidence from charities and food banks suggests many are staying, paying more rent and just getting poorer. But the number of those forced out is still increasing substantially. Many who are placed in temporary accommodation in outer London are travelling enormous distances to work or school. As the critic Jonathan Meades wrote in 2006: 'Privilege is centripetal. Want is centrifugal ... in the future, deprivation, crime and riots will be comfortably confined to outside the ring road.'

The architects of gentrification are extremely careful not to talk about it. Given that the word was coined by a Marxist, and is most often used by opponents of the property industry, this is good common sense on their part. When in 2014 I was asked to interview a property developer about the issue, I worked through seven or eight before someone at property giant Bouygues Development agreed to speak to me.

Richard Fagg, deputy managing director, was neither hostile nor evasive, but still chose his words carefully. He denied that their building of expensive new blocks of flats would lead to any displacement. Instead, he suggested that poorer areas would benefit from becoming 'blended communities'.

'In the poor parts of London where we've been working in the past, they have been – and I use this term politely – but they have been social enclaves,' Fagg said. 'No one buys homes there, because your money will probably depreciate. But that's changing. So hopefully, the likes of where we're working in Barking, people are taking their hard-earned cash, investing it in a mortgage, buying a property because there you're getting good capital growth over time in the future. Yes, it's starting at a low base. But you're going to get good growth, because the whole area is changing. It's not gentrification. It's just becoming a more balanced community.'

Fagg was not factually wrong about what is happening to the demographic composition of London areas such as Barking, north Peckham or Elephant and Castle. As the 1950s and 1960s tower blocks reach the end of their life – a decline hastened by years of disinvestment and failure to address poverty – one popular development model says they should be demolished and replaced with 'mixed use' developments. Social problems are supposedly reduced if you don't have 'enclaves'.

Simon Elmer from Architects for Social Housing points to Andrew Adonis's report 'City villages: More homes, better communities', which is the basis for Conservative housing plans. The report recommends re-categorising all social housing estates as brownfield land. In greater London, that amounts to 3,500 estates, 360,000 homes and more than one million people. The concern, says Elmer in a paper entitled 'The London Clearances', is that these ageing estates will be demolished and replaced with the same mix of luxury flats and 'affordable' housing that have cropped up in Elephant Park – the new private development being built in place of Elephant and Castle's Heygate Estate – where a two-bedroom flat will set you back £659,000. Last weekend David Cameron gave further shape to this plan when he announced a 'blitz' on poverty, suggesting the demolition of 'sink estates' in favour of more homes for private rent.

The property industry, meanwhile, has become markedly more sophisticated at engineering the change in atmosphere that will draw in young creatives to a 'new' area. (Again, the colonial language is always bubbling just under the surface.) Sometimes this is called place-making, and amounts to extravagant marketing exercises that seek to brand (or rebrand) an area, selling not just bricks and mortar, but an entire aspirational lifestyle. In some cases, place-making has meant going to extraordinary lengths: in poor parts of Harlem, estate agents bought up vacant street-front commercial properties and opened four trendy coffee shops, in an unabashed attempt to instigate gentrification themselves.

The cereal cafes and the hipster baristas are largely a distraction from the real pain of gentrification, which often resides in less glamorous and headline-grabbing developments, such as the granting of planning permission, the cynical redefining of 'affordable housing' to mean 80 per cent of market rate (it used to be more like 50 per cent), the payment of cash to struggling councils by developers wishing to avoid their legal Section 106 requirement to build affordable housing, or the eviction of poor families with no access to the media.

Saying that, the cultural manifestations of gentrification do matter. It is partly about symbolism, about a change in atmosphere that tells poorer residents that, soon, they will no longer belong. Or, in areas with an explosion of attractive bars and clubs, it is about the behaviour of the new arrivals – where that sense of belonging is indirectly seized from poorer families by revellers, students and nightlife tourists who drunkenly smash their beer bottles on the pavement.

A new independent boutique coffee shop may be benign in itself, but does it help usher in a new clientele to the area? Will other hipster businesses follow suit? Will this surge lead to a 'buzz', to press coverage in newspapers aimed at middle classes with the money to buy property? As the hugely telling place-making videos make abundantly clear, for the money men, a proliferation of art galleries, hipsters and small independent businesses is a great sign. Indeed, for the sharper investors, by the time Starbucks arrives, you're already too late.

I think I first noticed gentrification before I'd ever heard the word, when the branch of the discount supermarket Iceland in Balham, where I grew up in the 1980s, was replaced by an organic supermarket called As Nature Intended. In my childhood, this part of London was neither particularly posh nor poor, central but not that central, mixed by race and class and age, the kind of area that thrived precisely because it didn't have a particularly clear identity. A couple of years after the organic supermarket opened, I saw a property advert on the tube that had created annoying alliterative labels out of different London place names. Balham was 'Bankers' Balham'. I have rarely felt so ashamed. But I also know that none of this is important in the scheme of things – that places change, and they should change, and getting a bit sentimental about the fact you can't go home again is part of growing up.

The challenge for the citizens of the 21st century is to decouple this kind of personal sentiment from the generally unheard or ignored stories of displacement and suffering, from the resounding triumph of private profit in civic life over everything else – trampling, in particular, on the idea that shelter and access to the city ought to be fundamental human rights.

As rich and poor people alike continue to flock to cities like London, Berlin and San Francisco, either for work or a better quality of life, the controversies will only intensify and multiply. Apologists can continue to pretend a city is a force of nature, and displacement of poor people from their homes just ripples on the tide, but the rising popular sentiment against social cleansing is not merely a fabrication of leftwing activists, academics or journalists. The anger is real, and the determination to resist is growing. Gentrification is becoming one of the defining issues of our age.

16 January

'We can do it this evening, if you like,' the vet says

TIM DOWLING

My phone rings while I'm putting on my socks. It's a neighbour, calling on my wife's mobile. The old dog, she says, has had some kind of fit at the far end of the park. When I get there, the dog is lying on the grass, foaming at the mouth, with my wife kneeling alongside.

'What are we going to do?' my wife says. She is, I realise, speaking logistically.

'It's fine,' I say. 'I can manage.'

I scoop up the dog and we set off for home, taking a shortcut through the brambles. Once we regain the path, we are waylaid by other dog owners coming the other way, tilting their heads to one side and making sympathetic faces.

'Such a lovely dog,' one woman says, stopping to scratch the dog's ears, her eyes brimming.

Yes, I think, but also heavy.

At the park entrance, I have to pause to rest my back for a minute. The dog, when I set it down, stays upright on its legs. Back home, it walks in circles around the kitchen anticlockwise, disoriented and exhausted.

'Should we go to the vet?' I say.

'If we take that dog to the vet now, they'll put it down,' my wife says. 'Are you ready for that?'

'I don't know,' I say.

'Let's wait two hours, and see what happens,' she says.

After making several dozen circuits of the kitchen, the old dog hauls itself up on to the sofa and falls asleep. Four hours later, it comes to find me because it's hungry.

The next day, the youngest one catches me in front of the TV with tears streaming down my face.

'Are you watching *Marley & Me*?' he asks.

'It was on,' I say. 'It's the worst film I've ever seen.'

'Why are you doing that to yourself?' he says.

'A newspaper columnist who writes about his dog,' I say. 'Who makes a movie out of that?'

A week passes, then another. The dog shows some initial improvement, but the overall arc is gently downhill.

When I take the dogs to the park after Christmas, I get into a lot of end-of-life conversations with the former owners of old dogs. Some are of the opinion that any dog with an appetite has something to live for; others say that, looking back, they left it too long before intervening. Meanwhile, the old dog circles, nose to the ground.

'How old?' says one man, out with his new puppy.

'Sixteen,' I say.

'That is old,' he says.

On the Monday after New Year, my wife comes up to my office.

'I've made an appointment,' she says. '5.15pm.'

'Fine,' I say.

That evening my wife, two of my sons and I crowd into the vet's consulting room. We have a halting conversation about options, about quality of life, about what the future means to a dog. Everyone's eyes are red. The old dog circles.

'How soon are we talking?' I say with a weird quaver in my voice.

'We can do it this evening, if you like,' the vet says.

OK, we say.

We're left to say goodbye while a man with two yapping dachshunds is seen. As soon as he leaves, we're called back in. I'm of two minds as I hold the old dog still: if the act itself is humane, my complicity seems monstrous. It's quiet and quick, but it's not like in *Marley & Me*.

Afterwards, scratching those old ears one last time, I don't feel too bad. It's oddly reassuring to see the dog at peace. Everything seems as it should be, until I realise that in a minute I'm going to have to stand up and walk out, leaving her there on the floor.

19 JANUARY

The secret GP's diary: 'The headache has gone. We both breathe a sigh of relief'

A GENERAL PRACTITIONER

Monday

My morning surgery is a whirlwind of a suspected forearm fracture, gallstones, viral illnesses, an alcoholic wanting help to stop drinking and a young woman with a new diagnosis of diabetes. A severely depressed teenager with telltale bruising on his neck from attempted suicide by hanging leaves me shaking. It is not always possible to stick to the 10 minutes we are allotted for each patient. By the end of the morning I am exhausted, elated, sad and excited, and running half an hour late.

Tuesday

I visit the local nursing home where staff are concerned that one of their residents has developed Parkinson's disease. I observe her slow movements and flat facial features, an eternity away from the vibrant lady smiling back at me in a photo on her bedside table, taken on her 90th birthday only a few months ago. I study her medication chart and identify a potential culprit. I think her medication is causing side-effects resembling Parkinson's.

Wednesday

A heavily pregnant woman walks into the surgery with a bad headache. She describes tunnel vision in one eye and sickness. I examine her: blood pressure is fine, no other signs of pregnancy complications. It's probably a migraine, I say. But what if it's not? I phone the hospital. The obstetric registrar reassures me that it won't be pre-eclampsia, which can be fatal. The medical team won't commit to any advice without blood tests and a scan, so 30 minutes later I am no further forward. I decide to send her home. I ring her a few hours later and the headache has gone. We both breathe a sigh of relief.

Thursday

Two cases stand out today. I visit an elderly gentleman with end-stage lung disease and an aneurysm threatening to burst. He is deteriorating rapidly. I talk to his wife on leaving their house at lunchtime. Does she know who to contact when the time comes? Has she got the support she needs? I get an eerie feeling this discussion is timely.

A young woman complains of a sore throat that started this morning. She booked an emergency appointment because she didn't want to be ill for her weekend away. I tell her I don't have a magic wand that cures all, and viral infections do not know time or convenience, nor do they respond to antibiotics. 'I'm not leaving until you give me antibiotics,' she states aggressively. She leaves empty-handed, shouting abuse down the corridor. It leaves me upset.

Friday

Thirty-eight face-to-face consultations, 11 telephone calls, one home visit, 30 medication queries, 76 prescriptions to sign, two referrals to dictate, 55 lab results and 24 clinic letters to read and file – that's roughly an average day. Today's highlight was a repeat prescription request – a special infant formula for a young baby I saw last week with constant diarrhoea, who cried all the time and was driving her parents sick with worry. I call the mother and ask, 'So you think the milk change helped?' She replies, 'Thank you, doctor. I could kiss you!' (Diagnosis: cow's milk protein allergy; the baby is recovering with appropriate milk.) Occasionally, life as a GP is as simple and wonderful as that.

MOST DIFFICULT DECISION: Not sending the pregnant woman to hospital was a challenging decision. As a GP I need to be able to take risks, manage uncertainty and tolerate not having all the answers.

MOST SATISFYING RESULT: Finding out that a simple change in milk for a sick baby had made life better for all involved.

This piece ran as part of 'This Is the NHS', the story of one of the most complex organisations in the world told through the voices of those on the frontline.

22 JANUARY

Lake Road Kitchen, Ambleside, Cumbria: restaurant review – 'It's all a gal could hope for'

MARINA O'LOUGHLIN

Not enough attention is paid to bread in restaurants. The new Nordic practice of delivering it as its own course with all due ceremony is fine by me. Bread is both signifier and statement of intent, be it Michelin-chirpsing pancetta-studded brioche, or heated-up industrial baguette that might as well have 'avoid' stamped through it like a stick of seaside rock.

The bread at Lake Road Kitchen is perfect: not-sour sourdough (it's to do with keeping the starter out of the fridge, apparently, and checking it as regularly as a mother does a newborn). The crumb is enchantingly springy, the crust all satisfying, well-fired crunch. It comes with 'virgin' butter: newly churned, slightly granular from the buttermilk, a lactic, creamy joy with the shelf life of a mayfly. Spooned thickly on to the bread and sprinkled with rock salt – paradise.

That virgin butter, for spods like me, is a thundering klaxon. Yes, chef/owner James Cross has the almost inevitable Noma background. (One of these days I'm going to be able to write about a Nordic-inclined restaurant without referencing Noma; today ain't that day.) With its Scandi lake-shack look, its locavorism, its fermenting, pickling and foraging, the restaurant wears its credentials as proudly as a toddler with a birthday badge.

Hot on the heels of the bread come meaty little snails, crowned with bitter watercress, leaching sticky, dark sauce and dotted on a plate half-painted with something green; it's miso, made in-house not from soy beans but beans, peas and, I think, barley. This is just fierce: it tastes thrilling, resonant, alive.

We've chosen the five-course tasting menu; there's also an eight-course, and à la carte. It has been devised with real insight into the pace of a meal, the progression of tastes and ingredients. Delicate scallop might have struggled after the snail blockbuster, but this fat number is cooked until caramelised, and comes with fermented apple puree spiked by dill oil and the odd, cucumber-scented leaf of salad burnet: small, exciting jolts of flavour in each mouthful. Then a mighty assault on the taste buds: duck egg in a cradle of charred-edge onion petals, the allium theme continued with surprisingly classic sauce soubise and a powerhouse dressing of ramsons and capers.

By comparison, Scottish red deer with leeks vinaigrette seems almost ascetic – just the meat and veg, a gloss of meat jus, dots of sheeny black winter-truffle puree. But any sense of restraint flees at first bite: sweet, gamey meat; smoky, acerbic vegetable; the sexy reek of fungus.

Finally, not one of those modish, deconstructed desserts that look to have been dropped from a great height, but a perfect sliver of sea-buckthorn tart: fragrant curd and fragile, just-bitter buckwheat crust, with Italian meringue and a slick of the berries' virtually unsweetened puree. An electrifying, pleasurable slap in the chops.

Yes, I've been sniffy about foraging in the past – I've suffered desserts lavishly dandruffed with weeds – but here it's less trend-based box-ticking, more way of life. During my trip to Cumbria, I also go to L'Enclume (two Michelin stars), given that there's a real overlap in ethos. But while L'Enclume's undeniably exquisite food makes me less of a Simon Rogan agnostic, the newcomer's simplicity of approach and purity of delivery makes its stellar colleague's bells and whistles look a bit last century. You sense that nobody here is breathing heavily over the tweezers.

A meal without a single missed beat is as unusual as a non-menopausal Paul Hollywood fan. But this is one of them. Service, produce, timing, execution, beautifully kept cheeses, clever wine list: it's all a gal could hope for.

Look, I'll confess my visit was motivated by the floods, by wanting to do my bit for Cumbria in a way that didn't involve sandbags, fully anticipating a scrabble to be positive without being patronising. Instead, I'm silenced by my own prejudice: this talented team would be stars wherever they landed. That they have chosen to land in a small town given to Gore-Tex retailers and tearooms (one local stalwart offers 'Classic Prawn cocktail topped with Rocker Fellow sauce') is cause to marvel. And to travel: Ambleside also has the excellent Old Stamp House to make a weekend of it. Lake Road Kitchen is that rarest of things, the genuine destination restaurant.

23 JANUARY

Five years on from the Arab Spring: 'I was terribly wrong'

ROBIN YASSIN-KASSAB

Five years ago, the *Guardian* asked me to evaluate the effects of the Tunisian uprising on the rest of the Arab world, and specifically Syria. I recognised the country was 'by no means exempt from the pan-Arab crisis of unemployment, low wages and the stifling of civil society', but nevertheless argued that 'in the short to medium term, it seems highly unlikely that the Syrian regime will face a Tunisia-style challenge'.

That was published on 28 January 2011. On the same day, a Syrian called Hasan Ali Akleh set himself alight in protest against the Assad regime, in imitation of Mohamed Bouazizi's self-immolation in Tunisia the previous month. Akleh's act went largely unremarked, but on 17 February tradesmen in the Hareeqa area of Damascus responded to police brutality by gathering in their thousands to chant that 'the Syrian people won't be humiliated'. This was unprecedented. Soon afterwards, a number of Daraa schoolboys were arrested and tortured for writing anti-regime graffiti. When their relatives protested on 18 March, and at least four were killed, a spiralling cycle of funerals, protests and gunfire was unleashed.

In 2011, I wrote that Syrian president Bashar al-Assad personally was popular, and so he remained until his 30 March speech to the ill-named People's Assembly. Very many had suspended judgment until that moment, expecting an apology for the killings and an announcement of serious reforms. Instead, Assad threatened, indulged in conspiracy theories and, worse, giggled repeatedly.

I underestimated the disastrous effects of Assad's neoliberal/crony-capitalist restructuring during the previous decade. I was soon to be wrong about many other things too. In April 2011 the regime made conciliatory gestures to Islamists and Kurds. At first I thought this showed how hopelessly out of touch it was – the protest movement at that stage was pan-Syrian and non-sectarian. Then I understood its misinterpretation was deliberate. In the following years, the regime would stick to reading the revolution through ethnic and sectarian lenses; and largely due to its own efforts, these eventually came to dominate the field.

'Bashar al-Assad is the leader of the revolution,' one young Damascene told me. 'Every time he kills someone, every time he tortures, he creates 10 more men determined to destroy him.' At first the regime's resort to the 'security solution' made me think I had overestimated its intelligence. Then I realised I had underestimated it. Knowing it couldn't survive a genuine reform process, the regime provoked a civil war.

First, the savage repression of peaceful, non-sectarian activists. Tens of thousands were rounded up, tortured, killed or disappeared. At the same time, jihadists were released from prison. Then, in response to the revolution's inevitable militarisation, the regime applied a scorched earth policy. Soldiers burned crops and killed livestock. Civilian neighbourhoods were blasted by artillery, fighter jets, Scud missiles, barrel bombs and sarin gas. A string of regime-organised sectarian massacres in 2012 irretrievably hardened the mood.

The Syrian people's supposed 'friends' failed to seriously arm the revolution or protect the people from slaughter. With Assad's indirect aid, foreign jihadists stepped into the vacuum. Until July 2014, the regime and Islamic State enjoyed an unstated non-aggression pact. Even today, when Isis is fighting the Free Syrian Army, the regime (and Russia) bombs the Free Army.

An arsonist posing as a fireman, Assad tells the world his survival is indispensable to the defeat of jihadism. Too many commentators agree with him, perhaps because commentary in general has tended to ignore the travails and achievements of the Syrian people in favour of the terrorism story and proxy-war chess. As a result, the general public in the west seems to think Syria's choice is between, as one man recently told me, 'President Assad' and 'the nutters'.

Since 2011, I have learned to distrust the grand pre-existent narratives of both left and right, to fear the dead(ly) ends of identity politics and to focus instead on the human facts. Such as the 300,000 dead and 11 million displaced (the worst refugee crisis since the second world war) – the vast majority at Assad's hand. Plus the more positive realities, like the revolutionary local councils (usually democratically elected) that do their best to keep life going and which should be part of any settlement. Or the revolution in culture that has produced groundbreaking music, poetry, critical radio stations and newspapers.

The people practised democracy where they could. Yet by August 2013, counter-revolution seemed to have won, both regionally and globally. In Egypt, that month's Rabaa massacre began the liquidation of the Muslim Brotherhood, then the repression of everyone else. In Syria, as Barack Obama's chemical 'red line' vanished, Assad killed 1,400 people with chemical weapons. He continued to receive Russian weapons; the Egyptian army received theirs from America.

Iran and then Russia rescued the Assad regime from military collapse, although in a way it has collapsed already, subcontracting its powers to foreign states and local warlords. And it has lost four-fifths of the country. Some of 'liberated Syria' is held by beleaguered democratic nationalists – Arab or Kurdish – and a lot is strangled by transnational jihadists. The crisis increases exponentially. The only thing sure about Russia's invasion is that it is expanding the war in space and time.

So, a five-year accounting: friends and relatives have lost homes, witnessed atrocities, been forced into clandestine migration. Nothing unusual – every Syrian family, from whatever side, has trauma tales to tell. Most are mourning their dead. I will never show Palmyra's temples or Aleppo's Umayyad mosque's minaret to my children – these monuments that survived earthquakes and Mongol invasions are now razed, and the complex social fabric of the country irreparably torn.

Syria has witnessed the depths of human depravity. Syrians have also demonstrated the most inspiring creativity and resilience in the most terrible of circumstances.

Change in Syria and the wider region is running at breakneck pace, and heading in contradictory directions. As to the final results, this time I'll say it is far, far too early to tell.

This article was part of a Saturday Review feature in which 10 writers looked back at the Arab Spring five years on.

8 FEBRUARY

'My life is basically over' – 14 days on a sugar-free diet

SUZANNE MOORE

Day 1: 'I spiralise a courgette'

I wake up alarmed and dehydrated with a deep sense of dread. This is not just a hangover – I have agreed to give up sugar and keep a food diary. All I can think is: 'Thank God I'm starting today, as yesterday's would have been truly embarrassing. Crisps. KFC. Vodka.'

It's not my fault. I am clearly not an adult capable of making informed choices. So I resemble most overweight and overwrought people. My fat and my sluggishness are not a mystery to me: I eat and drink too much and my January was not dry.

Sugar is the source of all evil, so much so that a sugar tax is now being mooted. But how easy is it to give it up? I call a man who is going to help me, and I make a cheese omelette – I'm not sure what I can eat, but assume it is a low-carb diet, so this will be OK.

I arrange to meet personal trainer Nyambe Ikasaya for advice. He has – and I'm getting technical here – a lard-testing machine, and I'm too lardy. Also dehydrated. I explain about the vodka. He points out this is not the result of just one night's drinking. He gives me what he calls 'a nutritional protocol' and what I call 'a diet'.

Things I can't have: bread, booze, carrots – really? – and all fruit. I don't care about the fruit. He asks me what I want to achieve, and I enjoy whingeing on at him.

At home, I begin reading books about detoxing and giving up sugar. You know how they go: three or four days in, most people feel terrible and then suddenly brilliant. This is the detox narrative. Mostly, they seem to be written by 20- or 30-something women who apparently believe they are what they eat and who don't seem to have to feed anyone but themselves. Maybe my terrible attitude is toxic, but few of these books speak to me at all.

Apparently I should have cleaned out my cupboards of all the bad food and freshly stocked them. But I haven't done this because: life. I buy lots of vegetables and order my teenager a take-away while I spiralise a courgette. Someone says on the news that it's Blue Monday. It certainly is.

Day 2: 'Giving up sugar means giving up my social life'

I'm very confused about everything. Am I trying to lose weight or merely go cold turkey (apparently permissible as it is lean protein) on my sugar 'addiction'? Or is this, in fact, the same thing? All advice on giving up sugar ends with a similar testimony: 'Incidentally, I lost two stone, got glowy skin and my entire life was better.' Sugar ages us as well as making us obese, they say. Willpower is no match for the food industry and we are sold more and more detoxes. Also, I am very confused about breakfast. I never normally want it but have been told it's better to have it than not. But not coffee. Have mushrooms got sugar in them? Apparently I can have a few.

It seems to me I am doing a modified Atkins diet. Not so high in fat and dairyish, which is good as that made me feel dreadful. I have to go to a meeting so I take some smoked salmon and avocado with me to avoid an illegal sandwich. It goes to mush in my bag and tastes only of foil.

This diet requires me to plan all my meals. Do I seriously have to read all food labels? A bit of mustard with my steak is surely not the end of the world? I cook separate dinners for myself and my family. Well, why not, as I have cancelled going out. Giving up sugar means giving up my social life, as I am not one of those people who can stand around with a glass of sparkling water pretending this is just what they have been looking forward to ALL DAY.

There are now competing voices in my head: 'This is the most self-indulgent thing you have ever done.' 'Why can you not look after yourself properly and see that cutting down sugar makes sense health-wise?'

Is sugar an actual drug? Does resisting it make you morally superior? I just don't know.

Day 3: 'I don't want to sit there with freak food'

Been sticking with it, but tonight I have to cook dinner for family and friends. I need to be able to eat the same stuff as everyone else as I don't want to sit there with freak food. I get around this by not having rice, but inevitably I go on about it. My eldest, who is fit and health-conscious, says: 'Mum, I have a friend doing this. It's just really boring.' Explaining to other people what I can and cannot eat and how sugar is in everything is, I realise, not a dazzling topic of conversation.

Day 4: 'My mind is full of information about the curing of smoked salmon'

Terrible night's sleep. I feel anxious and have to go to the loo, a lot – I have never drunk so much water. Eat leftover salmon for breakfast. Do some light exercise: stretches, step (horror) and weights. Nyambe teaches me some stretches for my lower back pain while I spaff on about seeds.

These stretches are a revelation and I'm happy to learn them. Really help. But my mind is full of information about food, about sugar and the curing of smoked salmon. My mental space is crammed, because essentially all diets make you preoccupied with food. I want a break.

Day 5: 'It's all so dull that I go to a shop and try on clothes'

Slept 10 hours. Think about how much money I have already spent. Organic salmon. Steak. Sea bass. Parmesan. This is a very expensive 'protocol'. Go to a Turkish cafe and the woman offers me hummus and all sorts, but I order an egg salad. She brings it over and says: 'Darling, I made it nice for you. I put pomegranate in. You know?' I do know, and this is where I differ from some of the low-sugar gurus. I don't decline it or scream, 'Get behind me, you Sugar Satan.' I just think: 'A bit of pomegranate won't kill me.' Likewise, the rogue lentils that have also found their way into the salad.

In any case, it's all so dull that I go to a shop and try on clothes. Another unrewarding thing.

Day 6: 'Meet friends in a pub and drink water. My life is basically over'

What I crave is not sweetness per se, but texture: doughiness, crumbliness, softness. Meet friends in a pub and drink water. My life is basically over.

Days 7–8: 'I Google the carb value of capers. FFS'

Two days have blurred into one. I bump into people and talk about tomatoes. What have I become?

My personal trainer Nyambe is constantly supportive and realistic, which is great. The books are strict and hard to relate to. He is the opposite. I am eating a lot of eggs but have given up proper cooking altogether. Spend a fortune in the health food shop. One day I have stomach cramps. Is it because of the protocol?

My middle daughter says she is going to move back home as her flatshare situation is precarious. 'Don't worry,' she says, 'I can cook for you all the time.' I haven't the heart to tell her this is well-nigh impossible.

One evening I Google the carb value of capers. FFS. Still unsure about demonising a whole food group. Sins, points, values, forbidden foods. Still, I have stopped snacking and opening wine when making dinner.

Day 9: 'Gin is the way forward'

Fall off the wagon in a Spanish restaurant that does the most amazing gin and tonics. Decide that gin is the way forward as I genuinely don't care about food. Just order a courgette flower and more gin. This strikes me as a brilliant way to eat. Not the epiphany of a Gwyneth, and God knows it costs a fortune, but at least it's not quark.

Day 10: 'I have lost a couple of kilos of fat'

Spectacularly hungover and I have to get weighed. I have lost a couple of kilos of fat. So, if weight loss is the measure of all things, then something's working ...

Days 11–12: 'Eat celeriac'

Go to Copenhagen for the weekend. Drink wine and eat celeriac, which they seem to put in everything. But I don't go mad.

Day 13: 'I reach for the prosecco'

Do go mad. We are burgled and fined on the same day in Denmark. (That's another story.) We lose our laptops and all our valuables. Fly home stressed and, once there, I reach for the prosecco. Find some horrible chocolates that no one ate at Christmas. Have an out-of-body experience as I watch myself shovelling them all in.

Day 14: 'I have lost more fat and increased muscle'

Explain all this to Nyambe as I have another check-in. The weekend has not ruined everything, though, as I have lost more fat and increased muscle. This is heartening; there is no way I can live sugar-free full time.

Day 15: 'Life is too short to stuff a lentil'

Reflecting back. Yes, it is possible to give up sugar but, for me, it required too much planning and is very expensive. Carbs are cheap and everywhere. Clever cooks may be able to do this on a budget, but life is too short to stuff a lentil. Such an attitude may well shorten my life. Right now I don't want to be cooking separate meals from my family. It feels antisocial, and I don't want to stop my teenager eating an entire food group. I don't think I have ever spent so much on food just for myself.

Looking back, perhaps I entered ketosis (where the body burns fat) after a few days. This state is described with almost religious reverence by the low-sugar/carb crew. Certainly, I had no ecstatic experience, except a flattening-out of appetite. But while you might stop caring about food, being on a diet still takes up a lot of mental activity.

Do I feel better? Yes, actually, and here is the bit where I'm meant to say it's all down to stopping the sugar poison. But what I feel has made the difference are the stretches and bits of exercises Nyambe has taught me.

For all of my tussling, this experience has acted as a brake on my bad habits. How long will it last? Certainly I realise we all need to eat less sugar, and that even natural sugars (such as honey, agave syrup and fruit) are still, in the end, just sugar.

But no, I can't imagine my life becoming sugar-free – it's too difficult and dull. Instead I will try to cut down, without boring on. Cutting carbs/sugar is helpful at my age, when going through hormonal changes, as it levels your blood sugar spikes. Likewise losing fat and building muscle. Otherwise a lot of this is surely about calorie restriction. The weight loss bit is the sweetener of a no-sugar regime.

For this to be more achievable we need a fundamental rejigging of food pricing, or a different understanding of what percentage of our income we spend on food. Processed food is full of sugar, and it's cheap. Carbs bulk out everything, even ourselves, in the end. Food is everyday and special, fuel and celebration. Our skewed relationship with all of this is unhealthy. Mine is, for sure. But it's not just me, is it? This isn't just about my sad struggle with a courgette flower ... A workable, affordable diet that is not downright antisocial is now the thing I crave most of all.

Spring

Me! Me! Me! Are we living through a narcissism epidemic?

ZOE WILLIAMS

'They unconsciously deny an unstated and intolerably poor self-image through inflation. They turn themselves into glittering figures of immense grandeur surrounded by psychologically impenetrable walls. The goal of this self-deception is to be impervious to greatly feared external criticism and to their own roiling sea of doubts.' This is how Elan Golomb describes narcissistic personality disorder in her seminal book *Trapped in the Mirror*. She goes on to describe the central symptom of the disorder – the narcissist's failure to achieve intimacy with anyone – as the result of them seeing other people like items in a vending machine, using them to service their own needs, never being able to acknowledge that others might have needs of their own, still less guess what they might be. 'Full-bodied narcissistic personality disorder remains a fairly unusual diagnosis,' Pat MacDonald, author of the paper 'Narcissism in the Modern World', tells me. 'Traditionally, it is very difficult to reverse narcissistic personality disorder. It would take a long time and a lot of work.'

What we are talking about when we describe an explosion of modern narcissism is not the disorder but the rise in narcissistic traits. Examples are everywhere. Donald Trump epitomises the lack of empathy, the self-regard and, critically, the radical over-estimation of one's own talents and likability. Katie Hopkins personifies the perverse pride the narcissist takes in not caring for others. ('No,' she wrote in the *Sun* about the refugee crisis.

'I don't care. Show me pictures of coffins, show me bodies floating in water, play violins and show me skinny people looking sad. I still don't care.') Those are the loudest examples, blaring like sirens; there is a general hubbub of narcissism beneath, which is conveniently – for observation purposes, at least – broadcast on social media. Terrible tragedies, such as the attacks on Paris, are appropriated by people thousands of miles away and used as a backdrop to showcase their sensitivity. The death of David Bowie is mediated through its 'relevance' to voluble strangers.

It has become routine for celebrities to broadcast banal information and fill Instagram with the 'moments' that constitute their day, the tacit principle being that, once you are important enough, nothing is mundane. This delusion then spills out to the non-celebrity, and recording mundane events becomes proof of your importance. The dramatic rise in cosmetic surgery is part of the same effect; the celebrity fixates on his or her appearance to meet the demands of fame. Then vanity, being the only truly replicable trait, becomes the thing to emulate. Ordinary people start having treatments that only intense scrutiny would warrant: 2015 saw a 13 per cent increase in procedures in the UK, with the rise in cosmetic dentistry particularly marked, because people don't like their teeth in selfies. The solution – stop taking selfies – is apparently so 2014.

The compelling epidemiological evidence comes from *The Narcissism Epidemic*, in which the American academics Jean Twenge and Keith Campbell found that narcissistic personality traits have increased just as fast as obesity since the 1980s, with the shift in women particularly marked.

Campbell is also the author of a meta-analysis of three cohort studies that found rises in a self-esteem scale that was applied to US middle school, high school and college students in the two decades to 2008. By 2008, a score of 40 (perfect self-esteem) was the modal response of college students, chosen by 18 per cent of participants; 51 per cent scored 35 or over. At this point, the test has to change or the measurement has to stop: the self-esteem of nearly one in five college students could not get any higher.

One study, sponsored by the US National Institutes of Health, looks at lifetime prevalence: you'd expect any trait to become more pronounced over time, since people who have lived longer have more time to develop it. In fact, narcissistic traits afflict almost 10 per cent of people in their 20s, compared with 3 per cent of people in their 60s. Older people have more formed personalities and are less influenced by sociocultural pressures; when they were young, these pressures simply didn't exist.

The best-case scenario is disillusionment

Most of the traits have at their core the belief that one is extra-ordinary. The problem is obvious immediately: most people are not extraordinary.

The problem with narcissistic traits is that they're unreal-istic; the belief in one's own extraordinariness will sooner or later abut the world, and the result will be disillusionment in the best-case scenario or ever-greater fake grandeur in the worst. 'Especially when you're talking about traits and not the disorder, it's correlated in youth with less depression, less anxiety,' says Twenge. 'It wasn't until middle age that narcissists became depressed, because of their failed relationships.'

Your immediate worry, obviously, is that you have narcissistic traits yourself. Experiencing this anxiety means you don't, since true narcissists know it – and freely admit it. Another major figure in the narcissism field, Brad Bushman, has shown that agreeing with the statement 'I am a narcissist' correlates highly with narcissistic traits. They are proud of it: they would say it helps them succeed. They also relate proudly, in surveys, to the idea that they're low on empathy and caring isn't their thing. There's not much guilt in narcissism.

If you're still anxious, or just curious, you should take the narcissistic personality inventory (NPI). 'I made my husband take it on our fourth date,' says Twenge. 'I'm not joking.' And he passed with flying colours? She laughs. 'Yes. You don't have to score zero. A little above or a little below the average, you're fine. It's when people start scoring a 20 or above [out of 40] that there's some potential to worry.' It has seven strands: authority, self-sufficiency – a belief that you've achieved everything on your own – superiority, exhibitionism, exploitativeness, vanity and entitlement. I scored 11, mostly on exhibitionism. Now I'm worried that it's narcissistic even to tell you that. God, it's a swamp.

The damage narcissism brings can be quite amorphous and ill-defined. 'Much of our distress,' MacDonald notes, 'comes from a sense of disconnection. We have a narcissistic society where self-promotion and individuality seem to be essential, yet in our hearts that's not what we want. We want to be part of a community, we want to be supported when we're struggling, we want a sense of belonging. Being extraordinary is not a necessary component to being loved.'

The full-blown disorder is associated with harsh, critical parenting, but a mass rise in narcissistic traits is partly ascribed by MacDonald to lax and indulgent parenting: '[With] parents seeing their children as extensions of themselves – they want to be mates, the boundaries aren't set – the child gets very confused: "You're great, you're terrific." Maybe we're not, maybe we need to know we're just ordinary.'

This has been evinced – again by Bushman, alongside psychologist Eddie Brummelman – in a longitudinal study that found overpraised children showed more narcissistic traits than those who weren't overpraised six months to a year later. It's not so much a new kindness in parenting as a kind of lackadaisical positive assertion, where self-esteem can be conjured out of thin air simply by the people around you saying it's so. To a degree, MacDonald traces the new style of parenting back to new media: 'You see mums relating to the non-human other, the smart-phone, not the baby. The child is not getting a sense of self.' But the impact of social media is more pronounced – currently, at least – in the adult with narcissistic traits. 'There's a good accumulation of evidence that narcissists have more friends on Facebook,' Twenge says. 'We can't make the case definitively that social media causes narcissism, although it does certainly call for a certain type of attention-seeking. If you look at Twitter, and the quest for followers, that has a narcissistic ring to it.'

Our collective narcissism is destroying the planet

There is a context even broader than Twitter: a competitive culture in which asserting one's difference, one's specialness, is the bare minimum for being market-ready. Twenge is cautious: 'The market stuff hasn't been as closely examined. Certainly, individualism tends to be correlated with materialism, and so is narcissism. Economic prosperity does seem to be linked to individualism.' Yet it is hard to conceive of this mantra – you're special, you're worth it, you're different – arriving unrelated to the call of competitiveness. The idea that self-interest is benefi-cial, and that acting in self-interest will create better outcomes for all has been popularised by monetarist politicians since the late 1970s.

In a way, this is easier to see played out in group narcissism. 'Take, for example, members of parliament,' MacDonald says. 'It's not individual greed, is it? It's a culture of "let's grab it when we can". You walk into that culture when you become an MP, when you become a banker. Group narcissism is huge. And the worst thing our collective narcissism is doing is the destruction of the planet. Together, we're wiping out species after species after species, fuelled by consumerism, fuelled by our self-importance. Our narcissism may destroy us in the end.'

There is a natural human tendency to think that things are getting worse

One long-term study of narcissists and those with prominent narcissistic traits found that they do the most significant damage to those around them, over time. Among those with the full-blown disorder, this would relate to their failure to consider another person on an intimate level, seeing them only relation-ally: what can they do for me – or, in the case of their children, how do they reflect on me, or how have they disappointed me in what they've failed to reflect? Don't forget that, in the original myth, Narcissus is punished with a terminal fascination with his own reflection in revenge for his treatment of Echo, whom he despises for loving him. Narcissism is properly understood not as self-love, but emotionally monogamous self-love. Those with narcissistic traits may be more capable of considering others as discrete people, and it is this tendency to overreact to criticism that causes the damage over time.

So, let's say you have taken the NPI, haven't lied (because narcissists don't – at least, not about their own narcissism) and have scored relatively highly, and that this correlates with your observation that your high expectations of yourself are often not met, your relationships fail, and people who like you initially like you less four months later. All is not lost. MacDonald picks out five principles of self-improvement: gratitude, modesty, compassion (for self and others), mindfulness and community. Some of these are obvious – modesty as an antidote to self-love – and some have a practical application.

'If, for example, you write down at the end of the day three things you're grateful for, that can go a long way to reverse your narcissism,' he says. (This is huge in psycho-self-help at the moment: stimulating grateful thoughts also allays guilt. Hebb's law – neurones that fire together, wire together – suggests that your brain will always choose the more familiar pathway.) As for compassion: 'If we can remain more humble, we become kinder, too,' he says, but this is a two-way street. 'We need to have compassion for ourselves, as well. Compassion for others will follow.'

The interesting thing, as their prevalence increases, will be seeing whether society rebels against or accommodates narcissistic traits. 'There's a natural human tendency to think that things are getting worse, or at least they're not getting better, and you have to fight that tendency,' says Twenge. 'But you also have to fight the tendency to stick your head in the sand and say, "The kids are great and there's nothing wrong."'

3 MARCH

Why Botticelli's *Venus* is still fashion's favourite muse

JESS CARTNER-MORLEY

How long is a good innings as an iconic beauty, these days? Thirty years, like Cindy Crawford? Sixty-five, like Sophia Loren?

How about 530 years? That's how long Botticelli's women have been adored, desired and emulated. They have been muses to Bob Dylan and James Bond, Andy Warhol and Lady Gaga. Botticelli's Venus, rising from her seashell, is a poster girl not just for the Uffizi, but in teenage bedrooms all over the world. (She even appears on an Italian 10 cent euro coin.) Flora from the same painting inspired Elsa Schiaparelli in 1938, while the figure of Flora as seen in Botticelli's *Primavera* was brought to life on the Valentino catwalk last year.

The enduring charm of Botticelli's women – and how a painter who languished in obscurity for two centuries after his death came to set the bar for 20th-century beauty – is the subject of Botticelli Reimagined, which opens at the V&A in London on 5 March. The exhibition brings together 50 Botticelli works with 100 related works by artists who have interpreted him, from Dante Gabriel Rossetti and William Morris to René Magritte and Cindy Sherman. Martin Roth, director of the museum, hopes it will explain how and why Botticelli's legacy has 'suffused our collective visual memory'.

The Birth of Venus is 'an endlessly quotable metaphor for youth and beauty', Roth says. The original work is not included in the exhibition, being too delicate to be moved from Florence, but it dominates nonetheless. Two Andy Warhol silkscreens from 1984 permeate Venus with acid colours, turning a familiar image from a venerable museum work into a lurid billboard image. David LaChapelle's 2009 photograph of a heavily made-up, deeply tanned, bottle-blond model recreating the Venus pose makes explicit reference to the idea of Botticelli as setting an aspirational standard for female beauty.

But the extent to which we have internalised the image as a template is most striking in an accidental homage. In two photographs from Rineke Dijkstra's monumentally scaled but naturalistically posed Beach Portraits series, young girls pose on the shoreline unknowingly mirroring the posture and body language of Venus. One of the sitters, 14-year-old Erin Kinney, 'was trying so hard to answer to a specific image – trying to look like perfection,' Dijkstra told the *New York Times*. 'The girls were asked to pose on a beach, and they unconsciously assumed that pose,' says Ana Debenedetti, curator of the V&A's exhibition. 'Botticelli is so embedded in our visual culture that we know these images without even knowing that we know, in a way.'

There is a dancing quality to the way Botticelli's women stand, their weight off centre, which is seen today in the one-leg-forward pose that actresses adopt on the red carpet. (The standard red carpet pose is designed to make one look thinner. The Renaissance concept of *leggiadria* described figures drawn so as to appear light and graceful. Plus ça change.) There is a stillness, too – 'They are erotic objects, but peaceful,' Debenedetti says – which is recognisable in the tranquil half-smile that is today's standard celebrity look. They are blond, slender, with long hair. They illustrate an ideal woman of the 15th century, who turns out to look strikingly similar to our contemporary ideal. The exhibition includes footage of Ursula Andress emerging from the sea, 'a hint to the idea of love and beauty. She corresponds to a very classic western ideal of beauty: her colouring, her curves. She is erotic, but also has a very natural, earth mother appeal. You feel like she would have beautiful babies!' Debenedetti says.

There is something a little surreal about Botticelli's art, a dreamlike quality in which the boundary is blurred between human beings, in all their flesh and blood and complications, and nature in its innocent perfection. Elsa Schiaparelli tapped into this, transposing flowers from *Primavera* into embroidery in three dimensions, appearing to grow out of the fabric of an evening gown. The same tension between the ethereal and the hyperreal is there in Valentino's pre-fall 2015 collection, which features exquisite dresses that Flora herself could have worn.

Dolce & Gabbana used the image of Venus fractured and patchworked on to a dress that first appeared on the catwalk in

1993. Twenty years later, Lady Gaga wore the dress during her promotional tour for her album *Artpop*. 'What Dolce & Gabbana do is highlight the reproducibility of Botticelli,' Debenedetti says. 'They turn it into a fashion shoot.' Botticelli: the world's first fashion brand?

8 MARCH

Generation Y, Curling or Maybe: what the world calls millennials

KATE LYONS

They are Generation Curling in Sweden, Generation Serious in Norway, and Generation John Paul II in Poland. The Chinese call them *ken lao zu*, or 'the generation that eats the old', and the Japanese have a term scolding them for not giving undivided attention to anything: *nagara-zoku*, 'the people who are always doing two things at once'.

More prosaically, in the US they are called millennials and, in the UK and Australia, Generation Y. Around the world there is no shortage of descriptive epithets for those born between 1980 and the mid-1990s.

In many cases, the names reveal something of the specific problems they face, whether that is debt, lack of housing, unemployment, or something less tangible such as indecision.

For some, it is all of the above. In Spain, they call young adults *Generación Ni-Ni*, a demographic driven by national economic ruin into a limbo of neither work nor study – *ni trabaja, ni estudia*. The term even inspired a television show of the same name in the country where young people have suffered most in the recent financial crisis.

Spain's youth unemployment rate hit a peak of nearly 56 per cent in 2013 and has only recovered slightly. The number of Spaniards aged between 18 and 29 who experienced serious deprivation – meaning they couldn't afford to heat their home and buy meat or fish at least every second day – increased by 20 percentage points, from 8 per cent in 2007 to 28 per cent in 2011, the sharpest rise in the EU.

This group also goes by the name *mileuristas* because the average monthly salary for young people has dropped to €1,000 (*mil euros*) though, as Spanish millennial David Gonzalvo says, even this is optimistic: 'Before the 2008 crisis, it [€1,000] was considered a low salary, but now with €600 and €700 per month salaries, it is sadly considered a blessing, as is having a full-time job.'

It could be worse. In Greece they are the Generation of 500 euros, named after a scheme in which the Greek government employed young graduates on a salary of €500 (£395) a month.

In Germany, they have been called Generation Maybe – well educated, highly connected, multilingual, globally minded, with myriad opportunities, but overwhelmed by the possibilities, so they commit to nothing.

Thirty-year-old Sara Munder epitomises this. She had a stable job as a financial controller in Frankfurt, but felt trapped by the nine-to-five lifestyle and quit to move to Latin America. After holidays and volunteering in Brazil and Ecuador, she missed the stability and higher wages of Germany and returned home. Back in her old job, she immediately yearned for the laid-back lifestyle of South America. She is considering quitting again to run a hostel by the sea.

'We are sleepwalking through a networked world of opportunity and feel insecure in the face of the plethora of options ... We no longer know what to do,' wrote journalist Oliver Jeges, who coined the phrase Generation Maybe. 'We want to be there and not miss anything anywhere.'

It is perhaps these troubles, and a concern about the future, that lead millennials to be, by and large, a serious generation, less prone to the wild optimism or hedonism of their forebears. Norwegian millennials were christened *Generasjon Alvor*, or Generation Serious, in 2011.

After all, this is a group of people whose defining geopolitical moment was 9/11 and the 'war on terror' that followed. Terrorism is to them what the threat of nuclear war was to boomers and older members of Gen X. They have grown up with images of mass murder – in universities, nightclubs, army barracks, trains, buses, museums, cafes, beaches and city streets – and therefore have everywhere to fear. In some senses, this is Generation Terror.

'It's like our generation's JFK moment,' says Londoner Jac Husebo, 30, an actor and writer, of the day the twin towers fell. But terrorism soon became part of life. On 7/7, Husebo was 21. 'I was in a pizzeria in Budapest and the waiter turned around and said "London's been attacked", and we weren't surprised. It was the next place.'

Husebo says the terrorism has led to racism and fear – 'you do catch yourself on the tube, wondering about people' – but he acknowledges such fear is not unique to his generation. 'Now it's the Islamists, before that it was the Soviets.'

Few of the nicknames for Gen Y are sympathetic. In Sweden, this is the Curling Generation, named after the sport in which team-mates furiously sweep the ice in front of their stone to make sure its journey is smooth and unhindered. The parents of millennials have cleared any obstacles from their children's paths, allege their critics, and have refused to set boundaries, even going with them to job interviews.

'We pad their world in every possible way, we pamper them from the beginning,' says Swedish psychiatrist Dr David Eberhard, who argues this parental sweeping has led to a generation of mollycoddled people who are psychologically knocked out by relatively minor blows such as the death of a dog or a boss telling them off.

Yosuke Nishimura, a 27-year-old university graduate, is typical of Japan's *yutori sedai*, or relaxed generation. He has worked for a few different companies since university. He does not have a girlfriend and has never thought about settling down. And while the postwar generation were devout savers, Nishimura says his bank balance returns to close to zero every month.

'It's not about being selfish – I just belong to a generation that does things differently,' he says. 'The baby-boomer generation had everything mapped out for them, but, for good or bad, we are more interested in enjoying our moment of freedom.' Freedom only goes so far, however. Nishimura is a pseudonym. He does not want to be identified.

In China, they are a generation profoundly shaped by the politics of their country. The one-child policy, introduced in 1979, the year before the first millennials were born, means China's is a millennial generation that is unbalanced – with an estimated 33 million more men than women. These Chinese millennials without siblings are the 'little emperors' or *ken lao zu*, the generation that eats the old, because they are happy to live off their parents. One survey found that 70 per cent of young people in China thought nothing of asking their parents to give them money to buy a house.

For Poland's millennials, the death in 2005 of John Paul II, their home-grown pope, unified and defined them, the sociologist Paweł Śpiewak surmised, leading to them becoming known as *Pokolenie JPII* – Generation John Paul II.

Whether Generation JPII was a real phenomenon or just a media invention is up for debate. One Polish reader told the *Guardian*: 'It didn't really catch on. Maybe Poland is predominantly Catholic and the reaction to the pope's death was huge, but it wasn't a defining moment really. Important but not defining.'

Young adults in Britain have been hit on two fronts – by vertiginously steep house prices and by employment difficulties. In 1991, 67 per cent of 25- to 34-year-olds were homeowners in England; by 2011–12, this was 43 per cent. Those who cannot afford to buy must rent, with tenants spending an average of 47 per cent of their net income on rent – 72 per cent for those renting in London.

On top of this, young people in the UK are nearly three times more likely to be unemployed than those in other age groups, an inequality mirrored in most other countries. In all, 14.4 per cent of 16- to 24-year-olds are not in full-time education or employment, compared with 5.7 per cent of the total working population, the largest gap in more than 20 years.

In Australia, where the freestanding home on the quarter-acre block has long represented the Great Australian Dream, young people have found themselves locked out of the housing market. It took about four times the median household income to buy a home in Sydney in 1975; it now takes 12 times. Alexander Allen, 25, was only able to buy a property with a $50,000 (£26,000) loan from his parents. He had to work at three jobs to pay his mortgage.

In the US, the millennial generation is one defined by debt. More than 40 million people have student-loan debt, at an average of $29,000 (£21,000) each. The cost of education has skyrocketed, increasing 1,120 per cent from 1978 to 2010 and, in a perilous job market, they are finding it difficult to pay off their debts.

'[Millennials are] not only taking on debt at a higher rate, they're paying it off at a slower rate,' says Lucia Dunn, an economics professor at Ohio State University. 'These poor kids come out of college with the equivalent of a mortgage already.'

19 MARCH

It's great that a trans woman is celebrated. But is Caitlyn Jenner the best we can do?

HADLEY FREEMAN

It's been almost a year since Caitlyn Jenner came out as a trans woman in a TV interview, so let's keep up with this former Kardashian clan member and see how things have been going since. Just last week it was announced that she is to be the model for H&M Sport, the store's athletic-wear line. As is the modern way, Jenner announced the news on her Instagram account, praising the campaign as 'amazing and inspiring'. This follows an announcement last month that Jenner has partnered up with MAC cosmetics, for a charity lipstick to raise money for trans communities.

'Well done, everyone!' announced one website. Truly, the emoji of hands clapping could be the symbol for all coverage pertaining to Jenner. Sure, it's terrific to see a 60-something woman get modelling gigs. It's wonderful that a trans woman is being lauded as a beauty icon. It's flat-out fantastic that a fashion brand is making such an effort to support trans people. But. BUT.

The steep-curve rise of trans rights has been thrilling to witness as an outsider and, I can only imagine, extremely heartening to those in the trans community, who have for so long suffered outright abuse. Jenner has become the cipher through which media outlets prove how modern they are, lauding everything she does as 'inspirational', 'amazing', and all the other buzzwords of the BuzzFeed generation.

It could be argued that this rush to hyperbole is the due corrective for centuries of transphobia, which still very much exists. Yet not a single other trans person on this planet has enjoyed the privilege and public goodwill that Jenner has received since she came out. Moreover, true equality comes from being treated not as a special case, but as an equal. While the biggest issue for most trans people remains achieving acceptance, Jenner has long since sailed over that hurdle. So let's treat her as the equal she has said she desires to be.

Last February, Jenner was driving her SUV in Malibu and collided with two cars, killing 69-year-old Kim Howe. You probably haven't heard much about this sad mess, because it doesn't fit in with the media's nervy narrative about inspirational Caitlyn. If you have, it was likely through the joke Ricky Gervais cracked at the Golden Globes about Jenner 'not doing a lot for women drivers'. He was widely criticised for that, because apparently making a joke is worse than being involved in the death of a woman. After the accident Jenner said she was 'praying' for Howe's family. Of more comfort to them might have been the financial settlement she agreed to pay Howe's stepchildren.

Although investigators determined that Jenner had been travelling at an unsafe speed for the road conditions, prosecutors ultimately declined to bring charges against her, deciding there was not enough evidence to secure a conviction. But I'm curious to know how many other women who had been in an accident that left another woman dead are, nine months later, named one of *Glamour* magazine's Women Of The Year, as Jenner was.

But accidents happen. So let's get to know Jenner as a person, as opposed to deifying her as a plaster saint. On her reality TV show last week, *I Am Cait*, Jenner, a lifelong Republican, claimed that Donald Trump 'would be very good for women's rights'. This would be the Trump who is anti-abortion, calls women 'fat pigs', describes breastfeeding as 'disgusting', opposes marriage equality and once mocked a trans beauty contestant on TV. As a brand strongly associated with gay rights and equality, I'd love to know how many other Trump fans MAC hires for its advertisements.

No one should demand perfection of anyone. But one of the best things about the breathtakingly brilliant TV series *Transparent* was how the trans character, Maura, was depicted with all her human flaws: her prejudices, privileges and pettiness. By contrast, Jenner is treated like a cute trans pet, with the media patting her on the head and not listening to a word she's saying. They can't even hear her words over the applause they're giving themselves for being so open-minded. There are millions of trans people out there who don't endorse politicians actively oppressive to women, gay and trans people. But, dazzled by Jenner's proximity to the Kardashians, the broadcasters and the big brands keep staring at her above all, without actually seeing her.

'I am not a spokesperson for [the trans] community. I am not. Everybody in the media puts me in that position ... but I am only a spokesperson for me,' Jenner has said, with commendable self-awareness. It's not often I can say that anyone could learn from a Kardashian, but some people could take a lesson here.

19 March

Yes He Tried: the legacy of Barack Obama

GARY YOUNGE

When Ohio fell on election night 2008, President's Lounge, a bar on the overwhelmingly black south side of Chicago, erupted in jubilation. Corks popped, strangers hugged, police patrolling the streets yelled the freshly elected president's name from their loudhailers: 'Obama!'

As I scanned the faces at the bar, one woman looked at me, beaming, raised her margarita and shouted, 'My man's in Afghanistan. He's coming home!' Barack Obama had never said anything about ending the war in Afghanistan. Indeed, he had pledged to ramp up the US military effort there. But she had not misunderstood him; she had simply projected her hopes on to him and mistaken them for fact.

Obama had that kind of effect on people, back then. Often they weren't listening too closely to what he was saying, because they loved the way he was saying it. Measured, eloquent, informed; here was a politician who used full sentences with verbs. He was not just standing to be the successor to George W Bush. He was the anti-Bush.

And they loved the way Obama looked when he said it: tall, handsome, black – an understated, stylish presence from an under-represented, marginalised demographic. The notion that this man might lead the country, just three years after Hurricane Katrina, left many staring in awe when they might have been listening with intent. Details be damned: this man could be president.

Earlier on election day, I saw a grown man cry as he came out of the polling station. 'We've had attempts at black presidents before,' Howard Davis, an African American, told me, 'but they've never got this far. Deep in my heart, it's an emotional thing. I'm really excited about it.' His voice cracked, and he excused himself to dry his eyes.

I first heard about Barack Obama from my late mother-in-law, Janet Mack, who lived in Chicago and joined his campaign for the Senate in 2003. That was the year I moved to the US as a correspondent for the *Guardian*, first in New York and later in Chicago, before moving back to London last August.

Janet had seen Obama on local television a few times and thought he spoke a lot of sense. She attended the demonstration where he spoke, as a state senator, against the invasion of Iraq. When he first ran, she feared he would be assassinated, but became accustomed to him as a prime-time fixture. 'It's like living in California and the earthquakes,' she told me. 'You just can't worry about them all the time.'

We went to the south side of Chicago together to hear Obama's nomination speech in 2008, watching with a couple of hundred others on a big screen at the Regal Theater. People wept and punched the air. On the way home, Janet, a black woman raised in the Jim Crow south, punched my arm and laughed. Usually, she chatted a lot. But for most of the 30-minute ride she kept saying, to nobody in particular, 'I just can't believe it.'

In many ways Obama's campaign for the presidency was unremarkable. He had voted with Hillary Clinton in the Senate 90 per cent of the time. He stood on a Centrist Democratic platform, promising healthcare reform and moderate wealth redistribution – effectively the same programme that mainstream Democrats had stood on for a generation. But his rise was meteoric. His story was so compelling, his rhetoric so soaring, his base so passionate

– and his victory, when it came, so improbable – that reality was always going to be a buzzkill.

Obama had long been aware that voters saw what they wanted in him. 'I serve as a blank screen on which people of vastly different political stripes project their own views,' he wrote in *The Audacity of Hope* in 2006. 'As such, I am bound to disappoint some, if not all, of them.' But he was hardly blameless. He claimed to stand in the tradition of the suffragettes, the civil rights movement and the union organisers, evoking their speeches and positioning himself as a transformational figure. On the final primary night in June 2008, he literally promised the Earth to a crowd in St Paul, Minnesota: 'We will be able to look back and tell our children that this was the moment ... when the rise of the oceans began to slow and our planet began to heal.'

There was a lot of healing to do. When Obama came to power, the US had lost one war in the Gulf and was losing another in Afghanistan. In a poll of 19 countries, two-thirds had a negative view of America. Americans didn't have a much better view of themselves. The banking crisis had just sent the economy into freefall. Poverty was rising, share prices were nosediving, and just 13 per cent of the population thought the country was moving in the right direction.

This was the America Obama inherited when he strolled, victorious, on to the stage in Chicago's Grant Park with his family on election night in 2008 – a vision in black before a nation still in shock.

In Marshalltown, Iowa (population 27,800), on 26 January this year, a crowd waits in sub-zero temperatures for several hours to see Donald Trump while the hawkers enjoy a brisk trade. There are 'Make America Great Again' hats (made in China), badges stating 'Bomb The Shit Out Of Isis' and 'Hillary For Prison 2016'.

One man is carrying a poster with a picture of Hitler holding up a healthcare bill and saying, 'You've gone too far, Obama!' Across the road are protesters, most of them Hispanic. Over the previous six months, Trump has branded Mexicans rapists, promised to exclude all Muslims from the country, and insulted the Chinese, disabled people, women and Jews.

Inside, Sheriff Joe Arpaio from Arizona, an anti-immigrant zealot who still insists that Obama's birth certificate is a forgery, introduces Trump, who emerges from behind a curtain as though walking out on to a game show: 'Heeeeere's Donald!' As the crowd grows into the hundreds, they open up the bleachers on the upper level for the overflow. For the most part, Trump blathers like a drunk uncle at a barbecue. He calls Glenn Beck, who has endorsed his principal rival Ted Cruz, a 'nut job'. He brags about his wall to keep out the Mexicans. 'It's going to be a big wall,' he says. 'A big beautiful wall. You're gonna love this wall.' Afterwards, Brian Stevens, 37, tells me he thought Trump was impressive: 'I don't agree with everything he says. But I think he'll make a difference – he has to. Someone's got to stand up for America. We need him.'

Obama rocketed to national fame on the promise that there should be no more days like these. At the 2004 Democratic party convention, he described the nation's partisan divide as though it had been imposed from the outside, by cynical operatives and a simplistic media: 'spin masters and negative ad peddlers who embrace the politics of anything goes'. Back then, just over a year into the Iraq war, it looked as if America couldn't get much more polarised. But it did.

When Obama stood in 2008, one of the central pledges of his campaign was that he would rise above the fray in a spirit of bipartisan cooperation. That's not how it worked out. In 2010, the then Senate minority leader, Mitch McConnell, said the Republican party's 'top political priority over the next two years should be to deny President Obama a second term'. Republican congressmen, who refused to cooperate even with their own leadership, repeatedly threatened to bring the US to the brink of default, or simply shut the government down – unless Obama backed down from promises he'd made or laws that had already been passed. A few years ago, as the Republican-led House of Representatives engineered a brief government shutdown, congressman Marlin Stutzman illustrated how petulant Obama's opponents had become: 'We have to get something out of this,' he said. 'And I don't know what that even is.'

Regardless of what he said or did, President Obama was always going to be a lightning rod for political polarisation. Some argued that this was because the right could not come to terms with a black president, and there's probably something to that. At times, when the Republicans refused to return his calls or refer to him as president, or when someone shouted 'Liar!' during a presidential address, they appeared to refuse to recognise Obama as the legitimate holder of office.

But the issues go way beyond race: in all sorts of ways, he embodies the anxieties of a section of white America. He is the son of a Kenyan immigrant at a moment when America is struggling to come to terms with the impact of immigration and foreign trade. He is the son of a non-observant Muslim, and came to power as the country was losing wars in predominantly Muslim lands. He is the product of a mixed-race relationship at a time when one of the fastest-growing racial groups in the nation is those who identify as 'more than one race'. He is a non-white president who ends his term at a time when the majority of children aged five and under in America are not white.

Demographically and geopolitically, being a white American no longer means what it used to; Obama became a proxy for those who could not accept that decline, and who understood his very presence as both a threat and a humiliation. Trump, in many ways, is their response.

In his final state of the union address, in January, Obama conceded that he had not come close to achieving his dream of a more consensual political culture. 'It's one of the few regrets of my presidency,' he said, 'that the rancour and suspicion between the parties has gotten worse instead of better. I have no doubt a president with the gifts of Lincoln or Roosevelt might have better bridged the divide, and I guarantee I'll keep trying to be better so long as I hold this office.' With nine months left in an election year, it is difficult to see what would break the logjam.

By the end of Obama's first term in 2012, there was a general sense that things hadn't moved fast enough, that he had caved in to his opponents too easily. It was as though he negotiated with himself before reaching across the aisle, only to have his hand slapped away in disdain anyway. Having been elected on a mantle of hope, he seemed both aloof and adrift. Having moved people with his rhetoric, he was now failing to connect.

At a televised town hall meeting two years after his election, Obama was confronted by Velma Hart, an African American mother of two, who articulated the disappointments of many. 'I'm exhausted,' she told him. 'I'm exhausted of defending you, defending your administration, defending the mantle of change that I voted for, and deeply disappointed with where we are right now.'

A few months later, Hart lost her job as chief financial officer for a veterans' organisation. By the time I met her, in the summer of 2011, she was re-employed but still far from impressed. 'Here's the thing,' she told me. 'I didn't engage my president to hug and kiss me. But what I did think I'd be able to appreciate is the change he was talking about during the campaign. I want leadership and decisiveness and action that helps this country get better. That's what I want, because that benefits me, that benefits my circle and that benefits my children.'

'Do you think he's decisive?' I asked.

'Ummm, sometimes ...' she said. Like many, Hart wanted to support Obama, but felt he wasn't making it easy. 'Not always, no,' she added, after a pause.

The notion that strong individuals can bend the world to their will is compelling. It is also deeply flawed. 'That's what we're taught to believe from an early age,' Susan Aylward, who used to work in an Ohio food co-op, told me. 'We're taught that one man should be able to fix everything. Abe Lincoln, George Washington, Ronald Reagan – history's told as though it were all down to them. The world is way too complex for that.'

I first met Susan in 2004, coming out of the opening night of Michael Moore's *Fahrenheit 9/11* in Akron. Back then, she said she intended voting for John Kerry because he wasn't Bush, but she didn't love him. Four years later, we had breakfast just a week before Obama was elected and she could barely contain her excitement. She made her two-year-old granddaughter, Sasha, who's mixed race, sit up with her on election night. 'We wanted her to be able to say she saw it that day, even if she didn't really know what she was seeing.'

But when we caught up in 2012, Susan was processing her disappointment. 'It's not going to change my vote,' she said. 'I just wish he could have been better. I don't even know how, exactly. If you're going to be president, then I guess you obviously want to be in the history books. So what does he want to be in the history books for? I don't quite know the answer to that yet.'

When it comes to Obama, people have to own their disappointment. That doesn't mean it's not valid, just that it often says as much about them as it does about him. No individual can solve America's problems. Most radical change in the US, like elsewhere, comes from huge social movements from below. Poor people cannot simply elect a better life for themselves and expect that vested interests won't resist them at every turn: that's not how western democracy works.

I supported Obama against Hillary Clinton because he had opposed the war in Iraq at a time when that could have damaged his political career; she had supported it in order to sustain her own. I thought he was the most progressive candidate that could be elected, and while even his agenda was inadequate for the needs of the people I most care about – the poor and the marginalised – it could still make a difference. I got my disappointment in early, to avoid the rush.

I appreciated the racially symbolic importance of Obama's victory, and celebrated it. But I didn't fetishise it, because I never expected much that was substantial to emerge from it. He leveraged his racial identity for electoral gain, without promising much in return. As a candidate, race was central to his meaning, but absent from his message. When I read the transcript of the nomination speech I saw with my mother-in-law on the south side that night in 2008, I realised he had quoted Martin Luther King but declined to mention him by name, referring to him instead as the 'old preacher'. 'If a black candidate can't quote Martin Luther King by name,' I thought, 'who can they quote?' I jokingly referred to him as the 'incognegro'.

Obama never promised radical change and, given the institutions in which he was embedded, he was never going to be in a position to deliver it. You don't get to become president of the United States without raising millions from very wealthy people and corporations (or being a billionaire yourself), who will turn against you if you don't serve their interests. Congress, with which Obama spars, is similarly corrupted by money. Seats in the House of Representatives are openly and brazenly gerrymandered.

This excuses Obama nothing. On any number of fronts, particularly the economy, the banks and civil liberties, he could have done more, or better. He recognised this himself, and in 2011, shortly before his second election, produced a list of issues he felt he'd been holding back on: immigration reform, poverty, the Middle East, Guantanamo Bay and gay marriage.

By 2011, even those closest to Obama could see he was losing not only his base but his raison d'etre as an agent of change. 'You were seen as someone who would walk through the wall for the middle class,' his senior adviser David Axelrod told him that year. 'We need to get back to that.'

Back then, Obama's prospects looked slim. His campaign second time around was a far cry from the euphoria of the first. The president's argument boiled down to: 'Things were terrible when I came to power, are much better than they would have been were I not in power, and will get worse if I am removed from power.' What started as 'yes we can' had curdled into 'could be worse'.

But Obama has always been lucky in his enemies. The Republican party effectively undermined and humiliated their nominee, Mitt Romney, who then proved a terrible candidate. In 2012, I went to vote with Howard Davis, the man I'd met weeping at a Chicago polling station back in 2008, to vote Obama again. There were no tears this time. In the words of Sade, it's never as good as the first time.

As Obama's tenure ends, we are no longer confined to discussing what it means that he is president; we can now talk in definite terms about what he did. Everybody has their list. None is definitive. He withdrew US soldiers from Iraq (only to resume bombing later), relaxed relations with Cuba, executed Osama bin Laden, reached a nuclear deal with Iran and vastly improved America's standing in the world. Twenty million uninsured adults now have health insurance because of Obamacare. Unemployment was 7.8 per cent and rising when he came to power; today, it is 4.9 per cent and falling. He indefinitely deferred the deportation of the parents of children who are either US citizens or legal residents, and expanded that protection to children who entered the country illegally with their parents (the Dream Act). Wind and solar power are set to triple; the automobile industry was rescued. He eventually spoke out forcefully for gun control. He appointed two women to the Supreme Court, Elena Kagan and Sonia Sotomayor, the first Latina.

There are, of course, other facts to contend with. Obama escalated fighting in Afghanistan and the troops are still there; deported more people than any president in US history; used the 1917 Espionage Act to prosecute more than twice as many whistleblowers as all previous presidents combined; oversaw a 700 per cent increase in drone strikes in Pakistan (not to mention Yemen, Somalia and elsewhere), resulting in between 1,900 and 3,000 deaths, including more than 100 civilians. He executed US citizens without trial; saw wealth inequality and income inequality grow as corporate profits rocketed; led his party to some of the heaviest midterm defeats in history. In Syria, he drew a red line in the sand and then claimed he hadn't; he said he wouldn't put boots on the ground, and then he did.

The discrepancies between Obama's campaign promises and his record in office have been most glaring on matters of civil liberties. 'This administration puts forward a false choice between the liberties we cherish and the security we provide,' he said as a candidate on 1 August 2007. 'You can't have 100 per cent security and then 100 per cent privacy and zero inconvenience,' he said on 7 June 2013, during the Edward Snowden affair. 'We're going to have to make some choices.'

And finally, there are the things Obama didn't do. He didn't pursue a single intelligence officer over torture; didn't pursue a single finance executive for malfeasance in connection with the 2007/8 crash; didn't close Guantanamo Bay.

But a legacy is not a ledger. It is both less substantial than a list of things done, and more meaningful. 'At some point in Jackie Robinson's career, the point ceases to be how many hits he got or bases he stole,' Mitch Stewart, who played a leading role in both Obama campaigns, tells me. 'As great and important as all these stats were, there was a bigger picture.'

Legacies are about what people feel as well as what they know, about the present as much as the past. Aesthetically, there has always been something retro about Obama's public profile. The original campaign posters announcing 'Hope' and 'Change'; the black-and-white video clips in will.i.am's 'Yes We Can' video. With his family at his side, his brand offered not glamour exactly, but chic. Like John F Kennedy, he projected an image that enough Americans either wanted or needed, or both: a young, good-looking family, a bright future. He offered Camelot without the castle: no ties to the old, all about the future.

Photographs of Obama at the White House suggest both he and Michelle grew into this role quite happily. Whether it was Michelle dancing with kids on the White House lawn, or Barack making faces at babies and chasing toddlers around the Oval Office, they returned a sense of playful normality to the White House: an unforced conviviality that did not detract from the gravity of office.

'It's important to remember that he was more recently a normal person than most people at that level,' one veteran member of his team told me. 'For the 2000 convention, he couldn't even get a floor credential. In 2004, he introduced the presidential nominee. In 2008, he was the nominee. It's tough to see him and Michelle, and not give him that benefit of the doubt. He's had small kids in the White House. I think people will remember that as a moment and an era.'

When Virginia McLaurin, a 106-year-old African American woman, was granted her lifelong dream to visit the White House earlier this year, the president and his wife danced with her quite unselfconsciously. 'Slow down now, don't go too fast,' Obama joked. As the second term has progressed, they have seemed happy in their skin – and, for many, the novelty that it is black skin has not worn off. 'I thought I would never live to get in the White House,' McLaurin said, looking up at her hosts. 'I am so happy. A black president, a black wife, and I'm here to celebrate black history.'

Legacies are never settled; they are constantly evolving. A few years before he died, almost two-thirds of Americans disapproved of Martin Luther King, because of his stance against the Vietnam war and in favour of the redistribution of wealth. Yet within a generation, his birthday was a national holiday. When Americans ranked the most admired public figures of the 20th century in 1999, King came second only to Mother Teresa. Ronald Reagan is now hailed as a conservative hero, even though he supported amnesty for undocumented migrants and massively inflated the government deficit. During the final year of Bill Clinton's presidency, most guessed that his legacy would be one of scandal. Instead, he was hailed for presiding over a sustained economic recovery.

'History will be a far kinder judge than the current Republican congress,' Stewart tells me. 'It will rest on the untold successes that this administration has had. Energy efficiency, carbon efficiency. He reformed the student loan programme, which is going to have an impact on a generation of students. He's catapulted the US forward in ways that will continue to pay dividends long after his presidency. His legacy will be about these smaller, unsung accomplishments that will have a generational impact.'

Paradoxically, the element of Obama's legacy for which he will be best remembered – being the first black president – relates to an area that has seen little substantial headway: racial equality. The wealth gap between black and white Americans has grown, as have the unemployment gap and black poverty; black income has stagnated. That's not to suggest he has done nothing. He has appointed an unprecedented number of black judges, released several thousand non-violent drug offenders, reduced the disparity in sentencing for crack and powder cocaine. Anything he did that helped the poor, like Obamacare, will disproportionately help African Americans.

But, broadly speaking, Obama's racial legacy is symbolic, not substantial. The fact that he could be president challenged how African Americans saw their country. The fact that their lives did not radically improve as a result did not shift their understanding of how America works. When he was contemplating a run for the White House, his wife asked him what he thought he could accomplish if he won. 'The day I take the oath of office,' he replied, 'the world will look at us differently. And millions of kids across this country will look at themselves differently. That alone is something.'

The imagery did not, in the end, translate quite so neatly. True, when Trayvon Martin was shot dead by George Zimmerman in 2012, Obama was able to say what no other president could have said: 'Trayvon Martin could have been my son.' Nonetheless, it is unlikely that Zimmerman looked at Trayvon and thought, 'There goes the future president of America.' Thanks to Obama, Americans see racism differently; they do not, however, view black people differently.

Obama leaves office during a period of heightened racial tension over police shootings. 'His presidency was supposed to pass into an era of post-racism and colour blindness,' Keeanga-Yamahtta Taylor, Princeton professor and author of *From #BlackLivesMatter to Black Liberation*, tells me. 'Yet it was under his administration that the Black Lives Matter movement erupted. In many ways, it's the most significant anti-racist movement in the last 40 years, and it happens under the first black president. The eruption of this movement can be interpreted as a disappointment in the limitations of the Barack Obama presidency. And some of those limitations can be explained externally, by the hostility with which he's been met by the mostly Republican congress. But some of it lies in the limitations of his own policies.'

Over the past couple of years, the #BlackLivesMatter debate has taken place almost without reference to Obama. It suggests that, on one level, his relationship to some of the key issues surrounding black life is almost ornamental. He is the framed poster in the barbershop or the nail salon, the mural on the underpass, the picture in the diner or bodega – an aspiration not to be mistaken for the attrition of daily life. The question as to whether America can elect a black president has been answered; the issue of the sanctity of black life has yet to be settled.

His second term, however, has been more sure-footed than his first. Following the Sandy Hook shootings, when 20-year-old Adam Lanza killed 20 schoolchildren, six adult staff, his mother and himself, Obama finally vowed to challenge the legislative inertia on gun control and has not stopped since. As the Republicans have proven themselves incapable of compromise, Obama has felt more licence to stamp his authority on the political culture. A few months after the midterms, he signed the Dream Act; last November, he vetoed the Keystone Pipeline, from Canada to the Mexican Gulf, because of environmental concerns. While other presidents use the lame-duck portion of their tenure to get to work on their presidential libraries, Obama has been tying up loose ends. 'He'll be a blueprint for how you have a second term,' Mitch Stewart thinks.

As his term comes to an end and the fractured, volatile nature of the country's electoral politics is once again laid bare, Americans may be coming to realise that, in Obama, it had an adult in the room. As violence erupts at election rallies and spills over into the streets, they may come to appreciate the absence of scandal and drama from the White House. As their wages stagnated, industries collapsed, insecurities grew and hopes faded, he tried to get something done. Not much, not enough – but something. It is possible to have serious, moral criticisms of Obama and his legacy, and still appreciate his value, given the alternatives.

Americans are losing someone who took both public service and the public seriously; someone who stood for something bigger and more important than himself. This is the end of the line for a leader who believed that facts mattered; that Americans were not fools; that their democracy meant something and that government had a role: that America could be better than this.

24 MARCH

The aggressive, outrageous, infuriating (and ingenious) rise of BrewDog (extract)

JON HENLEY

In July 2010, a small brewery in the Scottish fishing port of Fraserburgh produced what was, at the time, the world's strongest beer. Named after the Francis Fukuyama book that declared liberal capitalist democracy the peak of human political evolution, The End of History was – according to its makers – in a sense, the end of beer.

At 55 per cent alcohol by volume, the brew, a 'blond Belgian ale ... infused with nettles from the Scottish Highlands and fresh juniper berries', was stronger than most whiskies, vodkas and gins. It sold in a limited run of 11 bottles, each artfully stuffed inside a deceased wild animal – seven stoats, four grey squirrels – costing between £500 and £700.

One of the brewery's two founders, James Watt, pronounced the drink 'an audacious blend of eccentricity, artistry and rebellion'. In their 'striking packaging', Watt said, the bottles 'disrupt conventions and break taboos – just like the beer they hold within them'. Not everyone agreed. Although the stoats and squirrels in question had died of natural causes, the charity Advocates for Animals denounced 'perverse' and 'out-of-date shock tactics' that 'exploited and degraded animals'. Alcohol action groups deplored a 'cheap marketing stunt' that was deliberately promoting excess in a nation with a well-known drink problem.

Watt and Martin Dickie, who met at school and launched their upstart brewery in 2007, then both aged 24, stood by their creation, which they had made in a local ice-cream factory by repeatedly chilling the brew and skimming off the ice to separate the water and concentrate the alcohol (which freezes at a lower temperature).

The End of History would clearly only ever be consumed in 'very small servings', Watt said. The brewery was simply showing people that beer could be something more than Stella, Carling or Tennent's – that it could, in fact, be 'something they had never imagined' (such as stronger than whisky). The company, he pointed out, also made a highly flavoured beer with a very *low* alcohol content.

Besides, Watt could think of no better way to celebrate the lives of 11 fine specimens of dead British wildlife than ensuring that, rather than being left to rot, their perfectly preserved corpses, stuffed by a master taxidermist from Doncaster, would be 'forever cherished' by the buyers of what was without doubt the most expensive beer in the world.

The End of History happened six years ago. It was a gimmick, a stunt, obviously. It also, sort of, was not. The company that pulled it, BrewDog, is a serial offender: it has, among other antics, driven a tank down Camden High Street; named a beer after the heroin-and-cocaine cocktail that killed River Phoenix and John Belushi; projected naked images of its two founders on to the Houses of Parliament; brewed beer at the bottom of the Atlantic Ocean; dropped stuffed cats from a helicopter on to the City of London; employed a dwarf to petition parliament for the introduction of a two-thirds pint glass; and released, for the royal wedding of 2011, a beer called Royal Virility Performance, which contained so-called natural aphrodisiacs such as 'herbal Viagra', chocolate and horny goat weed.

BrewDog has described itself as a 'post-punk, apocalyptic, motherfucker of a craft brewery' and urged its customers to 'ride toward anarchy'. Its slogans include 'In hops we trust', 'This is the revolution – so help me Dog', and 'Changing the world, one glass at a time'. It has a document that it calls its charter, which contains phrases such as: 'We bleed craft beer', 'We blow shit up', and 'Without us, we are nothing. We are BrewDog'.

BrewDog embodies, in short, much about modern life that many people love to hate: you don't have to search far to find someone on the internet calling BrewDog 'hipsters', 'pretentious', 'wankers', 'arseholes' or simply 'full of shit'. In the small but passionate world of British beer nerds, few subjects arouse stronger feelings than BrewDog: 'an instinctively repulsive ...

operation of expanding beards and stupidly named gaseous beverages', as one blogger put it.

Nonetheless, for the past four years, this has been the fastest-growing food and drinks producer in Britain, and the fastest-growing bar and restaurant operator. Since it was founded less than nine years ago, BrewDog has grown from two employees to 580. It has opened 30-odd highly successful bars – bare brick, exposed ironwork, spray-painted graffiti – across the UK, from Aberdeen to Bristol and Manchester to Clerkenwell. And there are 15 more around the world: Helsinki, Tokyo, Rome, São Paulo. Last year, the company's sales grew by more than 50 per cent, to £45m – more than half booked abroad – and BrewDog now exports to more than 50 countries. Solidly profitable every year since its inception, BrewDog's trading profit hit £5.5m in 2015.

For all the annoyance at their strategically deployed antics, BrewDog have built a hugely successful business on the loud and repeated pronouncement of their own authenticity: that all they truly care about is their beer. Their mission from the beginning, Watt told me last November in the company's bar in Shoreditch, over a glass of the company's flagship Punk IPA – the biggest-selling craft beer in the UK and Scandinavia – has been 'to revolutionise the British beer industry, and redefine British beer-drinking culture'.

Everything BrewDog does, he said with great earnestness, 'is about the beer. Everything. We want to make people as passionate about great beer as we are. Change perceptions, challenge conventions, but do it on our terms. We've always said we'll either succeed, or be some massive great crash-and-burn failure. But that's fine, because the space in between is really fucking boring.'

This sort of overheated rhetoric is just the thing that gets Dickie and Watt called pretentious hipster douchebags on the internet. But BrewDog's astonishing growth may raise the uncomfortable possibility that in an age of media-savvy and brand-sceptical digital natives, ostentatious displays of 'authenticity' – known to some as acting like pretentious hipster douchebags – may have become a necessary condition for success. Is it possible that James Watt and Martin Dickie, who make something great but sell it with infuriating stunts and obsessive passion, might represent the future of business?

The moment that changed James Watt's life – his beer epiphany, which he recalls with surprising (or well-rehearsed) precision – did not arrive in the most auspicious venue: 'It was a Sierra Nevada Pale Ale from the States, bought at Tesco in Stonehaven to wash down some fish and chips. Just this total explosion, this bomb of flavour – this, like ... awakening. And all around, industrial lagers and conservative cask ales, and nothing in between.'

Watt's public persona is all up yours and in your face. In person, he is an affable, considerate, even a charming man, of little hair – aside from the mandatory five days' stubble – and open gaze. For our second meeting, he had remembered (and served me) the bar food I had most enjoyed at our first. He talks a mile a minute in wildly overegged adjectives and looks after the business side of BrewDog: money, marketing, strategy.

Dickie, who has rather more hair and an altogether more measured manner, but otherwise resembles Watt so strongly the pair could almost be brothers, is mainly in charge of the brewing: devising new recipes and overseeing a small team of master brewers. Both are ridiculously, obsessively knowledgable about beer and the brewing process. On a tour of the cavernous and gleaming BrewDog plant in Ellon, just north of Aberdeen, Dickie happily batted around terminology – IBU, ABV, pH, haze, present gravity, headspace oxygen – with PhD-level microbiologists working in the lab.

The son of an oil-industry personnel manager and a primary school teacher, Dickie had not followed most of his school friends into engineering, but studied brewing and distilling at Heriot-Watt University in Edinburgh, where he shared a flat with an old classmate from Peterhead Academy in Aberdeenshire, James Watt.

Watt and Dickie first began experimenting with their own brews because 'basically, we couldn't find anything we really wanted to drink', Watt said. Back then, in early 2006, Dickie was working at a brewery in Derbyshire called Thornbridge, where he had just helped concoct a groundbreaking beer called Jaipur that would go on to win nearly 80 awards in its first five years.

What seems to excite Watt and Dickie about brewing – above and beyond their fanatical obsession with beer itself – are its sheer, unending possibilities. 'What's good with beer, compared to spirits, is you can try stuff and get an outcome really quickly,' Dickie, in jeans and T-shirt, told me on a dark December afternoon in the BrewDog Taphouse, a warm, shed-like bar conveniently attached to the company's Ellon brewery and filled with dog walkers, office workers from a nearby business park, guys with tats and caps, and girls in woolly hats. 'You can put in, like, twice the malt, four times the hops, whatever, and two weeks later, you know the result. Whisky, you have to wait years.'

In 2006, Watt had lasted all of a month in a legal affairs job after earning his law and economics degree before fleeing to sea in a fishing boat. The last in a line of fishermen, his 87-year-old grandfather is still catching lobsters. 'In the North Atlantic, in mid-January,' Watt told me, 'you learn a lot of things about risk, fear, decision-making. Teamwork. It has influenced my attitude to business. We don't do scared much.'

With Watt at sea two weeks out of four, studying part-time for his captain's papers, and Dickie busy brewing 'nice, boutiquey, hop-infused beers' in Derbyshire, the two school friends got together when they could. They made the kind of beers they liked and would want to drink, that not many other people were making, and in early 2006 they took one of them – an imperial stout they had aged in a Scotch whisky barrel – to London, to a tasting organised by the late beer and whisky writer Michael Jackson, who Dickie had met a year earlier through his work at Thornbridge.

'Flavour was everything to Jackson, he was obsessed by it,' Dickie said, reverently. 'He wrote about it brilliantly; described it so ... differently. He was a pretty incredible guy. Anyway, he tried this beer we'd made, and he said, "Guys, you need to give up the day job." That was all we needed.'

Beer has come a long way since an Italian medic, Aldobrandino of Siena, published his influential treatise on health and diet in 1256. Here was a drink, Aldobrandino argued, that 'harms the head and the stomach, causes bad breath, ruins the teeth, and fills the gut with bad fumes'. (On the upside, he noted, it also 'facilitates urination, and makes the flesh white and smooth'.)

It was clear by the late middle ages – across northern Europe, at least – that Aldobrandino's views would not prevail. In Britain, the Low Countries, Germany, Scandinavia, beer became increasingly popular – partly because it is boiled during the brewing process; it was a lot safer than water. In Britain alone, we once drank 65 gallons per person every year; by the mid-1700s, major London breweries such as Whitbread and Truman were making a million barrels of dark porter beer annually.

But by the latter decades of the last century, beer was in a bad way. Traditional cask ale was vanishing from the country's pubs in favour of thin, industrial bitters and fizzy, low-strength lagers. 'Technology,' Watt told me in the BrewDog bar in Shoreditch, 'allowed the big beer companies to bastardise and commoditise their products like never before. They used advertising and big budgets to somehow convince people this bland, insipid parody of a product was what beer was supposed to be.'

The fightback in Britain began with the Campaign for Real Ale (Camra), which held its first AGM at the Rose Inn, Nuneaton, in 1972 and set out to save traditional cask or 'real' ale from destruction. It laid down strict rules: living, unfiltered, unpasteurised beer, served from a traditional cask in which it had continued to ferment, could be called real ale. The vast majority of beer in Britain – chilled, filtered and pasteurised (to kill the yeast and extend the shelf life), injected with CO_2 (to make it fizzy), served from a pressurised keg – could not.

At about the time Camra was getting under way in the UK, beer on the other side of the Atlantic was in an equally parlous state. There, an unholy trio of identikit brewing giants peddling variations on a Budweiser theme dominated the market. 'There's an American beer ad from the 1980s,' said Watt, 'that pretty much sums up everything that went wrong with the beer business, all round the world: "Coors Light. Everything you want from a beer – and less".'

With no real tradition of cask ale, the independent US brewers who set about challenging the status quo took another path, reviving long-forgotten beer styles after their own fashion and – crucially – using American, usually west coast hops, rich with heady, intense, bitter flavours and powerful aromas of citrus and pine resins all but unknown in Britain. They called what they were making 'craft beer'.

At the end of 2006, Dickie followed Michael Jackson's advice and quit his day job at the brewery (which also meant moving back in with his parents). Watt stuck with the fishing, to keep some money coming in. The pair pooled their minimal savings, negotiated a £20,000 bank loan, bought a pile of secondhand brewing equipment and rented, recalled Watt, a dilapidated unit from Aberdeenshire council on 'this dystopian industrial estate, in between a needle exchange and a guy who promoted himself as the godfather of carpets'.

They were part of the vanguard of a remarkable renaissance in British brewing. In 2002, the British chancellor, Gordon Brown, had introduced a progressive beer duty, which slashed the tax paid by British brewers who made fewer than 3 million litres of beer a year. Almost instantly, the number of small beer-makers began to climb.

Often born in garages or kitchens or spare rooms, Britain's new-wave pioneers – Meantime, Magic Rock, Camden Town, Kernel, Beavertown, BrewDog – are among some 1,420 breweries now operating in this country, more than 100 times as many as there were in 1970. And rather than to the purists of Camra, it was to the anything-goes craft brewers of America that many turned for their inspiration: to exuberant beers with exotic ingredients (chilli, honey, chocolate, hemp, mustard, even myrrh), but also to hip design, guerrilla marketing and social-media savvy. Over the past two years alone, an average of nearly three new breweries have opened in Britain every week, brewing an ever greater variety of styles: bitters, porters, stouts, pale ales, milds, pilsners, bocks, brown ales, lagers, altbiers, weissbiers, gueuzes, saisons.

Watt and Dickie's first brew was a strongly hopped India pale ale, a style formulated in the early 1800s to weather the sea voyage to India, but which had become, by the 1970s, 'just a lacklustre 3.5 per cent beer; a marketing term', Watt said. They called their brew Punk IPA, in the hope it would blow up British beer-drinking in the way punk once blew up popular music.

BrewDog's first two batches of Punk IPA failed; the first because a phone, a thermometer and a set of car keys ended up in the mash, and the second because Watt and Dickie had bought dirt-cheap garden hose for their brewhouse and the whole brew tasted, 'like, really strongly, of plastic'. The third, however, worked. 'We knew,' Dickie said, 'it was awesome. Now we just had to convince enough people they should feel the same way.'

It was tough going. They filled bottles by hand, sometimes through the night, catching a few hours' sleep on sacks of malt in the brewhouse. They crisscrossed north-east Scotland in an ancient Fiat Punto and an even older Skoda pickup, flogging their beer at farmers' markets and offering it to bars and pubs who showed 'zero interest in a 6 per cent, heavily hopped IPA with a really big and different flavour', Dickie said. 'We ... Well, we made no money. It was hard.'

But less than a year later, BrewDog had won its first major contract – a weekly order to supply Tesco with twice the quantity of Punk IPA it was then capable of producing. Watt and Dickie had entered four of their beers in a competition run by the super-market chain: the prize for the winner was a place on the shelves in every one of its UK stores.

'In a blind tasting by a panel of people who knew something about beer,' said Dickie, still savouring the moment, 'we came first, second, third and fourth. Yeah. It felt pretty amazing.'

Opinions of BrewDog tend to go one of four ways. The evangelists think the company can do no wrong. The haters cannot get past the relentless self-promotion, and loathe everything BrewDog stands for. The compromisers argue that yes, they might on the whole be happier if BrewDog toned down the language and cut the stunts, but hey, they brew such great beers you have to forgive them. 'Buy their Beer and Not their Hype', as one beer blogger put it.

The final group, let's call them the sceptics, reckon the beer and the hype are, in fact, inseparable. BrewDog's particular form of hype, they argue, is such an intrinsic part of the package that without it, we probably would not see – still less drink – the beer. Jon Kyme, a thoughtful, small real-ale brewer in Ulverston, Cumbria, is one such sceptic.

People 'like to identify strongly with something; hang their identity on it', Kyme said. BrewDog has set itself up – brilliantly – to embody that identity: young, hip, rebellious; championing quality, battling a mediocre status quo. In fact, Kyme said, while the brewer undeniably makes good beers, there are lots of people pushing the craft boundaries at the moment and 'very few are making beers that are vastly superior to anyone else's'.

And that, he reasoned, is why the hype is so crucially, critically important to BrewDog: 'In a sense, it's their main product. It's only in the hype that there is an absolute, quantum gap between BrewDog and the rest. Their entire existence, basically, is marketing.'

'They brought something new and original to a sector that has been quite ... traditional,' said Mike Benner, the softly spoken head of Siba, the Society of Independent Brewers, a man who was often on the receiving end of BrewDog's weaponised ire during his 10 years as the chief executive of Camra. 'They've made headlines. They've been hugely influential; no doubt.'

Even the sceptics tend to concede that Watt and Dickie – antics be damned – have helped cultivate a new generation of adventurous beer drinkers, many of them fired by fierce loyalty to BrewDog. In 2010, the company leveraged the intensity of its supporters into a new financing model, raising crowdfunded capital without having to bend itself to financial targets set by banks or investors.

Gautam Bhatnagar, a London IT worker, is one of 40,000 people who – in exchange for discounts in BrewDog's bars and online shop and an invite to the annual AGM, a beer and music-fuelled knees-up attended last year by 6,000 shareholders – have spent at least £95 on two BrewDog shares in the company's record-breaking Equity for Punks crowdfunding scheme. (The fourth round, in 2015, raised £5m in 20 days, which was what prompted Watt and Dickie to drop those stuffed 'fat cats' on to the City.)

This year, helped by more than £10m of new cash raised in a few months from the latest of these crowdfunding campaigns, BrewDog will open a brand-new brewery on its current site in Ellon, boosting capacity fivefold. It is also opening a whisky and vodka distillery on the same site, and building a major new production facility in the US – its biggest export market – where Watt and Dickie are the stars of an extreme-brewing reality show called *Brew Dogs*, which follows the pair around America as they visit craft breweries and make beer using outlandish ingredients ranging from a lobster to the world's hottest chilli.

In a move that has not received quite so much publicity, BrewDog also takes £200,000 out of its profits every year and gives it to startup breweries. 'We mentor them, donate equipment,' Watt told me. 'Is that a gimmick? Yeah, a lot of people do see us as stunt merchants. That's their prerogative.'

In its brief history, BrewDog has upset, variously and sometimes repeatedly, rival breweries, drink-industry associations, health organisations, the Advertising Standards Authority (for a blog-post advising drinkers of one of its products to 'let the sharp bitter finish rip you straight to the tits'), even LBGT groups: last summer, it released No Label, the world's first 'non-binary, transgender beer' – half lager, half ale, and brewed with hops that had 'undergone a gender change'. Profits went to charities working with LGBT people, some of whom did not fully appreciate their struggle being used to sell beer.

THE BEDSIDE GUARDIAN 2016

The first in BrewDog's long line of highly publicised spats came early in the company's life, and set a pattern for what followed. In 2008, shortly after two BrewDog beers had won medals at the Beer World Cup, a biennial US-based affair known as the Olympics of the beer world, Britain's self-regulating alcohol industry watchdog, the Portman Group, took umbrage at the language on the Punk IPA label.

Specifically, Portman – which was formed by the major drinks companies to promote responsible drinking and responsible marketing – disliked the phrase 'an aggressive beer', arguing that the word 'aggressive' was 'more likely to be seen applying to the drinker, rather than the drink'. BrewDog was ordered to change the branding of Punk IPA and two of its other beers, or retailers would be told to stop selling the offending bottles. The dispute quickly caught the eye of the media – with, perhaps, a little helpful prodding – and the minute it was resolved, BrewDog launched a new beer called Speedball (the name for a combination of heroin and cocaine), gleefully labelling it a 'class A strong ale' with 'a vicious cocktail of active ingredients'. It was banned almost immediately, generating more publicity. BrewDog renamed it Dogma.

The following year, Portman banned BrewDog's 18 per cent Tokyo imperial stout, amid shock-horror headlines about its strength – a single bottle, one tabloid noted, 'contains six units of alcohol, the equivalent of THREE PINTS of normal strength beer'. In response, the company unveiled a 1.1 per cent ale called Nanny State.

These duels were, on one level, a game, but on another, they were not. In his basement bar in Shoreditch, nursing a glass of Born To Die ('thirty-day shelf life; huge, huge hop aroma, way more bitter than Punk IPA; almost resinous on the tongue; it really hammers those bitter alpha acids – aggressive, assertive,

'The choice is clear.' Hillary Clinton celebrates winning the presidential nomination at the Democratic National Convention in Philadelphia, on 28 July. JIM YOUNG/REUTERS

'I don't have to be so nice any more.' Donald Trump goes walkabout after a speech in Colorado Springs on 29 July. STACIE SCOTT/THE GAZETTE/AP

Michael Gove and Boris Johnson – 'face ashen with the terror of victory', as Jonathan Freedland described it – on the morning after the EU referendum.
STEFAN ROUSSEAU/AFP/GETTY IMAGES

'Cameron leaves Downing Street with few admirers, a country in crisis, the central aims of his premiership in rubble,' wrote Owen Jones of his departure on 13 July. GRAEME ROBERTSON FOR THE *GUARDIAN*

Jeremy Corbyn in Grimsby on 28 April, just after the suspension of Ken Livingstone from the Labour party for making anti-semitic comments. CHRISTOPHER THOMOND FOR THE *GUARDIAN*

Celebrations for the Queen's 90th birthday took place in typical British summer weather. PETER NICHOLLS/REUTERS

Only 16 of the 39 horses that started the Grand National in April managed to make it to the end. Amazingly, given the drama of this picture, none were seriously hurt. TOM JENKINS FOR THE *GUARDIAN*

Welsh fans celebrate in Cardiff after watching their team score a third goal in the Euro 2016 quarter-final match against Belgium on 1 July. GEOFF CADDICK/AFP/GETTY IMAGES

Power couple Jason Kenny and Laura Trott share a golden moment at the Olympic Velodrome in Rio after both took top cycling medals.

BRYN LENNON/GETTY IMAGES

Simone Biles, who won four gold medals at Rio, on the balance beam. 'She's the best I've ever seen,' said gymnastics coach Christine Still.

DMITRI LOVETSKY/AP

In the aftermath of the Paris attacks in November 2015, French graphic designer Jean Jullien turned the peace symbol into a universal message of sympathy with France. ROGER TOOTH FOR THE *GUARDIAN*

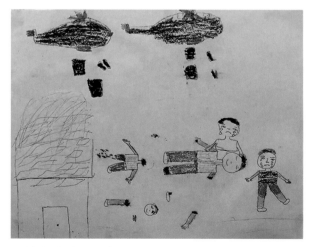

A child's depiction of living under siege in Aleppo. 'What is really shocking for me is that the dead children are smiling while the living ones are crying,' wrote volunteer physician Dr Zaher Sahloul.

Festival-goers at Glastonbury stage a memorial for Jo Cox, the Labour MP who was stabbed to death in Yorkshire on 16 June, a week before the EU referendum. DAVID LEVENE FOR THE *GUARDIAN*

'Baby, you were much too fast. The love, though? The love is going to last,' wrote Deborah Orr, on the news that Prince had died on 21 April.

In September, Grime star Skepta beat David Bowie and Radiohead to the Mercury prize. 'His win marks a celebrated second coming for the genre,' wrote Hannah Ellis-Petersen. OLIVIA ROSE FOR THE *GUARDIAN*

Ballet's golden couple Natalia Osipova and Sergei Polunin dancing together for the first time in the UK in a programme of new pieces commissioned by Osipova herself. TRISTRAM KENTON FOR THE *GUARDIAN*

palate-cleansing, refreshing'), Watt flatly accused the Portman Group of 'acting like a thinly veiled cartel. They have a vested interest in making sure their member companies entrench their market position.' (The Portman Group has consistently said it acts only to uphold its industry code, which is aimed solely at ensuring responsible drinking and drink marketing.)

Up in Ellon the following month, Dickie took a different tack. The 18 per cent Tokyo, he said, was a unique beer produced in very small quantities. 'We made one tankful, maybe 500 bottles. We sold 450 abroad – so there were, like, 50 on sale in the UK, at £18 each. To claim that's going to promote excess and irresponsible drinking ... Seriously? What about the brands selling 24 cans of lager for a tenner? That's excess.'

But the scandal of its banning, Dickie would concede, did generate amazing amounts of media coverage: 'Pictures of James in the *Sun* – "If Britain has a binge-drinking problem, blame this man" ... It meant we could explain what we were trying to do, talk about the six months it took to ferment this beer, do some evangelising.'

In 2009, the veteran beer writer and Camra grandee Roger Protz, who edits Camra's annual *Good Beer Guide*, tartly labelled Watt and Dickie 'lunatic self-publicists' and 'over-inflated ego-maniacs', unleashing a long-running feud with the custodians of real ale that resulted in BrewDog twice being excluded – for reasons still disputed – from the organisation's Great British Beer Festival.

Many craft beers, including BrewDog's, do not qualify as real ale under Camra's strict criteria simply because, although some are served from casks, most come in kegs, bottles and cans, and with added CO_2. Passions on both sides of this debate can run high. And for a thrusting young company eager to blow up a traditional market but without anything much in the way of an advertising budget, it seems no controversy – courted or not –

that allows you to play the plucky but oppressed newcomer, eager only to get on and do your thing, will do you much harm.

In May 2012, BrewDog was voted Scottish Bar Operator of the Year by the members of the British Institute of Innkeeping (BII). Just before the ceremony, an unidentified staffer from Diageo, the international drinks giant that sponsored the event, allegedly informed the organisers that no further backing would be forthcoming if the award went to BrewDog.

Amid scenes of high farce – the company that was declared the winner declined to collect the award after it saw BrewDog's name already engraved on the trophy – the multinational was forced to apologise. But BrewDog got to denounce Diageo as 'a band of dishonest hammerheads and dumb-ass corporate freaks' and affirm that the incident showed 'just how scared and jealous the gimp-like establishment are of the craft beer revolutionaries'. Within a few hours, its Twitter hashtag #andthewinnerisnot was trending around the world.

If some of these controversies were thrust upon BrewDog – who cannily took full advantage – others turned out to be rather more cynical. A few months after the spat over the high alcohol content in BrewDog's Tokyo imperial stout, it emerged that just one complaint from the public had led to the Portman Group ordering retailers to cease stocking the beer. It had been lodged by a Mr James Watt.

30 March

It's easy to sneer at US fringe politics, but the crackpots are gaining ground in the UK too

RAFAEL BEHR

On 27 April 2015, a white van was reported stolen in east London – inconvenient for the owner, but not politically significant. The theft only made the news because its cargo included 200,000 blank ballot papers, due for dispatch to Hastings and Eastbourne, in East Sussex, ahead of the general election the following week. Police believed that the vehicle was the target, and that the crime was not part of some larcenous automotive vote-rigging exercise.

It was a non-event. It wasn't even the best white-van-related story of the last parliament. I had forgotten all about it until a few weeks ago, when a resident of Eastbourne – a disappointed Labour supporter, a young man showing no outward symptoms of crackpottery – cited it as evidence that the election was fixed: 'I don't believe the Tories won,' he told me. (Historical note: the Tories won.) Opinion polls said one thing; results said another. It was all a bit mysterious until you considered the van, he added. 'The thing is, I'm a bit of a conspiracy theorist.' He made it sound like a professional qualification.

It is hard to measure paranoia but there is a lot of it about and – perhaps I am being paranoid here – it seems to be acquiring a more assertive character. Suspicion of politicians is not new. But I see more joining the dots of suspicion into elaborate constellations.

I have met Ukip supporters who believe that the Labour party is a vast paedophile protection racket. That is before they even get to European plans for the genetic dilution of Britain's indigenous population. The Scottish independence referendum spawned a multiverse of parallel realities, featuring secret oil fields, stolen ballot boxes, and collusion between the BBC, the Bank of England and Buckingham Palace to procure a false result on polling day.

There have been enough reports in recent weeks of Labour councillors and candidates peddling antisemitic mumbo-jumbo – Jews as puppetmasters behind 9/11, Isis and global capitalism – to suggest the party has an infestation on its hands. I must tread carefully here. I do not want to accuse everyone who yearns for an independent Scotland – or wants Britain to leave the EU, or voted for Jeremy Corbyn to become Labour leader – of indulging fanatics, let alone forming some combined assault on rational discourse. Millions of reasonable people support those propositions, and history might vindicate their judgment.

Those just happen to be the movements that have recently mined rich seams of social, cultural and economic alienation from the political centre, which they locate geographically in Westminster and which they define ideologically as soulless technocracy fiddling at the margins of globalisation.

Unrelated insurgencies can share a common idiom of dissent: rejection of 'mainstream media' as the propaganda tools of a self-serving elite; refusal to engage with evidence if the source is ideologically impure; inability to distinguish between reporting of news and malicious spreading of smears.

Those are also the components of a conspiracy theory: the self-reinforcing belief that attack and ridicule are precisely the weapons that rattled conspirators would use to sustain their conspiracy. Faith in the original proposition is strengthened when the establishment is depicted closing ranks to silence those who dare to speak out.

There is one place in particular where conspiracy theory and mainstream opposition politics cross-fertilise. It is the assumption that ministers spend their time lying because they dare not reveal their wicked true motives. You don't have to stray far along the spectrum of left opinion, for example, to encounter the view that Tories are evil. Not just incompetent or misguided, but thirsting for cruelty. Jeremy Hunt is presumed to wake up of a morning pondering ways to destroy the NHS, while Nicky Morgan masterminds the privatisation of childhood.

Few of us know anyone so systematically duplicitous or vindictive. It is possible that public office attracts sociopathic personality types. It seems more likely that most MPs come to the job with honest intentions, and unhappy outcomes are best explained by the mundane forces of stupidity and bad luck. Everyone who has worked in government reports that conspiracies are far too difficult to organise, that civil servants would bungle their implementation anyway, and that a lot more effort is spent trying to attract voters' attention to what ministers are doing than in throwing them off the scent.

The presumption that politicians are always up to something more sinister is a marker of what used to be the political fringe. That word seems inadequate now. It denotes a place on a spectrum that is, by definition, narrow and self-limiting. The fringe must be smaller than the mainstream to whose edges it is confined. But what if the fringe encroaches inwards on the centre, and the mainstream shrinks in proportion? What if 'fringe' politics denotes not a place but a habit of mind – a way of explaining the world, a set of rhetorical barricades against contradiction? The fringe can then overwhelm the mainstream.

For a taste of that, we can look across the Atlantic, at Donald Trump's march on the Republican presidential nomination. Here is a party that spent years campaigning against the morals and motives of its rivals, only to discover that it cannot control the audience it nurtured for that brand of politics. Trump was an avid promoter of the 'birther' proposition that President Obama was foreign-born, probably a secret Muslim, and so alien to the White House. Trump's rise erases a boundary between whack-job conspiracy theory and legitimate politics.

The US and British systems are only superficially alike. We do not have the same conservative traditions of bellicose illiberalism and messianic political religiosity. Nor do we have the same cult of wealthy bombast. It is hard to imagine a character with the sheer vulgarity of Trump appealing to a UK electorate.

We tell ourselves that we are smarter, more civilised, less credulous and worldlier than our American cousins. We want to congratulate ourselves on the certainty that it could not happen here, denying the possibility that, in an understated, low-key, parochial and idiosyncratically British kind of way, maybe it already has.

5 APRIL

The *Archers* torture is over – and only just begun

NANCY BANKS-SMITH

A peaceful Sunday in Ambridge. Helen, whose judgment is never likely to give Solomon sleepless nights, thought it a good idea to give her abusive husband, Rob, a simple Sunday supper – tuna bake with apple pie and custard – before announcing that she was leaving him. Wiser wives would prefer to break these glad tidings on a postcard from Ayers Rock.

It all led to what politicians call a full and frank exchange of views, and Rob pinned to the floor of Blossom Cottage with a knife. (This worried me for a while as it would have worried Miss Marple. Neither a fish knife nor a pie slice seemed quite cut out for the job.) Rob and Helen made it safely past the tuna bake but when the apple pie caught fire she spoke up. 'I don't care! I'm leaving and taking Henry with me.' Henry, for late arrivals at the scene of the crime, is her small son. They say everyone's for mother love, apple pie and tax relief, and here we have the first two in one explosive bundle.

Two and a half years of slow thumbscrew torture came to a helter-skelter, hugger-mugger confusing conclusion. Did Rob taunt Helen to kill herself? Or dare her to kill him?

Sunday night's episode was, unusually for the soap, a two-hander. One of those head-to-head encounters that are used sparingly but to great effect in *EastEnders* where Sean O'Connor, *The Archers*' exciting editor, comes from and where he is shortly returning. Ambridge, which allows no occasion to go uncelebrated, is even now planning a pageant.

Helen and Rob were alone as they have always been alone. A village where every second person is related to Helen and no one minds their own business has been blindingly oblivious to something very nasty going on in the woodshed. Coercive control is not an easy crime to spot or even spell. It's quite hard to put your finger on it. As Helen told a helpline, helplessly: 'I can't explain exactly what he does.' It is probably not unlike being married to Dr Jekyll. Everyone pities him for having such a twitchy wife.

Helen's pregnancy has lent a particular poignancy to her slavery. Now there is the question of the baby, Rob's unborn son. Just when you thought it was all over, it has barely begun.

9 APRIL

How do I tell our sons about their father's criminal past?

DECCA AITKENHEAD

I was driving through a local village with my children recently when we passed a sign for a prison. 'What does HMP stand for?' asked my son Jake. The explanation created a sensation. 'A prison?' gasped his brother, Joe. 'A real-life prison? Near our house!'

Before the recent purchase of a Lego Batman Batcave, featuring a jail 'with bars and everything', I'm not sure they were aware that such institutions existed. But the dangerous glamour of crime and punishment has electrified them and they can happily spend hours consigning delinquent toys to detention in their Lego jail. At six and four, the boys inhabit a universe of moral absolutes – goodies and baddies – in which inmates are obviously baddies. 'We live near actual baddies!' Joe exclaimed. 'What if one escaped?'

In hindsight, I should probably have let it go. But, without thinking, I heard myself say, 'Well, not everyone in prison is a baddie.' What did I mean? 'Well, some of my friends have been to prison. I even visited them. They weren't baddies. They were lovely people who just made a mistake and did something wrong.'

Jake asked if I'd ever been sent to prison and I laughed. 'No!'

Then he asked about his father – 'Was he ever locked up?' And I froze.

We all keep secrets about ourselves from our children. I don't think I knew this when I was a child. It was only when I became a parent myself that I began to scrutinise my biography and wonder which bits would best be kept to myself. Surprisingly few, was the answer, but not because I'd led an unusually virtuous life. It was just that my transgressions looked like minor misdemeanours compared with the X-rated rap sheet of their father's past.

Tony was just four when he burgled his first house. He stole compulsively, even from the family who adopted him, and locks had to be fitted to every bedroom door in their home except his. He spent much of his childhood behind bars for violence and theft, ran away to London at 15 to become a Soho hustler and lived in a squat with a prostitute. When he helped her escape her pimps, they broke in and beat Tony with iron bars, before carting his girlfriend off to resume her services. He tracked them down and shot them. No one died, but he went on the run. Arrested a year later, he was still in his teens when an Old Bailey judge sent him to prison for 14 years.

On release, Tony resumed his criminal career and became an accomplished gangster. Drug-dealing, gun-running, extortion and violence were all highly lucrative, but by 40 he had wound up his more ostentatiously lawless operations and confined his business to the discreet wholesale of cocaine. As he saw it, he had practically gone legit. More recreational crimes, such as football hooliganism, handling stolen goods or driving without a licence, he didn't even count as breaking the law. But he was heavily addicted to crack. Tony would smoke it every night, often until dawn, and was puzzled by my sense that it was neither normal nor ideal to sleep until 4pm.

When we first became a couple, it never occurred to me to worry about how this might one day be explained to our children. Only a lunatic would have predicted we would last long enough to make a family. I loved him, but failed to see how our relationship could work, and six months of anthropological novelty as a gangster's moll was enough for me. I told him I could not be with an addict and left him.

What happened next still astonishes me. Tony found a Narcotics Anonymous meeting that day and never touched crack again.

Once back together, he signed up for college classes, took an access course in humanities and won a scholarship to study psychology and criminology at university. The only father our two boys ever knew was a mature student who graduated with a first and went to work for Kids Company.

When our sons were born, I wondered how and when we would tell them about his past. When would be the right time for them to know their father used to be a criminal and a crack addict? At what point would we tell them he had been to prison? But the dilemma lay far ahead in the distance and would be faced together.

Two years ago, Tony drowned. We were on holiday in Jamaica and our four-year-old was swept out to sea by a riptide. Tony swam out and rescued him, but could not save himself. Now that he is gone, I am the gatekeeper of his past, in sole custody of a history the boys will never have the chance to integrate or reconcile with a father they know. Alive only in their imagination, he will always be a semi-mythical figure to them and this has transformed what used to be a distant, shared dilemma into an immediate problem for which I alone am responsible.

Disclosed too early, the risk is that the revelations will upset and confuse them. Left too late, they could devastate the boys' fantasies of a flawless hero. I can see how easily these fantasies will form. Tony gave his life to save his son; deification is inevitable – and he was a hero, it is true. But I don't want their image of their father to be a work of posthumous fiction that airbrushes out all his other truths. Neither do I want them to grow up under pressure to live up to the impossible standards of a ghost. Above all, I do not want Tony's past to become a toxic family secret. The truth always leaks out in the end and I want them to hear it from me.

It is very hard to see when the time would be right. If I tell them while they are children and see the world in black and white, good and bad, how will they be able to comprehend the complexity of Tony? If I wait until adolescence, will they glamorise his past and be drawn to emulate it? The friends I consulted all assumed the boys would be inspired by the redemptive triumph of Tony's life, but I worry that the message they would take from it as teenagers is that if their dad broke the law, they can too. He got away with it; why wouldn't they?

Adults understand how difficult and rare it is to turn around a life of crime and drugs – it's why they find Tony's story so inspiring. What they forget, I fear, is that we all mistake our own parents for the universal norm and can draw the most calamitously misleading assumptions from their unrepresentative example. But if I wait until Jake and Joe are adults, and sufficiently sophisticated to absorb his past without mistaking it for an indictment or a licence, I think they will be furious with me for keeping secrets and will feel betrayed.

All these thoughts made me very worried about whether it was wise to write a book about Tony's life and death. The price to be paid for the emotional catharsis of a memoir would be the surrender of editorial control; everything would be irretrievably known. Jake and Joe would be too young to read it, of course – but what if an older kid taunted them in the playground? 'Did you know your dad was a gangster? Your dad was a drug addict.' If I wrote the book, I would no longer be able to choose what and when to tell them.

In the end, that is precisely why I decided to write it. I do not ever want to lie to my children, but I can see the truth is so fraught with dangers that the temptation to edit or withhold may become irresistible. By relinquishing control, I forfeited that option and in the end this felt like the safest thing to do.

15 APRIL

The idealists of Lesbos: volunteers at the heart of the refugee crisis

HELENA SMITH

An air of expectancy hangs over Lesbos in advance of Pope Francis's visit today. Security is being tightened; beaches are being cleaned. In the island's town hall, the mayor, Spyros Galinos, has invested in a guestbook, which he hopes the pontiff will be the first to sign.

In the hillside village of Moria, home to the island's notorious, barbed-wire-topped detention centre, refugees are being prepped for Francis's arrival. 'It will be hugely symbolic,' says Galinos. 'For a few hours, the world's greatest humanitarian will be highlighting Europe's biggest humanitarian crisis.'

Few places conjure crisis as much as Lesbos. Since its emergence on the frontline of the greatest movement of people since the second world war, the Greek island has come to represent a spirit that goes well beyond its jagged coastline, an almost mystical rite of passage for vounteers wading in to help.

Pope Francis, the most prominent figure to fly in so far, takes a well-trodden path. More than 50,000 volunteers are thought to have passed through since men, women and children – the vast majority fleeing war in Syria – began to land on its shores in flimsy boats last summer. At no other time in modern history have NGOs or individuals stepped in to make up for the limited resources of a near-bankrupt country that has struggled to cope with the influx.

For human rights groups, the papal visit offers an opportunity to expose the plight of the thousands detained in Greece since Europe's controversial deal with Turkey to stem the flow. 'For everyone here, the experience is totally life-changing,' says Adil Izemrane, a Dutch volunteer who previously ran a property company in Amsterdam. 'Our hope is that Francis will be just as touched as we have, that the visit will open his heart and make him more proactive.'

Like many, Izemrane felt compelled to move to Lesbos when he saw the shocking image of the Syrian toddler Alan Kurdi lying limp and lifeless on a Turkish beach after his doomed family tried to reach the island of Kos last September. Before that, the 38-year-old had never heard of Lesbos. His favourite island was Ibiza, where every year he 'celebrated life' with friends. But by October he was in Greece, with what would soon be Europe's biggest food truck in tow.

'I see how much difference I can make for a lot of people and that's a thousand times more rewarding than selling condominiums,' says Izemrane, the son of Moroccan immigrants, who helped set up the humanitarian group Movement on the Ground. 'You may not be able to stop the [Syrian] war, but what this island does is make you realise you can change lives.'

If compassion is the volunteers' driving force, idealism is their staying power. So, too, is shock: the shock of experiencing the tragedy up close and, say nearly all, realising the lack of empathy displayed by governments back home.

When Steffi De Pous, who is also Dutch, arrived on Lesbos, she was by her own admission a yoga-teaching former model 'trying to do my bit' for peace, love and harmony. Being on a beach, alone, helping hundreds of drenched, exhausted refugees, was not what she had envisioned. But last summer, as the number of arrivals surged, that is exactly what happened. 'In the beginning, when there was almost no one here, you'd find yourself alone on some shore completely overwhelmed,' she recalled. 'One day I helped nine boats and about 450 people. It changes you for life,' says the 33-year-old, whose group Because We Carry initially distributed baby slings. 'I feel blessed. I never want to complain but I also have a burning fire inside because it doesn't feel fair. These people have risked everything to get here. And all Europe wants to do is deport them.'

Anger is a sentiment widely shared. At 25, Benjamin Julian, an Icelandic activist, is typical of the younger generation working with the solidarity movement in Greece. Like others, he has spent months travelling to and from island flashpoints, often dossing in anarchist-run squats. The refugee crisis is not only a just cause, he argues, but has radicalised western leftists just as Vietnam did. 'Sure, Greece is trendy, a once-in-a-decade networking festival for European anti-racist activists,' he says. 'But you know you are witnessing history too. Talking to volunteers who have seen the incompetence of the state and brutality of the state, it is very clear that even blue-eyed optimists leave as hardened political activists.'

There are few who do not believe that Europe – after its decision to deport 'non-asylum seekers' back to Turkey – is headed down a dark path. For Alison Terry-Evans, an Australian, Lesbos has borne witness to 'post-apocalyptic' scenes: howls in the night from those lucky enough to reach its shores; the terrifying silence of the hundreds who have ended up drowning along the way.

'You would hear the screaming before you would see those doing it,' she recollects. 'The children would cry, the women would shout, the men would be silent because they wanted to do both. It's very difficult after that to see the sea in the same way.'

Terry-Evans, a street photographer, founded Dirty Girls, an organisation that launders the wet clothes of arriving refugees.

Set in a remote olive grove up a long winding road in the north of the island, the laundry also washes the felt blankets handed out by the United Nations refugee agency – a move that has saved the UNHCR more than €1m (£800,000).

Susan Sarandon, the Hollywood star, has dropped by. Donations from actors and other people in the arts in Britain have poured in. 'We were in this privileged position of being in a place where we could be kind,' says Terry-Evans, who wants to establish laundries elsewhere to help the 53,000 migrants and refugees stranded in Greece since Macedonia and other Balkan states sealed their borders. 'After the EU's awful agreement, they have locked everyone up. Honestly, I don't think there is one refugee who is going to benefit from the pope's visit.'

The 'strange disconnect' between volunteers and the governments that represent them is not lost on Amed Khan, a long-time associate of the former US president Bill Clinton, who has also spent time on Lesbos. The investor, who bought Andy Warhol's *Mao* in 2011 but has since rejected consumerism for the world of philanthropy, has also been motivated by rage. 'I'm just furious about the callous indifference of the rich and gross incompetence of the powerful,' says the 44-year-old, who has funded a transit centre and search and rescue operations on the island.

'The whole thing is a disgrace, a self-induced faux crisis. Citizens' movements are good but where are the rich? In Rwanda we saw the same thing, people of limited means taking time out of their schedule to help. Here I hear of yachts being chartered for a million dollars a week; just the gas they use would be enough to educate refugee children for a year.'

Social media is the glue connecting young idealists. More than ever, they say, Facebook has highlighted the arbitrary nature of borders. 'I have sat on beaches with young Pakistanis and thought, "That could be me,"' says Kavita Kapur, an

American human rights lawyer helping on Lesbos. 'The only difference is my grandparents left and I have a passport that allows me to move on.'

But it is carefree Greece that has provided the backdrop for the idealists. 'It is easy, safe, accessible,' adds Kapur, admitting that it was her belief in the capacity of human beings that had brought her to the island. 'In a crisis of this magnitude, it is not Lesbos, it is Greece in general that has become a rite of passage for so many of us.'

16 APRIL

The Panama Papers: inside the *Guardian*'s investigation into offshore secrets

JULIETTE GARSIDE

The security guard handed over a key with a small yellow label. In 2013 the *Guardian*'s secure room had housed the team that worked through data leaked by Edward Snowden to expose unchecked surveillance by UK and US spy agencies. Now it was to be home to a small group of journalists gathered from all corners of the newsroom to work on a project code-named Prometheus. Our investigation into the murky world of tax havens, underpinned by the biggest leak in history, would surface eight months later with the publication of the Panama Papers.

The story began back in February 2015, with an article in *Süddeutsche Zeitung* that revealed the German newspaper had a slug of secret files about offshore companies on the books of the Panamanian law firm Mossack Fonseca. Some 80 gigabytes loaded on to a USB stick, the information related largely to the firm's Luxembourg customers.

Within weeks, the paper's investigative reporters, Bastian Obermayer and Frederik Obermaier, had been approached by a second source who had read their article and wanted to share more: 'Hello, this is John Doe. Interested in data?' The source demanded absolute anonymity. To this day, his or her identity remains unknown to the Panama Papers reporters. 'My life is in danger. We will only chat over encrypted files. No meeting ever.'

The *Guardian*'s involvement formally began in September 2015, when Katharine Viner, the paper's editor-in-chief, and Paul Johnson, deputy editor, flew to Munich to secure participation in the consortium of journalists around the world collaborating on the story. Back in London, the team began poring over the archives of Mossack Fonseca. These were being gradually uploaded to servers managed by the International Consortium of Investigative Journalists (ICIJ) in Washington. The database would eventually include 11.5 million emails, passport scans, contracts, share registers and even sound recordings.

As a business reporter tasked with unpicking tax-sheltering schemes used by California technology groups and London property developers, I have followed many trails to offshore dead ends. The Panama Papers meant that, for the first time, I was able to take a good look at what lay beyond the wall of secrecy.

It quickly became apparent that offshore agents such as Mossack Fonseca often have no special knowledge about their customers. Tax havens' lack of transparency may allow the keeping of secrets, but these secrets are often kept elsewhere. As a result, the database needed to be approached from multiple angles, whacked with many sticks until it could be cracked.

The *Guardian* brought together its specialists. Luke Harding, the paper's foremost Russia expert, took on the huge task of investigating Mossack Fonseca's many Russian and Ukrainian customers. Simon Bowers, a tax and fraud specialist from the City desk, picked apart the undeclared offshore holdings of Iceland's prime minister.

Holly Watt, who had previously exposed the MPs' expenses scandal for the *Daily Telegraph*, tracked down the files relating to members of parliament, peers and political donors. The *Guardian*'s chief sportswriter, Owen Gibson, delved into the world of sport, while reporters in our New York and Sydney offices hunted for stories of local interest.

David Pegg, with whom I had worked on the HSBC files, exposing tax evasion at the Swiss branch of Britain's biggest bank, matched land registry records with lists of Mossack Fonseca companies. He soon realised that the firm was acting for roughly 10 per cent of all offshore companies with land holdings in Britain.

Our colleague Helena Bengtsson, editor of the data projects team at the *Guardian*, compiled lists of tens of thousands of names, everyone from MPs to those wanted by Interpol or on sanctions orders. She then cross-matched these with the Panama Papers data, leaving her computer running all night so she could comb through the results in the morning.

We worked hard to keep the information safe. With investigative reporters looking into a $2bn Russian money-laundering scheme linked to Vladimir Putin, the threat of a hack by the FSB, Russia's security agency, was very real.

More than 140 high-ranking politicians and heads of state were uncovered in the data, leaving partners in less democratic countries at risk of government retaliation. Since the Panama Papers were published, Ecuador's president, Rafael Correa, has used Twitter to name and admonish local journalists for not handing over all the data. In Venezuela, a journalist has been fired for being part of the Panama Papers team. In Tunisia, the website Inkyfada has come under suspected cyberattack after naming an ex-presidential adviser.

The five reporters in the core team spent long days over the winter plugged into headphones and staring at screens. As we worked, more data was being leaked at regular intervals, with the last set dating from December 2015. In February, we began to approach those we intended to name, and our research began to collide with events in the outside world. Far away from Britain, the impact of the Panama Papers was beginning to be felt in apparently isolated political scandals.

In late January, two Mossack Fonseca representatives in Brazil had been arrested, and later released, by officials investigating the Petrobras affair. Two others fled the country. A prosecutor called the firm a 'money-washing machine'. On 4 March, the law firm received a letter from the ICIJ and *Süddeutsche Zeitung* stating that they had seen information concerning thousands of its companies.

On 11 March, TV crews from the consortium descended on Panama to film the firm's offices and ask for interviews. Later that day, founding partner Ramon Fonseca resigned as an official adviser to the Panamanian president, Juan Carlos Varela. In a parting shot, he tweeted: 'The pen is a powerful tool. It's sad when used for evil.'

On the same day, the Icelandic prime minister, Sigmundur Davíð Gunnlaugsson, walked out of a television interview with two Panama Papers reporters – the independent documentary-maker Jóhannes Kristjánsson, and Sven Bergman from Swedish TV. They had, on camera, named Wintris, the undeclared offshore company he had owned with his wife, and which his wife still owned. The film would not be released until 7pm GMT on Sunday 3 April, the date that all 110 news outlets brought together by the ICIJ had agreed to release their stories simultaneously.

But by the Monday before publication, the Kremlin was beginning to spin. Putin's spokesman held a press conference to warn that journalists were planning an 'information attack' on the Russian president, led by the ICIJ. Key names, including those of the banker Yuri Kovalchuk and the cellist Sergei Roldugin, were released.

The atmosphere inside the secure room at the *Guardian* was tense. We had been joined by the paper's investigations head Nick Hopkins, picture researchers, and a crack team of subeditors who moulded 33 articles into publishable form. Would the story hold? Should we bring publication forward? Requests for information flooded into the ICIJ. Like a general holding back his troops before the charge, the ICIJ's director, Gerard Ryle, hit the phones, talking editors into holding their nerve.

By the Friday, two days before we published, there were calls for a vote of no confidence in the Icelandic parliament. But the key data relating to Gunnlaugsson's offshore adventure remained unpublished, and so the embargo agreed months beforehand stayed in place.

After months working on our own, on 3 April the Panama Papers reporting team emerged from the locked office to gather around a desk in the centre of the newsroom. There were 11 items ready to be published. Viner and Johnson stood ready to give the signal.

At 6.48pm, Edward Snowden sent a Twitter message to his two million followers: 'The biggest leak in the history of data journalism just went live, and it's about corruption.' His tweet linked to a *Süddeutsche Zeitung* article headlined 'A Storm is Coming'. Within minutes, the Panama Papers whirlwind had struck. In 70 countries around the world, the reverberations are still being felt.

16 April

My working day: 'I'm a long thinker and a fast writer'

HILARY MANTEL

Some writers claim to extrude a book at an even rate like tooth-paste from a tube, or to build a story like a wall, so many feet per day. They sit at their desk and knock off their word quota, then frisk into their leisured evening, preening themselves.

This is so alien to me that it might be another trade entirely. Writing lectures or reviews – any kind of non-fiction – seems to me a job like any job: allocate your time, marshal your resources, just get on with it. But fiction makes me the servant of a process that has no clear beginning and end, or method of measuring achievement. I don't write in sequence. I may have a dozen versions of a single scene. I might spend a week threading an image through a story, but moving the narrative not an inch. A book grows according to a subtle and deep-laid plan. At the end, I see what the plan was.

I used to be a late starter, but now I get up in the dark like a medieval monk, commit unmediated scribble to a notebook, and go back to bed about six, hoping to sleep for another two hours and to wake slowly and in silence. Random noise, voices in other rooms, get me off to a savage, disorderly start, but if I am left in peace to reach for a pen, I feel through my fingertips what sort of day it is. Days of easy flow generate thousands of words across half a dozen projects – and perhaps new projects. Flow is like a mad party – it goes on till all hours and somebody must clear up afterwards. Stop-start days are not always shorter, are self-conscious and anxiety-ridden, and later turn out to have been productive and useful. I judge in retrospect. On flow days, I have no idea what I've written till I read it back. It's a life with shocks built in.

I don't mind whether I write by hand or on a keyboard. I don't mind anything, as long as I've woken up calmly in my own time. I'm a long thinker and a fast writer, so most days I don't spend much time at my desk. I concentrate well. I'm not tempted by the internet. If I'm redrafting, fine-tuning, I print the text and take it away to read on paper. But if I'm writing straight on to the screen, I tense up till my body locks into a struggling knot. I have to go and stand in a hot shower to unfreeze. I also stand in the shower if I get stuck. I am the cleanest person I know.

I am fuelled by tea. I don't want to break to eat. But after an intense bout of work I might fall asleep, which gets me fit for the next bout. I stop for the day when some inner falling-away says that's all there is. It feels like a page turning inside – the next page is empty. Nothing is left then but to go to bed and wait for dreams and for the next day.

About half my working year is like this. The rest involves talking, travelling, producing a public persona – but still with odd hours, and a constant output of ideas. The most frequent question writers are asked is some variant on 'Do you write every day, or do you just wait for inspiration to strike?' I want to snarl, 'Of course I write every day, what do you think I am, some kind of hobbyist?' But I understand the question is really about the central mystery – what is inspiration? Eternal vigilance, in my opinion. Being on the watch for your material, day or night, asleep or awake.

18 APRIL

Boaty McBoatface may not be the name of new polar research vessel after all

JESSICA ELGOT

It might be the democratic will of the people, but RRS *Boaty McBoatface* will probably never weigh anchor, the government has signalled.

The Natural Environment Research Council, which asked the public to vote on a name for its new £200m polar research vessel, confirmed on Sunday that the votes were overwhelmingly in favour of naming the state-of-the-art ship *Boaty McBoatface*. The suggestion received 124,109 votes, four times more than second-placed RRS *Poppy-Mai*, named after a 16-month-old girl with incurable cancer.

The chief executive of the NERC, Duncan Wingham, will have the final say in the naming of the boat, leaving him with a dilemma: delight the public and enrage the scientific establishment, or lose the goodwill the campaign has generated. Several PR experts have urged Wingham to keep the name to keep the momentum of public interest going.

However, Jo Johnson, the science minister, signalled the government was preparing to activate its get-out clause. 'The new royal research ship will be sailing into the world's iciest waters to address global challenges that affect the lives of hundreds of millions of people, including global warming, the melting of polar ice and rising sea levels,' he said.

'That's why we want a name that lasts longer than a social media news cycle and reflects the serious nature of the science it will be doing. There are many excellent suggestions among the 7,000 names put forward by members of the public and we'll make a decision as to which one should be put forward for the royal warrant when we've had a chance to review them all.'

Social media and science PR experts are divided as to how the NERC should respond to the poll.

'They should stick with the public decision,' said Bob Ward, policy and communications director for the Grantham research institute on climate change and the environment at the London School of Economics. 'If a new name is chosen, that is saying: "We don't trust the public", but people would soon forget about it.

'On the other hand, if they keep the name, then the interest in the vessel will also endure. It doesn't have to be a problem for them. And it makes no difference to the vital work the ship will be carrying out, but it does mean there is likely to be more public interest in that work.'

Other PR experts said the interest could be retained without having to give the boat a ridiculous name. Tom Sheldon, senior press officer at Science Media Centre, also emphasised how much the debacle had raised the organisation's profile. 'Lots of people in science seem to see this as a bit of a PR disaster, but I think the opposite,' he said.

'The entire nation have been discussing a polar research ship. And they've all heard of NERC. How many other scientific research councils could they name?'

Sheldon said he did not think any goodwill would be sacrificed if a different name was chosen. 'Even if NERC pick a name with more gravitas, I seriously doubt there will be any public indignation; we've had fun with this, and it will always be *Boaty McBoatface* to the nation,' he said.

'Presenter Evan Davis signed off the BBC2 flagship news programme with "Newsy McNewsnight". There is now a horse called Horsey McHorseFace. It even featured on Channel 4's *Gogglebox*. It's captured our attention, made us laugh, and spawned a new meme. How many science public engagement exercises can you say that about?'

Michael Tinmouth, a social media strategist who has worked with brands such as Vodafone and Microsoft, said he did not expect to see a glass of champagne being broken over the bow of *Boaty McBoatface* any time soon, but also urged the NERC to own the story.

'It's a childish name, so it's an opportunity to engage with a younger generation,' he said. 'If I was them, I would get a team of designers and brand experts together and do something like develop a cartoon or a project for younger children which features a character called *Boaty McBoatface*, even if the boat isn't actually called that.

'I think the worst way to handle it would be to ignore it, but to be fair to the PR team behind it, they haven't yet completely slammed the door shut and they should seize the opportunity.'

Ward said he hoped the NERC would not be deterred from public engagement by this saga. 'Some of the biggest science stories in recent years have been through making scientific discoveries into public events, like space shuttle launches or the [Large] Hadron Collider, where there was a real sense of theatre.

Most experts agree the name is a lucky choice in one way. 'It certainly would ruffle a few feathers in the traditional scientific community, but there's nothing offensive about it,' Ward said.

The name was first put forward by James Hand, a former BBC radio presenter, who expressed surprise at the furore *Boaty McBoatface* had caused.

Hand said he stood by *Boaty McBoatface* as a 'brilliant name' for the research ship, but he voted for RRS *David Attenborough*, which came in fifth with 10,284 votes. Another less serious name – RSS *It's Bloody Cold Here* – came fourth in the vote.

In May, the NERC duly decided to overrule the public vote and call the ship RRS David Attenborough. *The name* Boaty McBoatface *will be consigned to one of its remote-controlled submarines.*

21 APRIL

Here is the news: it's usually bad – and that's bad for us

SIMON JENKINS

If it bleeds, it leads. Fear projects. Bad news sells. Failure makes the front page, success goes to the back. So what is it this week with so many headlines about the Queen? I recall an edict once coming down from a newspaper proprietor that the boss was 'fed up with so much bad news'. He wanted a 'good-news paper'. We duly prepared a spoof front page: 'No crashes at Heathrow', 'Government doing well', and, in the gossip column, 'All celebrities slept in their own beds last night'.

But if laboured good news does not work, bad news has become a toxin of public debate. The order has gone out to Brexit spin-masters, on both sides, to push fear. Immigrants must swarm, crime must soar, wealth must plummet and influence fade. Foreign stories are always bad news, unless about animals.

This week we had migrant-deaths horror, Ecuador-quake horror and Kabul-bomb horror. At home we had pupil sex-harassment, online trolling and youthful depression. The BBC regional news ran four items: 'Dad killed girl after conviction U-turn', 'Gun attack victim was due in court', 'Man murdered mother with carving knife', and 'Boy made up toddler strangling story'.

Even an event as banal as a mayoral election in London – Europe's booming capital – is dominated by crisis and gloom. Across the land, Britain's schools face upheaval. The health service is in meltdown. Housing is a disaster. A Martian tuning in afresh to the British media would assume Britain was a failed state.

I used to believe that bad news would boost the morale of ordinary citizens. So much misfortune and misery in the outside world would be reassuring. As long as we personally are not experiencing an earthquake, a pogrom or matrimonial violence, we are doing better than most. Evil gossip about the lives of others reflects well on our own dull selves. A celebrity fallen from grace restores balance to the world. Fate comes to every Icarus.

Now I am not so sure. I recently looked back at the files of old newspapers. While good news sometimes read as propaganda, there was far less of today's relentless, 24/7 misery. The old journalistic rule of thumb, that bad news should be leavened with good, has died. Terrorism incidents are turned into week-long sagas of hysteria. This can only feed insecurity and risk-aversion.

As if in support, that other branch of entertainment, the film industry, is now unnervingly bleak. Two decades ago the American critic Michael Medved campaigned against the movie industry's implicit message that 'physical intimidation is irresistibly sexy, and violence offers an effective solution to all human problems'. Film-makers retorted that their products were simply 'escapist', and could not possibly lead to imitative behaviour.

If so, asked Medved, why was advertising so lucrative in shaping our behaviour? He was drummed out of Hollywood. Yet America's subsequent history of gun abuse and overseas belligerence suggests that Medved's question was at least worth asking – and it still is.

News media make the same excuse. They deny the reality of imitative crime, even when a murderer's hard drive is found stashed with violent images of the day's reporting. Demands for restraint and a sense of proportion are said to be spitting in the wind of reality. News values are determined in the marketplace. Bad news is the background noise of public life – 'a reflection of the values of a wider society'. Besides, this is about freedom of speech.

On this argument – as long as humans crave the thrill of the evil, the extraordinary and the weird – bad news will always drive out good. The cry of the politicians and the professions – 'Why don't you report the good work we do?' – is for the birds.

Yet the reality is that Britain's crime is falling, prosperity is increasing and people are living longer. Around the globe, diseases are defeated each year, technology liberates millions, and deaths in armed conflict are at an all-time low.

The American psychologist Steven Pinker has recorded that society is steadily evolving in a more peaceful and tolerant direction. The growth of information, civil rights and pacifism 'prompts us to feel the pain of others, and to align their interests with our own'. Europe's essentially humanitarian response to the migrant surge across the Mediterranean illustrates this philanthropic emotion, even if national governments struggle to honour it in practice. Pinker was widely ridiculed by media merchants of doom, as if for putting them out of business.

If we really take the view that viewing the world as awash in cruelty and misery does no harm, we should stop worrying over one set of indicators clearly moving in the wrong direction, that of mental depression. The tenfold rise in serious depression over the past half-century may have many causes, including improved diagnosis. But it appears to relate, in part, to social isolation and alienation.

We can claim that children have always been bullied, girls harassed, women abused and men stressed to suicide. We can demand that everyone stop being too sensitive about health and safety and show a bit of backbone. But the round-the-clock barrage of bad news is hardly likely to relieve depression. It induces the opposite: public anxiety and fear. That can only provide millions of votes for the world's Donald Trumps.

More strangely significant is the antithesis: the one unimpeachably 'good news' story of the week. I carry no banner for the monarchy, though it seems a harmless and lighthearted way of embodying state headship. Nor is the Queen's 90th birthday a surprise: it has been on the cards for 90 years.

What is clear is that a nation will grasp at any ray of sunshine in the darkness. It will overwhelmingly and happily honour the longevity of a woman who has been a dignified feature of the national scene for almost everyone. I don't know if any opinion poll of upward public contentment is planned but, like the Olympics, the royal birthday seems bound to relieve, however briefly, the black-dog mood. It is one good news story even the British media cannot ignore.

22 APRIL

Creating the web we want: how do we make the *Guardian* a better place for conversation?

KATHARINE VINER

Last year, a few weeks before I started as the new editor-in-chief of the *Guardian*, I read a review in the *New York Times* of Jon Ronson's *So You've Been Publicly Shamed*. The book looks at the emergence of public humiliations on social media, and the review ended by saying that 'the actual problem is that none of the men running those bazillion-dollar internet companies can think of one single thing to do about all the men who send women death threats'. Since I was about to become the first woman to run the *Guardian* (sadly not a bazillion-dollar internet company), I decided I had a responsibility to try to do something about it.

That's why, over the past two weeks, the *Guardian* has published a series of articles looking at online abuse, with more to follow in the coming months. You might have read our interview with Monica Lewinsky, in which she described the trauma of being subjected to what could be called the first great internet shaming, and how she still has to think of the consequences of talking about her past – whether, by misspeaking, she could trigger a whole new round of abuse.

Lewinsky's experience has prompted her to tackle online harassment head-on: she is now a respected anti-bullying advocate. But as we've considered online abuse in all its forms – the rape and death threats; the sexist, racist and ad hominem attacks;

the widespread lack of empathy – it has become clear that some of the institutions that most need to follow Lewinsky's lead do not police, that tech companies are failing to keep on top of the problem and victims are being abandoned to their abusers.

We've called our series 'The Web We Want'. It's an attempt to imagine what the digital world could and should be: a public space that reflects our humanity, our civility and who we want to be. It asks big questions of all of us: as platform providers, as users and readers, as people who write things online that they would never say in real life. It also asks big questions of the *Guardian*.

Online abuse has been a problem since the earliest days of the web. Since the *Guardian* opened up its articles to comments, tens of thousands of conversations have taken place below the line between readers and journalists, and between readers and other readers. Many of these conversations have been excellent: thoughtful, engaged and rewarding. But some subjects – latterly Islam, refugees and immigration – have become magnets for racism and hate speech, while others – feminism, domestic violence and rape – can attract highly misogynistic responses. Across the internet, we have now reached a tipping point. For women, the abuse is often violent and sexualised, with direct threats to rape and mutilate. For non-white people, the abuse is often racist; for Jews, it is antisemitic; for Muslims, it is Islamophobic. To some extent, everyone online is affected. To the extent that our lives are conducted online, this is the water in which we all swim: it's horribly polluted and it's making a lot of us sick.

The focus is beginning to shift towards what we can do to reduce abuse and who should be taking responsibility for ensuring that this happens. *Guardian* political editor Anushka Asthana this week reported that the Labour MP Yvette Cooper has called on police and prosecutors to unmask the true extent of online harassment, describing it as 'stifling debate and ruining lives'.

Sandra Laville, a senior reporter in our London newsroom, helped launch 'The Web We Want' with a piece about attempts by Facebook, Google and Twitter to fight online abuse by fostering a 'counter-speech' movement. Many people, including some of the communities that these tech companies are attempting to empower, have questioned whether they are dodging their responsibilities and providing too little support to victims of abuse.

I would argue that the big digital players still need to bear more of the burden of the social costs of what they do (they have the deep pockets to pay for this). But news organisations aren't blameless. With this series, we are acknowledging that the *Guardian* has a problem with abuse and harassment. That is why we took the very unusual step of publishing research on our moderation data – the first media or tech organisation to do so – and engaged readers in a discussion about how to have better conversations.

The editor of 'The Web We Want', Becky Gardiner, and Mahana Mansfield, the *Guardian*'s senior data scientist, examined the 70 million comments left on the *Guardian* since 1999, particularly those blocked by our moderators for abuse or derailing the conversation, and reported on what they found. The stark results offer proof of what many have long suspected: of the 10 regular writers whose articles had the most comments blocked, eight are women (four white and four non-white; one Muslim and one Jewish) and two are black men. Three of the 10 most abused writers are gay.

The response to this work has been fantastic – some commentators called it historic – and we hope that others will follow our lead in looking at their own comments, as effective solutions will be hard to find without data and dialogue. We are exploring the possibility of sharing our data with academics in this area, and hope others will do the same.

'The Web We Want' is not just about identifying the problem: it is also about trying to work out how to make it better. Extreme abuse is rare on the *Guardian*, thanks to our highly skilled moderators, whose work ensures that comments abide by the community standards that are there to keep conversation respectful and constructive. But we need to maintain a supportive working environment for *Guardian* moderators and writers, and even low-level abuse can have a chilling effect on journalists and participants in the comments.

As editor, I think we need to act more decisively on what material appears on the *Guardian*. Those who argue that this is an affront to freedom of speech miss the point. That freedom counts for little if it is used to silence others. When women and minorities don't feel able to speak their mind for fear of insult, threat or humiliation, no such freedom exists.

In a video we made for the series, *Guardian* columnist Jessica Valenti described it this way: 'Imagine going to work every day and walking through a gauntlet of 100 people saying "You're stupid", "You're terrible", "You suck", "I can't believe you get paid for this". It's a terrible way to go to work.'

Over the next few months, the *Guardian* will continue to explore, with our readers, the questions and challenges raised by these issues. Should we look at stricter moderation, or more ways of rewarding positive contributions to our site? Should we limit the number of comments we host, or make them a privilege of membership? In a time of challenge to the business model of journalism, moderation is not cheap.

In her book *Hate Crimes in Cyberspace*, Danielle Keats Citron compares contemporary attitudes to online abuse with attitudes to workplace sexual harassment in the 1970s. Then, it was normal to have your bottom pinched at work. It isn't any more. Today, all kinds of bullying and aggression dominate much online conversation. Sadly, we can't eliminate bigotry. But that doesn't mean we have to tolerate it, much less give it a platform on which to thrive.

26 APRIL

Hillsborough disaster: deadly mistakes and lies that lasted decades (extract)

DAVID CONN

It was a year into these inquests, and 26 years since David Duckenfield, as a South Yorkshire police chief superintendent, took command of the FA Cup semi-final at Hillsborough between Liverpool and Nottingham Forest, that he finally, devastatingly, admitted his serious failures directly caused the deaths of 96 people there.

Duckenfield had arrived at the converted courtroom in Warrington with traces of his former authority, but over seven airless, agonisingly tense days in the witness box last March, he was steadily worn down, surrendering slowly into a crumpled heap. From his concession that he'd had inadequate experience to oversee the safety of 54,000 people, to finally accepting responsibility for the deaths, Duckenfield's admissions were shockingly complete.

He also admitted at the inquests that even as the event was descending into horror and death, he had infamously lied, telling Graham Kelly, then secretary of the Football Association, that Liverpool fans were to blame, for gaining unauthorised entry through a large exit gate. Duckenfield had in fact himself ordered the gate to be opened, to relieve a crush in the bottleneck approach to the Leppings Lane turnstiles.

The chief constable, Peter Wright, had to state that evening that police had authorised the opening of the gate, but as these inquests – at two years the longest jury case in British history – heard in voluminous detail, Duckenfield's lie endured. It set the template for the South Yorkshire police stance: to deny any mistakes, and instead to virulently project blame on to the people who had paid to attend a football match and been plunged into hell.

The evidence built into a startling indictment of South York-shire police, their chain of command and conduct – a relentlessly detailed evisceration of a British police force. Responsible for an English county at the jeans-and-trainers end of the 1980s, the force had brutally policed the miners' strike, and was described by some of its own former officers as 'regimented', with morning parade and saluting of officers, ruled by an 'iron fist' institution-ally unable to admit mistakes.

The dominance of Wright, a decorated career police officer who died in 2011, loomed over the catastrophe. He was depicted as a frighteningly authoritarian figure who treated the force 'like his own personal territory' and whose orders nobody – tragically – dared debate.

The families of those killed in the 'pens' of Hillsborough's Leppings Lane terrace, who have had to fight 27 years for justice and accountability, recalled the appalling way the South York-shire police treated them, even when breaking the news of loved ones' deaths. Relatives and survivors recalled indifference, even hostility, in the unfolding horror – although the families' lawyers thanked individual officers who did their valiant best to help victims. Then there was the unspeakably heartless identification process in the football club gymnasium, after which CID officers immediately grilled families about how much they and their dead loved ones had had to drink.

The families, and many survivors, spoke up in the witness box at these inquests to reclaim the good names of the people, mostly young, who went to Hillsborough that sunny April day, to watch Kenny Dalglish's brilliant Liverpool team.

The overwhelming evidence, shown in BBC colour footage of the horrific scene and contrary to the lurid, defamatory tales spun afterwards by the police, was of Liverpool supporters heroically helping. The 'fans' – a label too often applied to depict a dehumanised mob – included doctors, nurses and police officers, alongside scores of people with no medical training who, once they had escaped themselves, fought instinctively to save lives.

The 96 people who died or were fatally injured in 'pens' three and four, standing right behind the goal, so by definition Liverpool's hard core of support, were honoured by their families in achingly tender personal statements read out in court. They came from all walks of life: working class, middle class, wealthy, hard up; from Liverpool, the Midlands, London and around the country. They included a heartbreakingly large number of young people – 37 were teenagers – because to watch an FA Cup semifinal then cost only £6. They were sons, daughters, brothers, sisters, husbands, one wife – Christine Jones, 27 – and partners. Twenty-five were fathers; one, 38-year-old Inger Shah, was a single mother with two teenagers; altogether, 58 children lost a parent.

The horror the victims suffered and the generally abject response of the police and the South Yorkshire Metropolitan Ambulance Service (Symas) were exposed in greater detail than ever before, in months of film and photographic evidence, from cameras that had been at Hillsborough to cover a football match. Survivors of the lethal crush bore tearful witness to the vice-like squeeze, the cracking of ribs, arms and legs, faces losing colour, the vomiting and emptying of bowels and bladders, relatives and friends dying next to them, the still barely believable piles of dead bodies at the front of the 'pens'.

One doctor said the crush, which caused death by compression asphyxia as people could not expand their chests to breathe in, was 'like a constrictor snake'. Survivors recalled their own helpless entrapment, the agonising suffocation, the eye-popping panic, the terrible screams for help, the delayed reaction of South Yorkshire police officers on the other side of the metal perimeter fence.

The makeshift courtroom, assembled within the ground floor of a plate-glass office block on a Warrington business park, often felt blankly incongruous for stories of such human extremes. Yet the remnants of the police effort to blame the supporters were on show even here, despite the families' long, exhausting battle against it, and despite the lord chief justice, Igor Judge, having stated when he quashed the verdict of the first inquest that the narrative was false.

Duckenfield's own barrister, John Beggs QC, an advocate instructed by police forces nationwide, pressed the case most forcefully that supporters had misbehaved, persistently introducing as context into his questioning notorious previous episodes of football hooliganism, his manner often repellent to the families attending.

But Beggs was not alone. The present-day South Yorkshire police force itself and the Police Federation also argued that Liverpool supporters outside the Leppings Lane end could be found to have contributed to the disaster because 'a significant minority' were alleged to have been drunk and 'non-compliant' with police orders to move back. Yet survivors gave evidence of chaos at the Leppings Lane approach, no atmosphere of drunkenness or misbehaviour, and no meaningful police activity to make orderly queueing possible in that nasty space.

Even as the terrible failures of Hillsborough were being laid bare at the inquests, the South Yorkshire police culture of the 1980s – and its other infamous scandal, Orgreave – was being further exposed. In July, the Independent Police Complaints Commission decided not to formally investigate the force for its alleged assaults on striking miners picketing the Orgreave coking plant in June 1984, or for alleged perjury and perverting the course of justice a year later, during the collapsed prosecutions of 95 miners.

However, the IPCC's review found 'support for the allegation' that three senior South Yorkshire officers had 'made up an untrue account exaggerating the degree of violence' from miners, to justify the police's own actions that day. It revealed that senior officers and the force's own solicitor privately recognised there had been some excessive police violence, as well as perjury in the 1985 trial, but never acknowledged it publicly, and settled 39 miners' civil claims, paying £425,000 without admitting liability. The IPCC said the evidence 'raises ... doubts about the ethical standards and complicity of officers high up in [the South Yorkshire police]'.

Wright never doubted the rightness of the violent defeat meted out to the miners, and when the prosecutions collapsed he adamantly denied any malpractice. No police officer was ever disciplined or held accountable, and there was no reform.

Four years later, on 15 April 1989, 24,000 Liverpool supporters set off in high spirits for the semi-final in Sheffield, their safety dependent on that same police force.

Wright's high-handed rule was at the root of the disaster, the inquests heard. Just 19 days before the semi-final, he abruptly moved his seasoned, expert, popular commander at Sheffield

Wednesday's Hillsborough stadium, Chief Superintendent Brian Mole. In Mole's place, Wright promoted Duckenfield, who had never commanded a match at Hillsborough before, nor even been on duty there for 10 years.

A trail of former officers bleakly confirmed the farce behind the switch: a bullying prank played on a probationary constable by officers in Mole's division the previous October. Reportedly to teach him a lesson because they felt he was making radio distress calls too readily, the officers put on balaclavas and terrified the probationer with a mock armed holdup. On 20 February 1989, Wright personally sacked four officers and disciplined four more for this excessive internal prank. But Wright's disastrous decision to move Mole was never questioned by senior officers.

Duckenfield turned up to command the semi-final, he admitted, knowing very little about Hillsborough's safety history: about the crushes at the 1981 and 1988 semi-finals, or that the approach to the Leppings Lane end was a 'natural geographical bottleneck' to which Mole had carefully managed supporters' entry.

Duckenfield admitted he had not familiarised himself in any detail with the ground's layout or the capacities of its different sections. He did not know the seven turnstiles – through which 10,100 Liverpool supporters with standing tickets had to be funnelled to gain access to the Leppings Lane terrace – opened opposite a large tunnel leading straight to the central pens, three and four. He did not even know that the police were responsible for monitoring overcrowding, nor that the police had a tactic, named after a superintendent, John Freeman, of closing the tunnel when the central pens were full, and directing supporters to the sides. He admitted his focus before the match had been on dealing with misbehaviour, and he had not considered the need to protect people from overcrowding or crushing.

The families of the people who were ushered into that terrifyingly unsafe situation and died read shattering personal statements, many remembering their loved ones' casual goodbyes. Irene McGlone recalled her husband Alan, 24, skipping with their daughters – Amy, then five, and two-year-old Claire – before driving to Hillsborough with three friends, including Joseph Clark, 29, another father of two, who also died. Amy asked if her dad could wake them up when he came home that night.

'I am still waiting to wake my girls up from this nightmare, and send their daddy in to them,' McGlone wrote.

Having failed to prepare, Duckenfield admitted 26 years later that he also failed profoundly at the match itself. He did not know what he was doing. While Mole used to be driven all over Sheffield before a big match to check on traffic flows, then, closer to the 3pm kick-off, patrol around the ground, Duckenfield said he still could not remember at all what he did in the more than two hours between concluding his briefing of officers and arriving in the control box at 2pm. Once in the small control room, he stayed there.

Superintendent Roger Marshall, put in charge outside, was new to the role. In his evidence, he accepted the police had no plan to filter people's entry into the Leppings Lane bottleneck, using police horses or cordons, beyond 'some random ticket checking and ... some checks for drunkenness'. Repeatedly played footage of the mass congestion that developed, Marshall admitted that it was a problem starting at 2.15pm, with thousands more people still arriving, and by 2.35pm, police had 'completely lost control'.

By 2.48pm, the crowd at the turnstiles had compacted into a dangerous crush, and Marshall radioed the control room, asking if the large exit gate C could be opened. Duckenfield did not respond until Marshall said somebody would die outside if he did not open the gate. At 2.52pm, Duckenfield ordered it open.

At these inquests, he admitted he had given 'no thought' to where the people would go if he opened the gate. He had not considered the risk of overcrowding. He had not foreseen that people would naturally go down the tunnel to the central pens right in front of them. He had not realised he should do anything to close off that tunnel. The majority of the 2,000 people allowed in through gate C went straight down the tunnel to the central pens, and gross overcrowding there caused the terrible crush. Of the 96 people who died, 30 were still outside the turnstiles at 2.52pm. They went in through gate C when invited by police, and were crushed in the central pens barely 10 minutes later.

Paul Greaney QC, representing the Police Federation – who on behalf of the rank and file principally sought to emphasise senior officers' lack of leadership – took his turn on Duckenfield's sixth day. Standing three rows of lawyers back, he elicited from Duckenfield admissions that he lacked competence and experience, that his knowledge of the ground was 'wholly inadequate'.

In tense, charged exchanges, Greaney asked Duckenfield if he had frozen in the crucial minutes when making the decision to open the gate. Duckenfield denied this four times. Then Greaney asked again: 'Mr Duckenfield, you know what was in your mind. I will ask you just one last time. Will you accept that, in fact, you froze?'

Slumped in his seat, Duckenfield replied, 'Yes, sir.'

Then Greaney put to him: 'That failure [to close off the tunnel] was the direct cause of the deaths of 96 persons in the Hillsborough tragedy?'

'Yes, sir,' Duckenfield said.

The horror in pens three and four was described by traumatised survivors and police officers over subsequent months of graphic, terrible evidence.

A police constable, Andrew Eddison, who went into the pens to pull people out, said in his statement that 'everybody had urinated themselves' and defecated, and that vomit swirled over the bodies and around his feet. There were two piles of bodies at the front, and Eddison said a hand at the bottom of one was pulling at his trouser leg. Once the bodies were finally cleared, it turned out to be a child.

David Lackey, a man trapped in pen three, recalled Thomas Howard, 39, a married father of three who worked in a chemicals factory, crushed next to him, saying repeatedly: 'My son, my son.' Howard's 14-year-old son, Tommy Jr, died with him.

Duckenfield admitted quite readily in court that as people were suffering this terror, he told his lie to Kelly. This fiction, that fans without tickets had forced the gate, had already found its way to the BBC, reported as a version by John Motson, the television match commentator, at 3.13pm. Alan Green, commentator for BBC Radio 2, broadcast an unconfirmed report of 'a broken-down door' at 3.40pm, then at 4.30pm he reported that police had said 'a gate was forced' – the police story of misbehaviour settling on the initial public consciousness.

Walter Jackson, the assistant chief constable who was at the ground as a guest of Sheffield Wednesday, was in the control room and heard Duckenfield say it. It took an hour for Jackson to learn the truth, when Marshall told him, at 4.15pm, that Duckenfield himself had ordered the gate opened.

Yet, half an hour before that, when Jackson still believed – as he said in his evidence – that fans had 'stormed' the gate, he had ordered Chief Superintendent Terence Addis, head of CID, to set up an investigation into the deaths. Addis, under questioning, said he had arrived at Hillsborough and talked to Jackson at 4pm, but repeatedly said he could not remember what Jackson had told him; Addis said he did not think he even asked Jackson for an initial view of what had caused the unfolding disaster.

Addis also denied that he had instructed his CID officers in the gymnasium to ask relatives about alcohol, but his account did furnish the families with an explanation for how they were questioned. The Hillsborough gymnasium was designated as the place to house bodies in a fatal emergency. With only four ambulances making it on to the pitch, 82 bodies were taken by supporters and police officers to the gymnasium, using advertising hoardings and even a stepladder as makeshift stretchers. Addis set up the gymnasium, he revealed, not just as a place of identification, but as the CID 'incident room' – the centre for his investigation – 'to try to identify the cause of the incident'.

He said he had talked to Detective Superintendent Graham McKay on the way to the gymnasium, and from McKay, Addis said, 'I got most of the gist of what happened.' Although Addis did not specify what he was told, McKay, who gave evidence at the inquests, has always vehemently made the case that Liverpool supporters misbehaved and were drunk.

An extraordinary revelation was that at 5.58pm, with so many people dead, injured and traumatised, a police inspector, Gordon Sykes, sent a force photographer to take pictures of litter outside. Mark George, QC for 22 bereaved families, accused him of 'digging for dirt' to establish evidence of drinking by supporters. Sykes denied that, but admitted it was 'to gain evidence of what's been happening, one way or the other'.

In fact, the photographs showed the bins outside the Leppings Lane end – which 24,000 Liverpool supporters had passed – about a third full, mostly of soft drinks cans including Vimto, Sprite and Coke, with a few beer bottles or cans.

Addis decided all the identification should take place in one location, so he ordered the bodies of 12 people who had been taken to hospital and certified dead to be taken back to Hillsborough, where the other 82 bodies were being kept. The other two victims were Lee Nicol, 14, who was pronounced dead two days later, and Tony Bland, then 18, who was kept on life support for four years before he died in 1993.

At the gymnasium, families were made to queue outside in the cold, clear night, then eventually brought in and told to look through Polaroid photographs of all those who had died, not grouped by age or gender. Families whose loved ones had bus passes or other identifying documents on them were also made to go through this process. When their dead relatives were brought out to them, several parents testified that they were told they could not hold or kiss their dead children because they were 'the property of the coroner'.

Dr Stefan Popper, the coroner, who approved the arrangements, ordered blood samples to be taken from all victims and tested for alcohol – even the children, including Jon-Paul Gilhooley, the youngest, aged 10. It has now been revealed that some people lying injured in hospital also had their blood taken and tested for alcohol. Popper has never fully explained why he decided it was appropriate to take and test people's blood.

The story that the disaster should be blamed on the supporters was, meanwhile, being spread throughout that night by South Yorkshire police officers in their sports and social club, the Niagara – including the most lurid tales that would be published by the *Sun*, under the headline 'The Truth', during the week. It emerged at the inquests that one of the nastiest stories, that fans had picked the pockets of the dead, was not just untrue, but that the police had evidence that it was untrue from the beginning because they had made routine logs of all the cash and other property found on each person.

Sykes confirmed that in the Niagara he had seen a local Conservative MP, Irvine Patnick, and asked him if he wanted to know 'the truth'. He then took Patnick to several officers who told him that some supporters were 'pissed out of their minds', and that they were 'pissing on us' and kicking and punching police during the rescue operation.

'It was booze that did it,' Patnick, in a note, recorded Sykes telling him. 'You speak up for us to tell them in parliament what happened.'

The astounding hypocrisy of this became plain as Sykes admitted it in court: this was all said in the bar. Even with the deaths of so many people who had been in their care, and with their distraught relatives and friends still strung all over Sheffield desperate for news, many police officers went for a drink when their shifts officially ended. Those at the Niagara club included Duckenfield, Supt Bernard Murray and other senior officers. Sykes confirmed, almost casually, that the police were 'upset, shocked, and having a drink, and talking about their experiences'.

A picture emerged in glimpses, of a drinking culture in the South Yorkshire police, with most stations at the time having a bar. Police Federation minutes noted that officers 'got considerably drunk' that night while bereaved relatives were queueing outside to enter the hell of the gymnasium – where police would interrogate them about drinking.

Duckenfield was one of several officers who developed a drink problem afterwards, describing himself sinking 'half tumblers of whisky' in the mornings to enable him to read documentation for the Taylor inquiry.

That put into perspective the relentless police allegations about people who had a drink before a football match, the po-faced assertions that people smelled of 'intoxicants' or were, in the odd phrase favoured by Beggs, 'in drink'.

Wright had opened a fact-finding meeting at 9am on 16 April 1989, the day after the disaster, by immediately exonerating his force. 'I'm not in the business of questioning decisions,' the minutes record him saying, to a group including Duckenfield and all the senior officers responsible for the match.

They then told him stories against the fans: they were not inside the ground by 2.30pm because there were 'hordes of people drinking'; they were 'not normal'. Not one officer mentioned the actual cause of the deaths – the failure to close the tunnel – or the horror people suffered. Nobody mentioned Mole's removal, and nobody, Duckenfield included, accepted any responsibility. Wright told his officers: 'You did a good job.'

He moved on to discuss how the story of 'drunken, marauding fans' would be got out, saying the force could not do it too publicly because it had to respond 'professionally'. But, he said, the 'animalistic' behaviour of fans would emerge.

Later that day, the then prime minister, Margaret Thatcher, and her press secretary, Bernard Ingham, visited Hillsborough. Wright briefed them. Ingham has always since said of Hillsborough that he 'learned on the day' it was caused by a 'tanked-up mob'. The South Yorkshire Police Federation secretary, Paul Middup, widely quoted in the media at the time, used the same phrase: 'A tanked-up mob.' In a television interview played in court, Middup said the disaster was not the police's fault, and criticised supporters' behaviour, saying they would not follow officers' instructions.

The *Sun* quoted him in its article, published on Wednesday, 19 April 1989, saying 'I'm sick of hearing of how good the crowd were' and adding that he did not doubt the notorious police stories that fans had urinated on and assaulted the 'brave cops'. Giving evidence, Middup said he was only reporting to the media what police officers had told him.

That same day, Wright attended a Police Federation meeting at the Pickwick restaurant in Sheffield. Far from condemning the stories, the minutes record Wright congratulating Middup for the case he had been making. Wright actually said of Duckenfield in that meeting that 'unfamiliarity' as a match commander could be an advantage, because an inexperienced officer would be 'more on their mettle'. Wright told the meeting: 'If anybody should be blamed, it should be the drunken, ticketless individuals.'

The South Yorkshire police officers were ordered, contrary to all regular practice, to record their Hillsborough experiences not in their official pocketbooks but on plain paper. A series of officers acknowledged at the inquests that this was unprecedented: it was a disciplinary offence not to write in a pocketbook, which is a contemporaneous note, very difficult to amend without it being obvious, and is therefore persuasive, credible evidence in a courtroom. Accounts on plain paper could be – and infamously were – amended before going to the official public inquiry headed by Lord Justice Taylor.

Some officers did write in their pocketbooks. Some, including Marshall, said they handed theirs in, but they have not been found by the force or given to the investigations. Most wrote on plain paper, the majority including descriptions of supporters drinking and misbehaving. Many made a similar observation: that the pens, even when they went in after the crush, 'smelt of alcohol'.

Barrister Stephen Simblet, representing bereaved families, suggested to one of these officers, Alan Ramsden, that that was 'a surprising observation' to have made about that place of disaster. Ramsden replied: 'Yes, I did make reference to that. But in hindsight, which we are all blessed with, it could be the smell of death.'

The plain-paper accounts were amended before they went to the Taylor inquiry. The Hillsborough Independent Panel reported in 2012 that 164 statements had been altered. In 116 of these, criticisms of the police operation and senior officers' lack of leadership were removed. Pete Weatherby, QC for 22 bereaved families, questioned Peter Metcalf, the solicitor for South Yorkshire police who implemented this process, and Chief Superintendent Donald Denton, who headed the police's amendment operation. Weatherby concentrated on just a few of the 164 statements, showing that all references to the 'Freeman tactic' (closing the tunnel to the central pens) were deleted.

Weatherby put to Metcalf that this was concealing important evidence from Taylor. Metcalf denied it, saying he was advising on statements being in suitable form for Taylor. He told the coroner, Sir John Goldring: 'I think I was serving the interests of truth, sir.'

Denton actually admitted that removing the evidence about previous tunnel closures 'impeded' Taylor's inquiry, which was kept 'in the dark'. But to his own barrister, Christopher Daw QC, Denton said he was following legal advice, that while changing officers' statements was 'unorthodox', he believed everything he did was 'proper, lawful and in good faith'.

In August 1989, at a time when football supporters were still being collectively stigmatised for the hooliganism of a few, Taylor found completely against the police case, and criticised the force for making it. Publicly, Wright accepted the Taylor report; privately, his force redoubled its efforts at the first inquest to blame supporters. Their relative success at doing that, securing a verdict of accidental death in March 1991, fuelled the families' continuing trauma, and their long campaign for justice.

The final verdict, when it eventually arrived, represented the most thorough vindication imaginable for the families of the dead, and an equally damning indictment of the South Yorkshire police. The jury supplanted the 1991 verdict with one of unlawful killing, laying blame squarely on the police in the process. Critically, it agreed that Liverpool fans had in no way contributed to the disaster. The families gathered outside the Warrington courtroom and sang 'You'll Never Walk Alone' before a throng of media.

At last, after 27 years of horror, heartbreak and struggle, the families have seen a jury deliver the verdict that they, their loved ones, and those who suffered and survived but found themselves targets of the South Yorkshire police's ferocious campaign required. The families were people mostly trusting of the police, who after their horrific loss found themselves in a nightmare, fighting the police's false case and repeated letdowns by the legal system. Derided and denigrated as 'animalistic', they were ultimately driven on by the power of human love and loyalty, and the bonds of family.

The lessons for British policing from this needless devastation of so many lives stretch far beyond the failings of one out-of-his-depth officer who took 26 years to fully confess. The police have a difficult, vital job: to keep society safe. However here, where they failed, their use of the word 'animals' documented an inability to see a group of citizens even as people.

They came to the Warrington business park mostly as old men, with hearing problems, impaired memories, illness and trauma. Yet many seemed oddly still like a force apart, speaking a macabre, dehumanised language: males, youths, casualties, intoxicants. Some did make expressions of empathy, but not many – Duckenfield, blunderingly, was one; Jackson and Marshall were others. Some junior officers were clearly moved; several criticised the police operation and process of changing statements. Others, with bereaved families sitting feet away, repeated their original allegations and went no further.

There were some police officers whose decency stood out. One was Russell Greaves, a detective constable who tried to revive Sarah Hicks, 19, on the pitch after she had been brought out of the crush next to her sister Vicki, 15. Trevor and Jenni Hicks, the girls' parents, had given heart-wrenching evidence. Trevor was said by witnesses to have been running between the girls, as desperate attempts were made to revive them, shouting and pleading: 'Not both of them; they're all I've got.'

Trevor Hicks himself tried to perform mouth-to-mouth resuscitation on Vicki, which involved, he testified, sucking vomit from her mouth, then he went with her in an ambulance – another scene of hell, with a teenage crush victim, Gary Jones, on the floor, and Hicks trying not to stand on him. He believed another ambulance would be along for Sarah but, as Greaves recalled, no ambulance came. They carried Sarah on an advertising hoarding to the gymnasium, but there were no ambulances there either, so they laid her on the pitch and performed CPR again. Eventually, qualified medical staff told them she was dead. Greaves recalled that he closed Sarah's eyes.

At the end of his evidence, Greaves asked if he could say a few words. A big man with a moustache, overcome with emotion, he then read something he had prepared, to a rapt courtroom. 'Just mere words cannot comfort Trevor or Jenni Hicks, or remove their sense of loss, pain and utter devastation,' he said. 'But I would like to take this opportunity to say to them that I did my very best for Sarah in the circumstances. I could not have done more. For the time I was with Sarah, Sarah was with someone who cared. Sarah was not alone.'

Greaves and his friend Fred Maddox were police officers, but they were off duty that day. They were there with other police colleagues to support Liverpool Football Club. They had gone for a drink before the match. They were 'fans'. Then when the disaster happened, they did everything citizens could expect of police officers, and of fellow human beings. As with many survivors who gave evidence a generation on, and the families who have endured an unimaginable ordeal, their honesty and humanity shone through.

6 MAY

So we're all Foxes now?
I've been one for 65 years

JULIAN BARNES

I haven't always been a Leicester City supporter: there was a time before I could read, or knew how to tune the Bakelite wireless to the voice of Raymond Glendenning on *Sports Report*. But from the moment I became sportingly sentient – say, the age of five or six – I have been (as they didn't much say then) a Fox. So, six and a half decades and counting. I did, initially, support a second team – Partick Thistle, from the grittier end of Glasgow. But that was because my infant mind believed they were called Patrick Thistle, and my middle name is Patrick. I eventually stopped supporting Thistle – such is the strange, irrational adhesiveness of fandom – when I was about 40, though of course I still instinctively check their results in my Sunday newspaper. But apart from this dalliance, I have been entirely monogamous.

Support for Leicester has been fashionable this season, of course: how many times have sympathetic voices spoken the words 'We are all Foxes now'? And generally, it's been heartfelt, as was the thumbs-up from my Kurdish greengrocer after he invited me to confess my football allegiance over a plastic basket of veg. We are all Foxes now: that's to say, this season Leicester became most football supporters' second team; if their own lot couldn't take the title, better Leicester than some hated and despised rival. 'Yes, I've been supporting the Foxes this season,' my friend Rachel Cooke confided. 'I mean, after Sunderland, and then the Blades, of course, and Liverpool.' But it's more than just a passing sentimental indulgence. Fandom routinely consists of a swirling mix of stupid love, howling despair and frantic self-loathing, but Leicester have also brought into violent focus what other supporters think of their own teams and managers. A long-standing Arsenal fan emailed me a couple of months ago – when everything could still have gone terribly, terribly wrong for Leicester – with his ideal scenario. 'I hope you win,' he wrote. 'And when you do, I hope that Arsenal fans, thinking of the £125,000 a week squandered on Per Mertesacker and Theo Walcott, will march on the Emirates and burn it down.' Well, I shan't feel responsible if that happens.

There are other reasons why we are all Foxes now. For a start, there is absolutely zero chance of Leicester winning the title again next year: it will be back to big money, big-city teams, Pep Guardiola, perhaps Mourinho, and so on. The Big Five (or Six) will once again be in charge. So we offer no long-term threat. But it is also because Leicester embody a kind of football – and ethos – which still speaks to the inner squaddie of most fans. They are – or at least, they seem to be – selfless, highly industrious, un-bigheaded, romantically all-for-one-and-one-for-all, and prepared to scrap till the last minute of added time: the puritan virtues dressed in blue. They don't have a bloated bench of internationals. They don't rotate because there isn't that much in the dressing room to rotate. They were all very cheap to buy: Riyad Mahrez, the players' player of the year, cost £400,000 when he arrived from Le Havre (whereas Manchester United are currently about to spend £46m on a Portuguese midfielder). And – another item of appeal to the romantic – the Foxes are proving that there are such things as second acts in the life of a footballer; in some cases, even third and fourth acts.

To be a lifelong supporter of Leicester is to have spent decades poised between mild hopefulness and draining disappointment. You learn to cultivate a shrugging ruefulness, to become familiar with the patronising nods of London cabbies, and to cling to an assortment of memories, of pluses and minuses, some comic, some less so. Yes, we have won promotion to the top division every so often; but the fact of promotion logically implies an earlier relegation. Yes, we did win the League Cup; but what burns the soul are the four times we reached the FA Cup final and the four times we lost. When asked to name my three sharpest Leicester memories, they are of varied texture: a pathetically heroic Len Chalmers, in the days before substitutes were allowed, hobbling around in an FA Cup final against Spurs back in the black-and-white days (he played 60 minutes with a broken leg, whereas today's softies collapse from the mildest case of ingrowing toenail); Keith Weller's hilariously unstoppable own goal, volleyed from near the halfway line, a clip of which used to be part of *Match of the Day*'s introductory collage; and the moment, deep into extra time, when we beat Crystal Palace in the play-off final at Wembley in 1996. I was seated among tiers of incredulous Palace fans as Steve Claridge shinned the ball in from a distance of at least several inches. Yes, there have been some fine managers, glorious moments, and players like Banks, Shilton and Lineker. But more typically I think of that year not so long ago, when, weeks into the season, the team's leading scorer was one of our defenders – with three own goals.

I long ago learned to rationalise the situation. 'Yes, Leicester City,' I would answer for the thousandth time. 'But you see, supporting Leicester is very good training for supporting England. You get hardened to the disappointment, so it doesn't hurt as much.' Actually, it probably hurts just as much when, every two years, England go out in the quarter-finals of this tournament, the preliminary rounds of that, or fail to qualify altogether. Which raises a dangerously alluring proposition. If Leicester can win the Premier League, why shouldn't England win the Euros on 10 July? There are good reasons, of course – called Germany, Spain, Italy and France – but then there were good reasons (Manchester City and United, Chelsea, Arsenal and Spurs) why the Foxes could never end up on top of the heap as king of the castle. And that's another thing I've been noticing this season: that it's impossible to talk about football except in cliches. This is not just the default linguistic position; it's the only one. And so, all those phrases have come tumbling out of my mouth: 'It's been a rollercoaster of a season', 'It's a massive six-pointer', 'They left absolutely everything out there on the pitch', 'I just hope we can dig out a result', 'We're hoping the Blues will do us a favour on Monday night'. Not to mention all the reynardine stuff about the flying Foxes and the Fox in the box. When asked, 'Are you still Dreaming the Dream?' I would automatically reply, 'Yes, but I'm also beginning to Feel the Fear.' Still, everyone in football, apart from Eric Cantona, speaks the same way. Verbally, it's a truly democratic sport.

A few weeks ago, as the sharp-shirted buzzards of *Match of the Day* contemplated the season's run-in, Alan Shearer recalled the time he won the title with the last 'unfashionable' club to do so, Blackburn Rovers. Like Leicester, they had seemed to be moving effortlessly towards the title, but in the last weeks jitteriness took hold, until in the end, as Shearer put it, 'we fell over the line'. This seemed an all too plausible parallel and, being a realist (ie pessimist), I naturally pushed the prediction further: the Foxes would fall not over but just before the line, trampled into the May mud by Harry Kane and company. But that didn't happen either. When Leicester took the title, it was with a lead of seven points and two games to go. There are going to be a lot of little boys in Leicester over the next few years bearing the names of Kasper and Wes and Robert and Danny and Riyad and Jamie, I can tell you.

The team did it; Ranieri did it; Pearson began it all; the fans did it; the owners helped. Even Richard III is being given some talismanic credit for the spectacular change of fortune. But I would also like to claim a small assist myself. In March of last year, when the Foxes were mired at bottom of the table and seemingly bereft of all hope, I found myself in Santiago de Compostela. Behind the cathedral's high altar is a gilt and bejewelled life-size bust of Saint James, reached from either side by a set of steps. Apparently it is traditional for hopeful and credulous petitioners to embrace the saint from behind while making a wish. This is not my kind of thing at all. But then it was explained that before setting off for each World Cup or European Championship, the Spanish squad climbs the steps, embraces the bust and asks the saint for victory. So, in fully ironic mode, I gave old James a hug and requested him to ensure that Leicester City escaped relegation. As I came down the other side, I said to him under my breath, 'And if you can do that, I might have to believe in you.' When the season ended with the Foxes not just safe but lower-mid-table, I felt a certain moral queasiness. And now look what he's gone and done: talk about Saint James the Over-Deliverer. In which case – and this might be pushing our theological luck – there is the small matter of the Champions League next season. Then I'd really believe in you.

10 MAY

Tax avoidance: for 'fantastically corrupt', David Cameron should look closer to home

GUARDIAN LEADER

There are times when a manual earth-restructuring implement is best referred to as a spade, so let us speak plainly. A summit on corruption will be held tomorrow in a city that is internationally recognised (by the IMF, among others) as a tax haven. It is being hosted by a politician who admitted last month that he has personally profited from offshore finance and whose party is bankrolled by an industry that makes extravagant use of those same tax havens. Not only that, he has intervened to aid tax avoiders. That's right, David Cameron is holding a meeting on corruption.

The prime minister is not personally corrupt – but he is certainly guilty of epic hypocrisy. So, for that matter, are Britain and the west. They have spent decades ordering poor countries and failed states to sort out their problems with dodgy money, even while taking much of that dodgy money and ploughing it through their banks, their ritzy stores, their estate agents, and their offshore tax havens – with barely any questions asked or eyebrows raised. When Mr Cameron was caught on camera yesterday boasting to the Queen of the 'fantastically corrupt countries' turning up at Lancaster House this week, he might have mentioned that Afghanistan is a failed state that did not get any less failed over 13 years of British intervention. And he should certainly have mentioned that the president of Nigeria, Muhammadu Buhari, is coming to

London to lobby it to sort out the tax havens in its own backyard. Indeed, Mr Cameron might have quoted a letter sent to him a fortnight ago by campaigners in Nigeria.

'We are embarked on a nationwide anti-corruption campaign,' the letter said. 'But these efforts are sadly undermined if countries such as your own are welcoming our corrupt to hide their ill-gotten gains in your luxury homes, department stores, car dealerships, private schools and anywhere else that will accept their cash with no questions asked. The role of London's property market as vessels to conceal stolen wealth has been exposed in court documents, reports, documentaries and more.' So the president of the Nigerian senate, Bukola Saraki, currently facing allegations that he failed to declare his assets, owns a property in London's Belgravia in his own name. But last month's Panama Papers revealed that the £5.7m property next door is owned by companies incorporated in the Seychelles and British Virgin Islands, whose respective shareholders are Saraki's wife and former special assistant. And a £1.65m townhouse in Kensington is shown as belonging to a BVI company whose sole shareholder is Folorunsho Coker, former head of the number-plate production authority of the state of Lagos and currently business adviser to the governor of Lagos. It may be that none of these individuals have done anything wrong, but the charge from those campaigners is hard to duck. Under successive governments, from Thatcher to Blair to Cameron, London has become the financial centre for the world's dirty money.

A third of all the trillions hiding offshore is sitting in tax havens linked to the UK, according to Oxfam. These havens rely on Britain for security and protection. The Jersey pound note features the Queen. On the Caymans, they sing as the national anthem 'God Save the Queen'. Yet Whitehall persists in pretending they are autonomous – even though London has overridden them before, on the abolition of capital punishment, say, or the decriminalising of homosexual acts. It will not do so on shady finance, however. The result is that Britain will soon bring in a public register of who ultimately owns the companies listed here – even while its overseas territories won't. The Caymans and the rest claim that this is because they are home to perfectly legitimate operations – in which case, what have they got to hide?

This fudge suits both the City and the havens. The accountancy firms and tax lawyers and wealth managers in London will continue to reap fat fees by using their branch offices scattered across offshore Britain to look after clients seeking low tax and secrecy – even while the UK can claim that its domestic financial industry is as clean as can be. Few will call this corruption or hypocrisy, as it wears a sharp suit and talks so nicely.

In Oscar Wilde's *The Importance of Being Earnest*, Cecily implores Gwendolen: 'This is no time for wearing the shallow mask of manners. When I see a spade I call it a spade.' The reply comes: 'I am glad to say that I have never seen a spade. It is obvious that our social spheres have been widely different.'

10 MAY

The dystopian world of Beatrix Potter

KATHRYN HUGHES

The 150th anniversary of Beatrix Potter's birth this summer is already kicking up a host of merchandising possibilities that might appear to come under the rubric of 'cashing in'. You'll be able to buy a copy of Potter's newly discovered and much-hyped late book, *The Tale of Kitty-in-Boots*, or put your children in fancy dress as Mrs Tiggy-Winkle or Samuel Whiskers. And that's not forgetting the new 50p Peter Rabbit coin, which is already in circulation and selling on eBay for 40 times its face value. Coloured versions of the coin, originally costing £55, are now changing hands for over £600.

But before we rush to condemn all this 'merch' as nothing but a tasteless desecration of childhood innocence, we need to remember that this is what Potter's world has always been about, from that moment in 1902 when she published her first animal tale. It's not simply that Potter was herself an eager marketeer, keen to sell the rights to her images for nursery wallpaper and christening beakers, so that when she died in 1943 she was a wealthy woman (and a public-spirited one, too – she bought 4,000 acres of the Lake District and then gifted them to the National Trust). It's that the world Potter created so compellingly in those 23 little books comprises nothing less than a clear-sighted primer for navigating the amoral world of mature capitalism.

Writing at a time when the human cost and economic vulnerability that underlay Britain's imperial project could no longer be ignored, Potter shows us a world where there is one cardinal rule: eat or be eaten. On the very first page of her very first book, Peter Rabbit is sent out to play with the terrible maternal warning to be careful, because 'your father had an accident ... he was put in a pie by Mrs McGregor'. Tom Kitten, meanwhile, is turned into a sausage roll, wrapped up in pastry by two triumphant-looking rats. Nor, in Potter's world, is there any point in looking to adult lawgivers to put things right and kiss things better. Jemima Puddle-Duck, an experienced mother, is obliged to stand by helplessly while her eggs are stolen by Mr Tod, 'a foxy person'.

Private property is constantly under threat in Potter's world – at risk of being taken over by someone who is bigger and stronger. The Two Bad Mice break into a doll's house and, when they find that they can't eat the pasteboard food, take malicious pleasure in trashing the place. Mr Tod, meanwhile, is a profligate capitalistic landlord who has 'half a dozen houses' but is 'seldom at home', and as a result is constantly watching out for opportunistic squatters.

Potter was writing as Darwin's earlier revelations about nature being a place of ceaseless, violent competition were being grafted on to the realisation that the 'survival of the fittest' applied as much to two-legged creatures as it did to those with tails and whiskers. Beneath our thin veneer of civilisation we are, Potter warns, nothing but beasts, red in tooth and claw. In *The Tale of Tom Kitten*, Tom and his sisters are told by their mother to walk on their hind legs while wearing their best clothes, like respectable, rational beings. Within minutes, though, they are scrapping in the dust, naked, while some thieving ducks make off with their clothes. Civilisation turns out to be an illusion, as much a matter of top dressing as Diggory Delvet's velvet coat.

Unlike virtually any other classic children's author, Potter didn't offer much in the way of happy endings. Although her heroes and heroines just about manage to escape with their lives, they mostly finish the story having lost something of value. (Squirrel Nutkin, indeed, is obliged to leave his tail behind on Owl Island.) Nor is there any sense of a moral lesson having been learned. Instead, Tom Kitten, Jemima Puddle-Duck and their friends will, we are led to believe, repeat their adventures tomorrow, and the day after, and the day after that. And at some point, they will almost certainly get killed and eaten.

So this summer, when you find yourself tutting over the way your childhood memories of mice in pinnies and ducks in bonnets have been desecrated by the dead hand of commercial exploitation, remember this: the reason why we still care so passionately about Beatrix Potter is not because she offers us an escape from the random cruelties that are part of decaying capitalism, but because she has the moral toughness to show us exactly what it feels like to be powerless and afraid.

19 MAY

It ain't easy being
a black Brexiteer

DREDA SAY MITCHELL

I'm on the left and I want out of the European Union. Although Paul Mason made the same case in the *Guardian* this week, it is a rather lonely position to take these days. A generation ago that wasn't the case. In the 1980s, 'Get Britain Out' was up there with 'Refuse Cruise' and 'Coal Not Dole' as the good lefty's badges of choice, and leaving the EU was part of the Labour party's programme until 1988. I think that the EU poses a direct threat to democracy and to the British working class; I thought so then and I think so now.

The trouble is that this means I am now on the same side of the argument as people I fundamentally disagree with, even on the subject of the EU itself. I have no problem debating with such people or sharing panels with them, but that does depend on showing a basic level of empathy and respect. And when it comes to Nigel Farage – I don't think he has it.

I was asked to appear on the same panel as Farage at a debate this week, organised by the *Daily Mirror*, on whether we should stay in or leave the EU. I realised that I might have some explaining to do when *Mirror* readers saw me on the same side as Farage, the Ukip leader, and the Tory MP Andrea Leadsom. Current and former Labour politicians Peter Mandelson, Ayesha Hazarika and John McDonnell were on the other side, though McDonnell has had profound differences with Mandelson on defining subjects such as New Labour and the Iraq war.

I expected all the issues to be examined in a free and lively debate but, perhaps naively, I was reckoning without Farage and the particular dynamic he brings to these occasions. He was civility personified before proceedings began – indeed, he was encouraging to some degree, recognising the challenges that face a non-politician like me on a highly charged political occasion.

But once we were under way, his tone was different, as was his demeanour. He seemed less concerned about a debate in terms of an exchange of thoughts or ideas, and more concerned – consumed perhaps – with scoring points. No blow too low. 'You wanted to rub our noses in diversity, didn't you, Lord Mandelson?' he said. The remainers were outraged and so, sitting right next to him, was I. You get a distinct, sinking feeling sat next to someone who wants to blame workers like your own parents for Britain's problems.

'Why shouldn't we have people of different ethnic backgrounds, different colours?' Mandelson shouted back at Farage, the two exchanging fire across me. 'You've shown your true colours and you owe her an apology,' Mandelson added.

Amid the hullabaloo, all the warnings from friends – who had cautioned, 'Don't get into this issue, Dreda, you'll be fitted up by rightwingers' – seemed right. I was also forced to take issue with Leadsom, my other fellow panellist, who spoke of public services being 'overwhelmed' as a result of immigration. Some Brexiteers may choose to speak this way, but not in my name.

When I suggested that the EU was actually a class issue, it was McDonnell, from the opposite camp, who picked up on the idea. I'm fed up with hearing about what's good for big business and high-flying professionals; at street level, views are far more mixed. I don't know many kids from the estates who are excited about starting their own media company in Milan. McDonnell believes in a different kind of EU. I respect that position; I just don't think it's possible. But at the same time, I was wondering if it was possible to swap chairs around so I could enjoy more congenial company.

Farage and I didn't speak again, and after the event I stayed up late into the night responding to criticism from angry Ukippers. They accused me of being there just to embarrass Farage. That wasn't my intention. But I hope that's what transpired.

I don't regret participating, and I'll be doing more debates, not least because I'm unwilling to give the impression that women can't hack a little argy-bargy on a panel. I am also unwilling to cede the leave argument to rightwing Conservatives when there's a long and proud tradition of leftwing opposition to the EU. The arguments made by Tony Benn, Barbara Castle and Peter Shore a generation ago still stand as far as I'm concerned. It's for other leftists to explain why they don't.

And if not me, who like me? For often, when I'm approached to appear on the media or at public events and have to decline, I am then asked: 'Do you know any other minority pundits who share your views?' Or any who are working-class, council-housed or comprehensive-educated? Whether we leave or remain, the issue of diversity in public life – or the lack of it – will run and run.

19 MAY

Being trans isn't a phase you go through

JACK MONROE

When the tabloids this week ran a story about a 19-year-old electing for a bilateral mastectomy, because they (the preferred pronoun) are non-binary transgender, there was the predictable pearl-clutching and rolling out of tired old tropes. Aspiring armchair psychiatrists were quick to denounce Opi Baron as 'obviously mentally ill', while accusations flew thick and fast that 'being transgender is fashionable'.

I bought my first chest binder at the age of 19, and it wasn't just a phase. Thousands of women have breast enhancement surgery every year to alter the 'natural' configuration of their chest to match the way they would prefer it to look. One of my cousins underwent breast enlargement a few years ago, and her family and friends were supportive, accepting her explanation that the procedure would increase her self-confidence.

Yet when I went public about wanting a chest reduction, it was met with horror. The writer James Delingpole proposed starting a petition for me to keep my breasts attached to my body, with the insistent headline: 'We need to talk about Dr Jack Monroe's breasts.' Another journalist suggested that there should be Kickstarter funding for my surgery.

I was heavily criticised by some users on Mumsnet for my 'proposed removal of a pair of healthy breasts', as though breasts were a trophy I would be a fool to part with. Perhaps so, but body dysphoria runs deep, and I would be a fool to tolerate it when I don't have to.

Sitting over breakfast with my mother a few months ago, I awkwardly tried to answer her questions about being transgender. 'I just don't want you to make any permanent changes that you might regret,' she started. I laughed and gestured to my 44 tattoos before gently countering that it might be too late. 'You dye your hair, Mum,' I pointed out.

This may be a startling confession for a food writer, but when I was younger I had a severe eating disorder. I struggled at school – socially, mentally and academically – and so I starved myself. It started with giving my lunch away, then skipping breakfast, then walking to and from school instead of catching three buses, in a bid to be thinner, which would solve everything, or so I thought.

When my parents realised how gaunt and exhausted I had become, I was told that if I didn't start eating properly again, I would be sent to hospital and forced to eat through tubes down my throat. I begrudgingly regained weight and confided in my food-technology teacher about the despair I felt. I loved food tech because of the precision and the creativity, the weights and measures, the tiny glimpses of flavour. In time, food was no longer an enemy, but a joy.

With my newfound love of food came puberty. My breasts began to develop and I hated it. I had been boyish and braless for 15 years and that's who I was. As a young woman, I pretended my name was Adam. I prayed to God at night that I would turn into a boy when I started to develop. Something was wrong, deep down, but I didn't know what it was or how to fix it.

I started to bind my breasts. I wrapped bandages round them to hold them down. I didn't want them at all. I thought they were ugly, messy and cumbersome. Not mine, not a part of me I wanted or identified as my own. I have no connection with them. I feel nothing there, which is something I have had to explain gently to various lovers over the years, who can't understand the disconnection.

When I had my first appointment at a gender clinic, I sat and talked completely openly to a doctor for the first time. That's the thing about being trans that the armchair commentators can't comprehend: it's a condition, just like any other. Although our experiences are all different, there are symptoms, questions that need to be asked, and criteria that need to be fulfilled in order to reach a diagnosis.

My medical report diagnosed me as transgender. I have been on hormones now for eight months. I walk taller, laugh more and feel like myself. I mostly, finally, fit into my own skin. Friends have commented on how much more confident I am. I eat whatever the hell I like. I like myself.

People can sit at home and pontificate about my body all they like. Free speech and all that. But it's mine. And I know what I'm doing with it, and why I'm doing it, and it's not up for debate.

You can tell me I'm not a boy until you're blue in the face but, to quote my friend, the author and trans activist Christine Burns, it's as good as saying that sugar is salt.

22 MAY

Black lives matter. So does Islamophobia. Beyoncé in a sari? Not so much

NOSHEEN IQBAL

'Is it OK to use the black emojis if you're not black?' As conversation starters about identity politics go, few seem more juvenile and current than this one. (FYI, to avoid the tedium of this real-life chat I had recently, it's easier to stick with your own skin tone.) And yet, here we are, at the frontier of 'being woke'. On one hand, this means being socially aware about issues such as #blacklivesmatter, racial profiling, privilege, Islamophobia etc – all the big guns. On the other? Not every battle is worth having. To clarify, this isn't a discussion about the very real and very insensitive cases of cultural appropriation in recent years – the most obvious being Native American headdresses, a sacred tradition regurgitated as cheap and crass festival costume fodder (so two summers ago; keep up). No, what we're seeing more and more of now are the minority voices within minorities who are policing communities and culture to the point of ridicule.

Take, for example, the #reclaimthebindi movement. I understand the frustration: having been embarrassed about your heritage and made fun of when you were younger for your mum's funny clothes and accent, it's jarring then to see Becky at Latitude co-opting sari tops and henna for that ethnic festival look a decade later. It's not necessarily racist, but it is definitely high on the scale of Dumb, Annoying Shit People Do. To be ranked in that same file: colour runs (the Hindu spring festival Holi reconfigured as an Instagram opportunity in Hyde Park); the fact that Black Twitter is rarely credited for setting the agenda for contemporary pop culture; Coldplay's cringe discovery of India on their last album. However, to claim that Beyoncé committed a heinous, culturally insensitive crime by wearing south Asian-style gold and henna in the video for Coldplay's 'Hymn for the Weekend', or that only African American women can truly appreciate *Lemonade*, segregates culture in an aggressively retro way. It's a parody of earnestness that does us no favours. How did we even get here?

Tribally marking off permission rights as to who can and who cannot enjoy certain music and certain fashion – both industries where creativity and innovation depend so much on borrowing from so-called 'other' cultures – is inane. It also distracts from bigger-picture arguments: say, the disproportionately high numbers of non-white deaths in police custody, or the rights of Bangladeshi factory workers, still stitching your H&M vests for less than a living wage.

See the energy expended on Blake Lively last week. A relatively innocuous actor slash lifestyle brand – the B-side to Gwyneth Paltrow, if you will – Lively was called out as a racist for posting a picture of her arse on Instagram with the caption: 'LA face with an Oakland booty.' Which is, for clarity's sake, a lyric from 'Baby Got Back' by the connoisseur of big butts, Sir Mix-A-Lot. Lively may well be dim to sensitivities around race and privilege (she did, after all, host her 2012 wedding to Ryan Reynolds at a plantation in South Carolina), but that's by the by. The alleged furore she sparked in this instance was because, to quote women's website Jezebel, she 'touts a diametrical opposition: that Los Angeles can be equated to elegance and/or beauty (read: whiteness) and that Oakland is its foil (read: blackness)'.

Sure, yes, I get it. But is this the hill we want to die on? The *Daily Mail* would like its readers to think so. Like many sections of the press, it will routinely, hysterically, report on tiny corners of the internet shrieking racism at every minor outrage – arguably, because it's easier then to undermine social justice warriors as sensitive keyboard ninnies even when they're battling legitimate prejudice.

Should we really be wearing out moral outrage and energy in pretending that Sir Mix-A-Lot belongs not to those coming of age in the 1990s, but exclusively to the African American experience? And, if so, where do we stop When Cultural Appropriation Goes Bad? Once you put down dodgy markers, where only people of colour have the right to write about race, only black people can rap, only my mum can make authentic palak gosht (that last one is true, actually), where do you draw the line? And at what point do we admit that the argument becomes less to do with being respectful of 'other' cultures and more about your own ego as a minority voice? While it's one thing to stick it to white privilege and remind the mainstream that not everything is made for and about white people, it's quite another to cordon off culture into ever tinier boxes, where the right to enjoy and be influenced by what you consume is narrow and prescriptive.

Suddenly, that utopian optimism about embracing, sharing and celebrating one another's differences seems so quaint. The struggle isn't about one-upmanship. Nor is it about the racial politics of your emoji.

23 MAY

Between a rock and a lard place – is fat good for us, or what?

PASS NOTES

AKA: Triglycerides.

Appearance: Three fatty acid chains attached to a glycerol molecule.

And if you zoom out a bit? Greasy/delicious.

Mmmm ... greasy/delicious. But is it healthy? Asking that question demonstrates that you don't understand what 'healthy' means.

Giving that answer demonstrates why you have no friends. Look, the point is that there are many different kinds of dietary fat, each of them with different effects on the body, effects that, in turn, vary according to how much of them you eat, which other things you eat, and the genetic, behavioural and other circumstances of your life.

Couldn't you just say, 'It depends'? I could, but then you wouldn't understand the full complexity of public nutrition.

Who says I want to? Just tell me what the experts have decided. Mostly, that they hate each other.

Eh? The National Obesity Forum has just published a report claiming that government advice to cut down on fat is having 'disastrous health consequences'. 'The change in dietary advice to promote low-fat foods is perhaps the biggest mistake in modern medical history,' says Dr Aseem Malhotra, a senior NOF adviser.

Is he right? Not according to Public Health England's chief nutritionist, Dr Alison Tedstone. 'It's a risk to the nation's health when potentially influential voices suggest people should eat a high-fat diet, especially saturated fat,' she says.

That's Dr Aseem Malhotra told! It probably isn't. The NOF report claims that the science behind the official guidelines has been 'corrupted by commercial influences'.

Take that Big, um, Farmer! Except Professor Simon Capewell from the Faculty of Public Health denies it. 'By contrast,' he adds, 'the report from the National Obesity Forum is not peer-reviewed. Furthermore, it does not indicate who wrote it or how it was funded.' The British Heart Foundation is on his side as well.

Look, can I jam my head into a bucket of doughnuts or can't I? Go for it. Just not too often.

How often is too often? Well, it's complicated and we don't really know.

Argh! Sorry.

Do say: Just eat a balanced diet, stay a healthy weight and do regular exercise.

No really, just say: Eat a balanced diet, stay a healthy weight and do regular exercise.

31 MAY

The new James Bond should get political and start taking on some real villains: first Trump, and then the oligarchs

PAUL MASON

Bond should be female. Bond should be black. Bond should be an actor famous for being posh, blond and perfect. Or an actress famous for asexual nudity in a shlock medieval mega-series. It could even, at a pinch, be Daniel Craig again; he has turned the role so dark that, in *Spectre*, the villains began to look less steel-eyed, Nordic and mentally tortured than the hero.

All these outcomes are possible. But I have a more radical proposal: politicise Bond.

Bond's raison d'etre was to defend the postwar order. He only survived the end of the cold war by morphing twice. First, into an all-purpose defender of decency against organised crime. And then into that ultimate postmodern signifier: the fashion model who runs about amid explosions.

The sight of Daniel Craig's physique forced into a suit made apparently one size too small by designer Tom Ford, and then trying to run with his jacket buttoned tight like a Russian oligarch's security detail, signalled that the end of the line must be close. On Sunday, the director, Sam Mendes, announced he is going to quit – so what should Bond become?

In Ian Fleming's novels, Bond's obsession with smart food, wine, cars and clothing symbolised fastidiousness in a dirty world. 'You must forgive me,' Bond tells Vesper Lynd in the novel *Casino Royale*, after informing her that Taittinger is the world's greatest champagne: 'I take a ridiculous pleasure in what I eat and drink. It comes partly from being a bachelor, but mostly from a habit of taking a lot of trouble over details.'

But that world is gone. Not only the class distinctions, blurred for ever by the 'mass luxury' brand empires; it is the concept of the west that is blurred, and that makes choosing the next Bond, and giving him or her a feasible plotline, almost impossible. The Bond franchise can only maintain its current formula – spectacular violence, bad couture and vanilla sex – if it completes its detachment from reality.

Instead, try this thought experiment. The Bond of *Casino Royale*, published in 1953, time-travels to London in 2016. Once he's got over the multi-ethnicity, the unacceptability of smoking and the proliferation of actual casinos, what does he do?

As a trained intelligence operative, he makes a summary of the threats. There is jihadism, prone to unleashing suicidal attacks on civilians in major cities. There is Russia, its nuclear-armed bombers buzzing the airspace of the west, its soft power invading the very heartlands of British decency – Mayfair and Knightsbridge – in a way no Soviet operation managed.

He mulls – over a dry martini, naturally – which is the greater threat, and which is more urgent. And then it hits him. It's not Russia, not Isis, not even the decadence that has turned western civilisation soft. The threat is that a madman from central casting gains control of the White House, becomes commander-in-chief of the US military and gets his hands on the nuclear arsenal of the world's only superpower. After that, the global order fragments; Nato becomes a sham; the Paris climate accord is ruined; the social fires raging in the developing world burn out of control, propelling millions of refugees northwards.

Bond comes to a swift conclusion: he must target Donald Trump. Somehow, I doubt Barbara Broccoli would entertain this scenario, whether starring Idris Elba, Tom Hiddleston or Emilia Clarke. So what, in reality, are the options?

Fleming's original Bond played on a subtext in postwar western life: that, during the war, ordinary, decent people had been forced to do thrilling, transgressive things they could not talk about. And then, in peacetime – that grey world of rationing and sexual conformity – some very lucky people got to live the dream some more.

The Bond of 1953 is clinically, violently polyamorous, with untrammelled access to the luxury world of the old elite without any need to observe the social conformity that elite membership demands. He has permission to break the rules of western civilisation in order to save it.

Since Craig took over the role in 2006, Bond's enemies have been members of Quantum, a kind of LinkedIn for the criminal business elite. In the latest movie, Quantum was revealed as a sub-branch of Spectre, run by arch-enemy Ernst Blofeld. But the franchise never embraced the full anti-capitalist potential of this storyline.

For the Bond genre to survive, Spectre would have to be portrayed, overtly, as the global oligarchy, ripping off the world. Bond would be tasked by MI6 to kill and maim members of the hedge fund industry, the fracking bosses and CEOs extorting financial rent from the rest of us.

He – or she – might start by having a quiet word with the man who tried to hike the price of HIV drugs from $13.50 to $750, and then move on to the Saudi millionaires who have bankrolled violent jihadism. The Panama Papers would leave such a Bond with no shortage of targets.

When the Bond films altered the hero's focus from anti-Soviet espionage to a fight against a global network of greed-inspired madmen, it was read as a cop-out. The Soviet threat had been real; supervillains such as Blofeld were not. But palaces and mansions of the world are now replete with cat-stroking sadists who would plunge us into war and climate chaos as long as it furnishes a batch of new Italian suits each year, and a different Breguet for every day of the week.

The next Bond – and the next director – must have a go at the real enemy. Or he must die trying. That would be a great finale.

31 MAY

We're watching the death of neoliberalism – from within

ADITYA CHAKRABORTTY

What does it look like when an ideology dies? As with most things, fiction can be the best guide. In *Red Plenty*, his magnificent novel-cum-history of the Soviet Union, Francis Spufford charts how the communist dream of building a better, fairer society fell apart.

Even while they censored their citizens' very thoughts, the communists dreamed big. Spufford's hero is Leonid Kantorovich, the only Soviet ever to win a Nobel prize for economics. Rattling along on the Moscow metro, he fantasises about what plenty will bring to his impoverished fellow commuters: 'The women's clothes all turning to quilted silk, the military uniforms melting into tailored grey and silver: and faces, faces the length of the car, relaxing, losing the worry lines and the hungry looks and all the assorted toothmarks of necessity.'

But reality makes swift work of such sandcastles. The numbers are increasingly disobedient. The beautiful plans can only be realised through cheating, and the draughtsmen know this better than any dissidents. This is one of Spufford's crucial insights: that long before any public protests, the insiders led the way in murmuring their disquiet. Whisper by whisper, memo by memo, the regime is steadily undermined from within. Its final toppling lies decades beyond the novel's close, yet can already be spotted.

When *Red Plenty* was published in 2010, it was clear the ideology underpinning contemporary capitalism was failing, but not that it was dying. Yet a similar process as that described in the novel appears to be happening now, in our crisis-hit capitalism. And it is the very technocrats in charge of the system who are slowly, reluctantly admitting that it is bust.

You hear it when the Bank of England's Mark Carney sounds the alarm about 'a low-growth, low-inflation, low-interest-rate equilibrium'. Or when the Bank of International Settlements, the central bank's central bank, warns that 'the global economy seems unable to return to sustainable and balanced growth'. And you saw it most clearly last Thursday from the IMF.

What makes the fund's intervention so remarkable is not what is being said – but who is saying it and just how bluntly. In the IMF's flagship publication, three of its top economists have written an essay titled 'Neoliberalism: Oversold?'

The very headline delivers a jolt. For so long, mainstream economists and policymakers have denied the very existence of neoliberalism, dismissing it as an insult invented by gap-toothed malcontents who understand neither economics nor capitalism. Now here comes the IMF, describing how a 'neoliberal agenda' has spread across the globe in the past 30 years. What they mean is that more and more states have remade their social and political institutions into pale copies of the market. Two British examples, suggests Will Davies – author of *The Limits of Neoliberalism* – would be the NHS and universities 'where classrooms are being transformed into supermarkets'. In this way, the public sector is replaced by private companies, and democracy is supplanted by mere competition.

The results, the IMF researchers concede, have been terrible. Neoliberalism hasn't delivered economic growth – it has only made a few people a lot better off. It causes epic crashes that leave behind human wreckage and cost billions to clean up. And while George Osborne might justify austerity as 'fixing the roof while the sun is shining', the fund team defines it as 'curbing the size of the state ... another aspect of the neoliberal agenda'. And, they say, its costs 'could be large – much larger than the benefit'.

Two things need to be borne in mind here. First, this study comes from the IMF's research division – not from those staffers who fly into bankrupt countries and administer the fiscal waterboarding. Since 2008, a big gap has opened up between what the IMF thinks and what it does. Second, while the researchers go much further than fund-watchers might have believed, they leave in some all-important get-out clauses. The authors even defend privatisation as leading to 'more efficient provision of services' and less government spending – to which the only response must be to offer them a train ride across to Hinkley Point C.

Even so, this is a remarkable breach of the neoliberal consensus by the IMF. Inequality and the uselessness of much modern finance: such topics have become regular chew toys for economists and politicians, who prefer to treat them as aberrations from the norm. At last a major institution is going after not only the symptoms but the cause – and it is naming that cause as political. No wonder the study's lead author says that this research wouldn't even have been published by the fund five years ago.

Since the 1980s, the policymaking elite have waved away the notion that they are acting ideologically – merely doing 'what works'. But you can only get away with that claim if what you're doing is actually working. Since the crash, central bankers, politicians and TV correspondents have tried to reassure the public that this wheeze or those billions would put the economy right again. They have riffled through the textbook – bank bailouts, spending cuts, wage freezes, pumping billions into financial markets – and still growth remains anaemic.

And the longer the slump goes on, the more the public tumbles to the fact that not only has growth been feebler, but ordinary workers have enjoyed much less of its benefits. Last year the rich countries' thinktank, the OECD, made a remarkable concession. It acknowledged that the share of UK economic growth enjoyed by workers is now at its lowest since the second world war. Even more remarkably, it said the same or worse applied to workers across the capitalist west.

Red Plenty ends with Nikita Khrushchev pacing outside his dacha, to where he has been forcibly retired. 'Paradise,' he exclaims, 'is a place where people want to end up, not a place they run from. What kind of socialism is that? What kind of shit is that, when you have to keep people in chains? What kind of social order? What kind of paradise?'

Economists don't talk like novelists, more's the pity, but what you're witnessing is the start of the long death of an ideology.

Summer

Fighter, joker, magician, religious disciple, preacher: Muhammad Ali

KEVIN MITCHELL

Muhammad Ali is dead. That is a sentence as difficult to write as it is to comprehend. At his loudest and most beautiful, he seemed, illogically, beyond destruction. Even in his palsied state in the championship rounds of his life, his eyes sparkled quietly and his wit remained as sharp as the punches with which he tormented nearly all of his opponents in 61 fights. So imperious was he that those of us who were entranced by him in the 1960s and 70s hoped against every rational expectation that he would never leave the party, even though he had used up his champagne moments a long time ago. Ali, a born illusionist, teased us to the end.

When the news arrived on Friday night that Ali had died, aged 74, surrounded by his immediate family in Scottsdale, Arizona, after his 32-year fight against Parkinson's disease, its inevitability did not soften the blow for admirers who once were numbered in their several millions. He lived in an era of mass communication that led John Lennon to claim the Beatles were more popular than Jesus Christ; Ali made a compelling case to push them into second and third place.

He housed such an improbable quantity of warmth that it seemed the love he generated could sustain the planet. For many, he was – as a gauche pop song of the 1970s went – the

Black Superman. Such adoration will appear ludicrous to a generation who knew him only as a sick old man, a long-retired famous fighter whose rare and faltering public appearances usually coincided with the death of one of his contemporaries, most notably Joe Frazier in November 2011. Yet, for those who saw him box, listened to him talk and watched him grow into a media phenomenon of his own creation, it was easy to regard Ali as unlike the rest of us. The paradox was he was like all of us, in one way or another.

Which brings to mind an oft-repeated Ali story. A nervous flyer but a bigger egoist, Ali once refused to buckle up when a flight attendant asked him to do so moments before takeoff. 'Superman don't need no seatbelt,' he protested in mock indignation. 'Superman don't need no airplane,' she is alleged to have replied. The anecdote describes both his ego and his attachment to mischief-making – and it might even be true, though the Ali myth-making machine was prodigious.

Ali was many things to many people. To older connoisseurs of boxing, to his mother Odessa and, until his own end, to Joe Frazier, he would always be Cassius Clay, whatever the public concessions to his demands for recognition as Ali. He was the brash and beautiful young black man from Kentucky who 'shook up the world'. He did that by beating the unbeatable beast that was Sonny Liston, in Miami in February 1964. He went to the ring as Cassius Clay and, after the muscular intervention of the Nation of Islam, left as a champion who would from that point onwards be known as Muhammad Ali.

To the United States government, defenders of the war in Vietnam and conservatives everywhere, Ali was the most dangerous of enemies, a converted zealot, the bombastic mouthpiece of a religion few until then had heard of and hardly any understood. His trainer, Angelo Dundee, once facetiously remarked that he thought a Muslim was the cloth used to cover a cheese plate. He was quickly disabused of that notion.

The Nation's hold on Ali was at first total, giving him the appearance of a scripted puppet rather than a man of his own convictions. In the days leading up to the first Liston fight, he was still Cassius Clay, and the promoter Bill McDonald begged him to postpone the confirmation of his conversion and name change until afterwards, fearing the news would hit the gate. He agreed, reluctantly. There was another impediment, however: the presence in town of Malcolm X, who had left the Nation a year before but remained an outspoken black radical regarded with suspicion by the white establishment. McDonald wanted him gone, as did the Nation. He was trouble. Clay, after consulting with his Nation bosses, told his one-time friend – who had inspired him to join the religion secretly when he was 18 years old – he had to leave.

A year after being run out of Miami, the gifted orator was in New York to address a meeting in the Audubon Ballroom in Washington Heights, where three hitmen with Nation affiliations emerged from the crowd and gunned him down, fatally. Did Ali know of the assassination plot? There is no conclusive evidence, but many inside and outside the movement reckoned he might have at least suspected, and they saw Ali's abandonment of his friend as treachery. Although it was claimed Ali might have been able to warn his former mentor of the attempt on his life, he probably was powerless. Such was the champion's growing aura, however, that the episode slipped quietly into the background as his own grand narrative unfolded.

The Nation for years sucked hard on the juice of Ali's celebrity but, over time, their hold on him ebbed. Like Malcolm X, he eventually saw them for what they were, hardline separatists whose ardour bordered on gangsterism, and he left, quietly, in 1975 to join the Sunni branch of Islam. What the Nation understood was that Ali was more famous and socially significant than they were. In 1975, his cutting free from the most dubious period of his career not only marginalised the Nation further, it brought Ali another kind of peace and opened his eyes to the folly of his earlier, strident views.

Ali soon was the darling of a white audience he had never courted in his radical days. His willingness to confront past mistakes, to sublimate his considerable ego, would compensate ultimately for the bellicose egomania that launched his career. By the muted end, the Louisville Lip trembled a little, but was as eloquent as ever.

Religion and politics aside, Ali remained a prisoner of his original vocation: boxing. When it was said and done, what he did best was knock out other fighters, some of the greatest from any era. To most (but not all) of those who did not have to suffer embarrassment against him in the ring, Ali was an inspiration. So many young men of his time all over the world took up boxing because they wanted to move like him, box like him, talk like him, be like him. That was impossible, however, because Ali dealt in a singular magic, inside and outside the ring. This most beguiling of dream-sellers bewitched opponents with the power of his personality, much as Mike Tyson did with his intimidating knockout power, and he had a similar effect on his audience.

Ali carried none of the practised menace of Tyson or Liston, however, taking instead an unusually theatrical, almost comical route towards intimidation and self-promotion. His air was invariably lighthearted, and his lifelong addiction to parlour tricks ensured he never lost his innocence or sense of wonder. He also loved attention and would tell some outrageous fibs to generate headlines. In a sport of lies, he was the ultimate deceiver.

An early example of his mischievous trickery was the iconic photo of a young Cassius Clay, posing as if sparring underwater, a striking image that graced the cover of *Life* magazine in 1961. The photographer, Flip Schulke, and the publishers were unaware at the time that Ali could not swim.

He performed similar legerdemain on dry land. As a ring artist, he was, for much of his career, peerless. Nobody – certainly at heavyweight – boxed so brilliantly and with such disregard for orthodoxy; he perplexed his opponents and annoyed the experts. He often led with his right hand, sometimes with both feet off the ground, as if levitating. He retreated in straight lines, contrary to the accepted wisdom of the sport. He kept his hands down and his chin perilously in the air. He would grab and hold, illegally, frustrating opponents and kidding referees. All these misdemeanours broke boxing's verities of technique and etiquette. Yet, until his legs and brain began to lose syncopation, he was untouchable, literally and metaphorically.

Probably the most dazzling single exhibition of Ali's genius was his three-round destruction of Cleveland 'Big Cat' Williams in November 1966, at the Astrodome in Houston, Texas (the city where he would be arrested five months later for refusing the draft). That night he hovered over the canvas like an angel and punched like the devil himself. The gathering anger in his heart, inspired by his fight against the US government, transmitted itself to his fists, and the energy he brought to his work was frightening. Williams, a street-toughened operator who carried an old bullet in his body, was rendered helpless in the face of Ali's venom.

Ali the fighter will be remembered best, probably, for: two controversial nights of high drama against Liston – the second containing the infamous phantom punch; the night at Wembley in 1963 when Henry Cooper embarrassed him with the sweetest of all his fabled left hooks; the first and last contests of his trilogy against Frazier, the Fight of the Century at Madison Square

Garden in 1971 and in Manila four years later; and his 1974 miracle after midnight in the jungle of Zaire, against George Foreman. To beat the ogre Foreman against universal expectation at 32 pleased him more than nearly any other victory.

It was a shame, yet inevitable, that he would carry on past the defining contest of his later days, the dismantling of Frazier in 1975 that left both of them physically and spiritually wrecked. In each of those performances – because that was what nearly every Ali fight was – his personality elevated mere boxing matches to stopping-off points in the history of the 20th century. He was not only a man for his times; he shaped those times and made them unforgettable.

There were inevitable lows: the embarrassment of his final two bouts: when Larry Holmes, his old friend and sparring partner, begged the referee to stop the slaughter of their 1980 mismatch; and when Trevor Berbick, a tradesman-like opponent of crude power, closed out the Ali CV on a wretched occasion in the Bahamas in 1981, within a week of Frazier's last fight. Joe and Ali left their dangerous business simultaneously but were separated by enduring acrimony; their periodic acts of reconciliation in subsequent years were as much exercises in public relations as genuine rapprochement.

As for his stand on Vietnam, that was not straightforward either. Some will say Ali's most lasting victory was away from his place of work, when he took on the United States government and ignored what, initially at least, was a clear consensus for military intervention to quell the spread of communism in south-east Asia. He was not always the most sophisticated thinker – more a quick-witted busker – but he would not be deterred by either the loss of acclaim (the very oxygen of his existence) or the threat of incarceration for his objection on religious grounds to being drafted for a war he initially knew little about.

Ali became a hate figure when he refused to fight, a court hearing finding him guilty after only 20 minutes' deliberation in 1967, on the very day that boxing authorities took away his title and banned him from fighting for three years.

While in legal limbo, he toured campuses across America under the aegis of the Nation, an entertaining advocate of insurrection in front of young audiences who were charmed by his off-the-cuff take on a subject that had obsessed his compatriots, but the nuances of which remained beyond his complete understanding.

Alerted to the injustice of his plight by Howard Cosell – a celebrated broadcaster with a bad wig, uncontrollable ego and a good conscience – as well as a coterie of concerned admirers that included boxing-fixated writers Norman Mailer and George Plimpton, others began to acknowledge the material sacrifice Ali had made: the best years of his career, from the age of 25 to 29. They recognised also that Ali risked five years' imprisonment, a sentence avoided with the high-profile support of those enlightened campaigners who brought their influence to bear in one of the most public discussions Americans engaged in over Vietnam. His exile encompassed a significant shift in image. In June 1971, the United States Supreme Court overturned his conviction, 8–0, a points decision as clearcut as any among the 56 victories of his boxing career, and he stood tall as a champion of free speech and self-determination.

Conflict in Ali's life was not confined to the courtroom and the ring. He was a father nine times and a husband to four women, but his many bedroom adventures left a trail of unhappiness. He showed disturbing insouciance in ignoring loud background rows with his spouses over his serial infidelity. For all of his propagation of the blessedness of Muslim womanhood, he indulged himself when it suited him, which was often – until Lonnie, who'd adored him from a distance as a teenager on the street where they grew up, settled on his shoulder in 1986 as his fourth and abiding guardian angel. They spent their recent years living in Scottsdale, while Lonnie, a fierce gatekeeper of his legend, kept an eye on the Muhammad Ali Center in Louisville. That was always their spiritual home, a city that did not always embrace its finest sporting representative.

Although he eventually discovered private contentment, Ali's gift for deception extended across all areas of his life when he was off the leash. Did somebody really steal his bicycle when he was 12, leading him into the arms of a local policeman, who set him off on his boxing career? Perhaps. To this day, nobody can be certain if he threw his Olympic gold medal into the Ohio river on his return from Rome in 1960, after being harassed by a white motorbike gang in a roadside cafe on the outskirts of Louisville. If you trawled the Ohio river for a thousand years, the sage American boxing writer Jerry Izenberg said once, you'd more likely find a mermaid than an Olympic gold medal.

As discordant as it sounded to white ears, self-mockery came easily to Ali. The photographer Andy Hall and myself spent an evening with Ali in a New York hotel room in 2004 that will live long in the memory. He performed his magic tricks, told bad jokes, had a long and hilarious phone conversation with the actor Will Smith (who played him in an eponymous movie) and, accompanied by his former promoter and sometime nemesis, Don King, sang an ordinary version of the old 1950s hit, 'Stagger Lee'. As we left, he drew King close and whispered, 'And still a nigger.' That is how the evening ended, a legend playing out the game he'd played all his life, a showman to the last curtain call – even if only for a small audience – and always conscious of the one thing he knew defined him more than boxing or even his penchant for entertainment: the colour of his skin.

Despite what some airline attendants might or might not think, Ali could, in a sense, fly. The Black Superman's presence was ethereal. He lit up rooms, rendered other conversations superfluous, made women's knees knock and prompted men to quietly wonder what it must be like to be him.

He was the funniest athlete of his era, of that there can be little argument. He used his illness to turn pity into love. He forgave anyone who ever did him down, and there have always been plenty of those scoundrels in professional boxing. He held not a single grudge, and gave away a thousand little bits of himself, from a smile to an autograph, unloading the tat of his trade – gloves, shorts, robes, even a signed cigarette paper – to those who valued such things. Everyone wanted a piece of Ali; and, in the end, he let them take what they wanted. He found riches elsewhere.

Sports Illustrated named him their Sportsman of the 20th Century. The BBC made him their Sports Personality of the Century. But those accolades, as well as his Olympic gold medal and all his professional titles, garlanded rather than defined his prowess, because his true genius extended beyond the boxing ring. 'I don't have to be what you want me to be,' he said once. And when one writer insisted on calling him Cassius Clay, he replied, 'I'm not your slave. I'm Muhammad Ali.'

Whoever Ali was, there was only one of the man with two names. Categorically, there will not be another. I doubt we could stand the excitement.

5 JUNE

Fasting for Ramadan won't be easy – it's the coffee I'll miss the most

SADIQ KHAN

Is it really that bold to be the first Muslim mayor and be unafraid to be Muslim? I don't call myself a Muslim politician; I'm not a Muslim spokesperson or leader, and it's important to clarify that because otherwise you're defined solely by your faith. We all have multiple identities – I'm a Londoner, a son and a father – and City Hall isn't a pulpit. But, as Ramadan starts, I'm aware that it's a great opportunity to do things in the community, and break down the mystique and suspicion around the religion. If you're someone who doesn't have Muslim friends and your only experience of Islam is what you see on the news – the angry man with a beard doing or saying something terrible – then you may inadvertently associate that with Islam and think that is what it's all about. So, I'm making it a priority this month to get out there and build bridges by hosting Ramadan meals around the city at synagogues, churches and mosques.

The best way for people to understand each other's faith is to share experiences. Fasting is a good way to do this because, when you're breaking bread with someone, inviting non-Muslims to have that iftar meal together, it shows that it's not a big deal, nor is it spooky or weird.

When I was growing up, you had to explain to people why you weren't eating. Now, in a cosmopolitan city such as London, where for 1,000 years there has been an open exchange of trade, ideas, people and culture, most people know someone – perhaps at work or through friends – who will be spending this month fasting. Ask them how they are! It makes a big difference when someone spends just a minute to see how you're doing. I've had friends fast through solidarity – they don't always make it through the whole day, but it's a kind gesture.

This year will be especially tough. Because of the lunar calendar, Ramadan moves back by 12 days each year and we're now at the peak of long summer days. A lot of these fasts are going to last for 19 hours. It's scary. My diary is still full during Ramadan – we've got the EU referendum coming up and I could even have to open my fast on stage with a glass of water at an event. Last year, we had a big selection campaign during Ramadan, so there were lots of very hot hustings, where I had to perform while fasting. That's part and parcel of it. What you don't want to do is try to completely change your lifestyle, because it sort of defeats the object of it and the sacrifice. Of course, there are Islamic injunctions in the event that fasting affects your performance as a brain surgeon or if you're in the armed forces, but it's impressive how much your body can and will endure – much more than you realise.

Anyone who knows me knows I'm miserable during Ramadan. Some would say I'm miserable all year round, but it does affect my mood. What I usually miss the most is caffeine; I go to lots and lots of boring meetings (not this year, of course, because now I have the best job in the world!) and I need caffeine to keep going. So this year, in preparation, I tried to cut down on coffee in the lead-up to it. Food isn't the issue – you get over that. The other big myth is that you lose weight in Ramadan. Not true. Part of me doing this is to show that it is possible to be someone with western, liberal values and be a mainstream Muslim. My election on 5 May proved that London believes you can do both at the same time.

According to research conducted by the polling company ICM a couple of years ago, British Muslims are the most charitable group in the country, and I believe a lot of that comes down to Ramadan – it's a month of sacrifice, reflection and humility. It's a real leveller, too – you can't not have empathy. For instance, as mayor of London, I'm more aware than ever that in this city, the fifth richest in the world, 100,000 people had to access a food bank last year – and I can, to a degree, understand that experience. (I say that with the recognition that, unlike people who are homeless, I get a big feast at the end of the day.)

There is a role that Muslims in the public eye play: to reassure people that we are OK. It's not because we're more responsible; it's because we're more effective. You don't have to shout it from the rooftops – it's about having shared experiences. We have the most diverse city in the world, but we don't have people mixing as much as they could. I want to enable people to have a sense of belonging.

14 JUNE

I'm being chased around the internet by a shed

STUART HERITAGE

A few weeks ago, I thought about buying a shed. I thought about buying a shed, and it was the most exciting thing I did that day, because I'm a hot-rod rebel and my entire life is a thrill-a-minute joyride of unimaginable debauchery.

In the end, however, I didn't buy a shed – mainly because it turns out that my tolerance for sheds is so abysmally low that I can only look at a maximum of three sheds before deciding that all sheds are stupid and only ninnies need them. However, that hasn't stopped me from being ambushed by adverts for sheds on a near-hourly basis ever since.

Thanks to a web cookie on the shed site telling an ad server that this is now my defining personality trait – Stuart Heritage: shed enjoyer – the vast majority of adverts I see online are for sheds. It feels as if I'm being stalked by sheds. It feels as if I'm living in the first draft of an Edgar Allan Poe poem, written in the days before he realised that ravens are scarier than sheds.

'Hey, shed guy!' the adverts scream. 'Remember those sheds you looked at the other week? They're still here! Look how boxy and mundane they still are. Come on, click it. Click the shed.'

Behavioural retargeting, this is called. Chances are you've encountered it, too. Maybe you once went on Amazon, purely to see whether the word 'singalongamax' had hyphens in it or not, and now you can't move for Max Bygraves adverts. Maybe you ordered your partner a NutriBullet for her birthday, and every site you subsequently visited carried an advert for NutriBullets, and you had to fling a coat over your screen every time she came in the room in case it ruined the surprise, and now she's convinced that you suffer from a crippling porn addiction. Behavioural retargeting is everywhere, and it's infuriating.

The easy way out would be for everyone to just install an adblocker and be done with it. Certainly, that's what people are doing in their droves – it's been estimated that up to a quarter of adults use them.

But this is where I have to draw a line in the sand, because I'm not a monster. If I use a site – any site: a news site or a forum or social media – it's because it has some worth to me, and I don't want to see it go anywhere. That's what adverts are for. You put up with a peripheral banner telling you how funny *The Book of*

Mormon is, and the site gets paid as a result. But when you install an adblocker, you remove this revenue stream and the sites you like begin to suffer. By installing an adblocker, you're actively contributing to the reduction of the internet. If you install an adblocker, one day everything you enjoy will be replaced by three rotating Facebook click-through galleries entitled 'The Industrial and Commercial Bank of China Presents 21 Funny Faces That Dogs Pull When They're Horny', and you'll have nobody to blame but yourself.

The problem I have isn't so much with adverts themselves, but with the specific adverts that follow you around from site to site like a wounded puppy, tugging on your trouser leg until you finally put it out of its misery. Before it was sheds, it was coats. Before it was coats, it was coffee tables. I'm also being stalked by a pair of shoes that I looked at once, and which now bloodlessly creep into my Facebook stream at every opportunity. They're nice shoes, too, but I refuse to buy them as a matter of principle. If those shoes ever go near my feet, the internet will have won and I'll be no better than a child.

Marketers know how infuriating retargeting is, too. In 2014, researchers found that people generally get more annoyed the more they see an ad for something they had previously looked at online. They overwhelmingly said that the adverts made them angry and, if they happened to see an advert for something they had already bought, they instantly became four times more likely to never buy it again.

Clearly, retargeting has its upsides – if they didn't increase sales on some level they wouldn't exist, plus it's now easier than ever to sweep through your office, clock everyone's retargeted banner ads and make a discreet inventory of all the perverts who've ever thought about buying adult-sized Peppa Pig duvet covers – but the downsides vastly outnumber them. If they annoy people so much that they would rather install an adblocker and choke their favourite sites to death in the process, then something needs to be done.

Luckily, something can be done. There's a little blue triangle in the corner of these adverts. Click it, and you'll be able to opt out of most retargeted ads. You'll still see adverts, but they won't be the same creepily omnipresent ads that would otherwise haunt your every move. And that's a win-win. You stop feeling like you're being stalked by a shed, the site still makes money, and nobody has to make the uncomfortable decision to install an adblocker. You're just left with the perfect, undiluted web experience you always wanted. Good writing, helpful debate and several dozen ill-advised '10 Celebrities You Didn't Know Were Jewish' sponsored-link galleries clogging up the bottom of every single article you ever read. Perfect.

16 JUNE

The mood is ugly, and an MP is dead

POLLY TOYNBEE

In an era when many question the validity of their elected officials, Jo Cox stood out. She rose to represent the area in which she was born. And she arrived at the Commons with hinterland, a career campaigning for Oxfam, Save the Children and the NSPCC. Today, shock among MPs was palpable.

This attack on a public official cannot be viewed in isolation. It occurs against a backdrop of an ugly public mood in which we have been told to despise the political class, to distrust those who serve, to dehumanise those with whom we do not readily identify.

There are many decent people involved in the campaign to secure Britain's withdrawal from the EU; many who respect the referendum as the exercise in democracy that it is. But there are others whose recklessness has been open and shocking. I believe they bear responsibility, not for the attack itself, but for the current mood: for the inflammatory language, for the finger-jabbing, the dog-whistling and the overt racism.

It's been part of a noxious brew, with a dangerous anti-politics and with anti-MP stereotypes fomented by leave and their media backers mixed in. Only an hour before this shooting, Nigel Farage unveiled a huge poster showing Syrian refugees fleeing to Slovenia last year – nothing to do with EU free movement – and none arriving here. Leave's poster read: 'Breaking Point. We must break free from the EU and take control of our borders.' Nicola Sturgeon, Caroline Lucas and many others condemned it as 'disgusting', and so it is.

At a ward meeting this week, my local Labour councillor in Camden, north London, showed us a sign that had been left on a member's car windscreen. The car had a remain poster and was parked round the corner from where I live. This is what the message said, in capitals (I've left the original spelling): 'This is a lave [leave] area. We hate the foriner. Nex time do not park your car with remain sign on. Hi Hitler. White Power' – accompanied by racist symbols. The owner had passed it on to the police.

Rude, crude Nazi-style extremism is mercifully rare. But the leavers have lifted several stones. How recklessly the decades of careful work and anti-racist laws to make those sentiments unacceptable have been overturned.

This campaign has stirred up anti-migrant sentiment that used to be confined to outbursts from the far fringes of British politics. The justice minister, Michael Gove, and the leader of the house, Chris Grayling – together with Boris Johnson, the recent mayor of London – have allied themselves to divisive anti-foreigner sentiment ramped up to a level unprecedented in our lifetime. Ted Heath expelled Enoch Powell from the Tory front ranks for it. Oswald Mosley was ejected from his party for it. Gove and Grayling remain in the cabinet.

When politicians from a mainstream party use immigration as their main weapon in a hotly fought campaign, they unleash something dark and hateful that in all countries always lurks not far beneath the surface.

Did we delude ourselves we were a tolerant country – or can we still save our better selves? Over recent years, struggling to identify 'Britishness' – to connect with a natural patriotic love of country that citizens have every right to feel – politicians have reached for the reassuring idea that this cradle of democracy is blessed with some special civility.

But if the vote is out, then out goes that impression of what kind of country we are. Around the world we will be seen as the island that cut itself off as a result of anti-foreigner feeling: that will identify us globally more than any other attribute. Our image, our reality, will change overnight.

Contempt for politics is dangerous and contagious, yet it has become a widespread default sneer. There was Jo Cox, a dedicated MP, going about her business, doing what good MPs do – making herself available to any constituents with any problems who drop into her surgery. Just why she became the victim of such a vicious attack, we may learn eventually. But in the aftermath of her death, there are truths of which we should remind ourselves right now.

Democracy is precious and precarious. It relies on a degree of respect for the opinions of others, soliciting support for political ideas without stirring up undue savagery and hatred against opponents. 'Elites' are under attack in an anarchic way, when the 'elite' justice minister can call on his supporters to ignore all experts.

As I listen to the anger aroused by this referendum campaign, it becomes clear that something close to a chilling culture-war is breaking out in Britain – a divide deeper than I have ever known. The air is corrosive; it has been rendered so. One can register shock at what has happened, but not complete surprise.

26 JUNE

When you wish upon a bra ...

VICTORIA COREN MITCHELL

Among all the surveys and polls and statistics of the past few days, I found one that really delighted me. Nearly 30 per cent of women, despite owning several bras, wear only two of them. Or, as the *Sun* put it: 'BRAVO TWO WEAR-O! WOMEN STICK TO THEIR FAVOURITE PAIR'.

This is in the general run of their lives, you understand. Not two bras at once. Although, in this changeable climate, never say never.

Meanwhile, 50 per cent of women admit to having a drawer full of new lingerie they never wear. A third of women reveal that they 'frequently' discard a bra immediately after purchase, shoving it into the drawer and never looking at it again.

I'm so relieved. This isn't something I've ever asked my friends about, for fear of being the only one. Also, most of my friends are men. It can be quite tricky, in the middle of a poker game where all the talk is of horses and goals and dog prices, to pipe up with:

'Is it just me or is satin a simply unrealistic fabric in a bra?' Not impossible, but tricky.

So it has remained the most secret of experiences: the moment where you slide open the underwear drawer and reach over the pricey ranks of shimmering, matching, handwash-only sets to grab one of the two baggy old friends you always wear, asking yourself nothing more complicated than: 'Black or white today?'

(As if they hadn't both gone beige with time anyway.)

For me, the donning of new bras is not exactly never. I'll wear a colourful matching set under a nice dress for a special occasion and I take armfuls of them on holiday. But they often do more harm than good. All very well if you get the chance to wander round in deshabille at bedtime ('What? Oh yes, I quite forgot to finish getting changed, as I reclined here doing the crossword in my peach silk smalls, sucking the pencil suggestively ...'), but for every time that happens there will be five occasions where I feel fat after dinner and hurry into a voluminous bathrobe, or my husband, who is slow to read underwear code and quick to make yet another doomed attempt at chapter 438 of *Wolf Hall*, falls unwittingly asleep.

On those nights, I feel at worst furious (I tend to prod him awake, shouting, 'Just about the companionship now, is it? Someone to grow old with? Allotments and cocoa? Perhaps you'd prefer me to turn a blind eye while you TAKE A LOVER?') and at best wistful as I think of the waste of time that still lies ahead, handwashing the blasted things.

I'm kidding myself. By 'handwashing', I mean putting the expensive underwear in the machine, where it will shrink without even a romantic memory to show for it. Whatever the label says, and whatever I promised myself at point of purchase, I know in my heart that I'll handwash a pair of pants the day my doctor tells me I have a thousand years to live.

It all comes back, as always, to the relationship between shopping and self-image. I'm afraid this is a predominantly female condition; it does apply to a certain sort of metrosexual man but, in the main, men still think in a straightforwardly acquisitive way: 'I want a burger ... I need socks ... I feel thirsty ... I'd like to grope a buttock.'

Women, however, think: 'I'm going to be the kind of person who has hummus. I will buy a tub of hummus to effect this.'

It's all a narrative. We picture ourselves flitting about in Italian shoes, carrying a bundle of newspapers under one arm, buying fresh bread, laughing as we pass a dog, exchanging a smile with an attractive passer-by, leaving a trace of floral scent on the breeze.

When we buy the new, satiny, pinchy bra-and-pants set, we might picture ourselves wearing nothing else as we crawl across the floor towards a dazzle-toothed Brazilian paramour – but we might just as easily imagine it completely hidden under a pencil skirt and tweed jacket as we sip a cappuccino in a town square while reading an improving novel on a Kindle. The question of whether the things fit ... well, that doesn't come into play until you're back home, hence the 30 per cent who 'frequently' discard a bra immediately on purchase.

It's not just clothes. I own, for example, an unused 'rice cooker'. That was never about cooking rice. It was about me laughing round a table with some witty yet intellectual friends, one of them perhaps in MI6, one of them a redhead and another Polish, all of us drinking bellinis and setting the world to rights as the risotto simmers gently on the stove. That's never happened. I sometimes stick some rice in an old saucepan when I'm eating alone, it's gone 9pm and there's no time to bake a potato.

I own several coloured-glass vases for the fresh flowers I never buy. I own a calf-length, pale cream woollen coat for the day I walk through Central Park with Robert Redford, cuddling en route to an art gallery. I own an old-fashioned ladies' bicycle for the day I freewheel around town with a basketful of books and cherries, miraculously sweat-free as I hop off at the library. I own many tiny beaded handbags, for those occasions when I have nothing to carry with me for the night but a handkerchief and a single aspirin.

I own an ankle bracelet. God knows what I pictured myself doing with that on.

And I own, I would say, 30 or 40 bras. I wear two. And, since having a baby, those two don't even really fit.

23 JUNE

Grieve now if you must – but prepare for the great challenges ahead

OWEN JONES

The lamps may not be going out all over Europe, but they're flickering. The continent is being tugged in different directions by competing forces, and it is unclear who will succeed. Two potentially historic events this week will help define its future.

Today Britain could choose to become the first nation to leave the European Union, the consequence of a campaign dripping in bigotry and the scapegoating of migrants. And, on Sunday, Spain goes to the polls for a rerun of an inconclusive election in December. The newcomer Unidos Podemos party, standing on a platform of opposing cuts and of democratising Spain and Europe, is attracting the support of millions of Spaniards. The votes highlight the competing visions of Europe's future.

There are three philosophies at play right now. The first blames migrants and people fleeing violence and poverty for the multiple problems afflicting European society, from the lack of secure jobs and houses to stagnating living standards to public services ravaged by cuts. The second seeks to build a Europe with shrivelled social protections, run ever more in the interest of major corporations, as exemplified by the notorious but embattled Transatlantic Trade and Investment Partnership. These two visions are far from mutually exclusive; they are frequently allied, or feed off each other. The third vision challenges them both: holding the powerful interests responsible for Europe's crisis to account, and aspiring to a democratised Europe that puts people before the need for profit.

I left Britain's poisonous referendum campaign for a few days to travel across northern Spain with Unidos Podemos. It didn't feel so much like entering another country as passing into a parallel universe. Spain shows there is nothing inevitable about people blaming migrants, rather than the people in charge, for their problems. And when it comes to problems, Spain is not lacking. A fifth of its workforce is unemployed, and nearly half of its young people are without work. Hundreds of thousands of Spaniards have been evicted from their homes. Child poverty has risen. Public services have been slashed. Yet in the working-class town of Torrelavega, a crowd roared with approval when told the problems facing Europeans are caused not by foreigners but by bankers, tax-dodgers and poverty-paying bosses.

There is no mass anti-immigration party contesting Spain's elections. Mainstream parties are not trying to outdo each other with anti-immigration vitriol. And it is not as though there is a lack of people entering the country: Spain experienced a sixfold increase in migrants in the 2000s. Immigration is simply not the prism through which people understand their problems.

Why? The memory of General Franco's dictatorship adds a layer of revulsion for the far right in the eyes of many Spaniards. Similarly, a history of Spanish emigration because of dictatorship, poverty and economic insecurity might mean more sympathy for people who travel to build a new life. But senior Podemos figures dismiss the idea that Spanish society is somehow culturally immune to anti-immigration hostility. Instead they point to the rise of the so-called 15-M movement in 2011.

An initial call on 15 May 2011 for Spaniards to mobilise against the country's political establishment attracted thousands of protesters. It was the catalyst for a phenomenon that has transformed Spanish politics. Over the course of many months, millions of Spaniards took part in protests and occupations.

It was this movement that laid the political foundations for the rise of Podemos. Its critical contribution was to ensure that the focus of Spanish anger was the powerful, rather than migrants. Podemos activists believe that without this movement, Spain could also have succumbed to anti-immigration sentiment.

Concerns about immigration should be debated. But in contrast to Spain, so many of Britain's problems are seen through the prism of immigration. The failure of a popular movement to organise meant that an alternative explanation for social ills never gained traction. Immigration was already the catch-all explanation for grievances; the referendum has only entrenched this view.

Across Europe, the visions represented by the rightwing Brexiteers in Britain and Podemos in Spain are locked in combat. If Britain leaves the EU as the result of a campaign whose core message is hostility to migrants, that will be a shot in the arm to already ascendant anti-immigration movements across Europe.

The question isn't whether France's far-right leader Marine Le Pen will celebrate Brexit, but how expensive the champagne she chooses to toast it with will be. The odds of the EU disintegrating amid anti-migrant and anti-refugee acrimony will increase. If Unidos Podemos do well in Spain on Sunday, that will be a significant boost to movements arguing for a Europe of public investment and workers' rights.

Europe has now endured years of cuts, regressive tax hikes and stagnating or falling living standards. The xenophobic right has feasted on the despair and grievances that have resulted. The antidote is movements such as Podemos: those that redirect anger at the correct targets, and propose an alternative Europe that doesn't breed insecurity. Greece's Syriza government was cowed by the EU because the bureaucrats could do so: Greece represents a tiny sliver of the eurozone economy. Spain, by contrast, can't be bullied in the same way: it is 'too big to fail'.

Our own government has led the attempts to drive the EU ever further down the road of servility to the interests of the market – by vetoing EU action to prevent Chinese steel-dumping, for example, and being the biggest cheerleader for the TTIP. That direction of travel makes the work of movements such as Podemos even more vital.

There have been many significant postwar moments in Europe, not least the fall of the Berlin Wall. But set against that backdrop, this remains a defining moment. Are we to have a disintegrating Europe characterised by widespread, destructive, anti-migrant resentment, corporate dominance and shredded social protection, or a democratic Europe run in the interests of the majority? The people of Britain and Spain can light the way.

23–24 JUNE

EU referendum night as it happened – 12 hours that changed the world (extract)

LIVEBLOG

20.13 In Cardiff, campaigners have set up next to the statue of Aneurin Bevan, Labour party icon and architect of the NHS. They believe the turnout in central Cardiff is very big – and think this is good news for remain – but worry that it may be a different story in the valleys and out in the countryside.

21.27 As any veteran of election/referendum all-nighters knows, it's crucial to have a ready supply of unhealthy sugary drinks and snacks close to hand. Bit worried about Robert Peston's paltry stock at ITV at this stage …

21.38 Ever the attention-grabber, live pictures are also now coming in of Boris Johnson leaving his vote until almost the last minute.

21.59 The polls are closing now following a campaign many believe was the most divisive in British politics.

22.06 YouGov has carried a poll of 5,000 people and YouGov's Joe Twyman has just announced the figures on Sky News. Here are the figures:

Remain: 52%   Leave: 48%

22.15 Peter Kellner, the former YouGov president, has come out with his final prediction. He thinks remain will have a lead over leave of about 8.5%.

22.23   The YouGov poll has seen the pound climb even higher, now up to a new high for the year of close to $1.50, while the FTSE 100 is forecast to open around 90 points higher tomorrow. Investors clearly like the idea that the remain campaign may be in the lead.

22.25   The first predictions from MPs are trickling through, and Labour's Chuka Umunna has said that he is 'reasonably confident' of the result he and the remain side have been campaigning for.

22.43   84 pro-Brexit Tory MPs sign a letter saying Cameron should stay as prime minister regardless of the result of the referendum.

23.43   The first result is in, from Gibraltar. It is a massive vote for remain.

23.46   On Sky News, Nigel Farage has just given what sounded a bit like a concession speech (even though he insisted that was not what it was).

00.05   Remain win in Newcastle, but by less than expected:
      Remain: 65,404 (50.7%)   Leave: 63,598 (49.3%)
This is a very good result for leave. Remain were expected to be comfortably ahead.

00.20   Leave win in Sunderland by more than expected:
      Remain: 51,930 (39%)   Leave: 82,394 (61%)
Leave were expected to win here, but not by a margin as big as this. It looks as if remain's early optimism was premature.

00.22   The leave victory in Sunderland has sent the pound plunging, down 3.5% to $1.435.

00.31   British emigrants in Berlin are gathered at the legendary Volksbühne theatre to watch the incoming first results. An overwhelming majority has voted remain – but not all of them did enthusiastically.

00.44 Cardiff South and Penarth Labour MP Stephen Doughty is cheerful about the chances of the Welsh capital returning a healthy remain vote.

01.03 Eddie Izzard has joined supporters of the Stronger In campaign as they gather to wait for the result of the EU referendum at the Royal Festival Hall.

01.06 Meanwhile, the count continues in Belfast, where Alasdair McDonnell MP is not looking as confident after the Sunderland result as he was earlier.

01.30 You can always tell who is losing on an election night – it's the side where they start blaming each other. Earlier, when it looked good for remain, we saw Vote Leave have a go at Nigel Farage. But now the recriminations are breaking out on the remain side, where Labour is blaming the government.

01.33 The fall in the pound is the third biggest move on record, after the 2008 financial crisis and Black Wednesday, when sterling left the Exchange Rate Mechanism.

01.38 One after another, leading remain figures have been telling broadcasters that the result is looking close, in interviews where they appear to be less optimistic than they were at about 10pm. John McDonnell, the shadow chancellor, said the results were 'exactly as predicted ... pretty close, whichever way', adding: 'I am hoping remain will win, but I think it will be one or two percentage points either way.'

01.43 Google says there has been a more than 250% increase in the number of searches for 'what happens if we leave the EU' in the past hour, as early results indicate stronger-than-expected results for Brexit campaigners.

02.05 Leave have now got more than 1 million votes, the BBC is reporting.

02.13 The pound is slumping now, down 5.5% at $1.408, as bookies now put leave as the favourite to win.

02.19 Professor Michael Thrasher, the Sky News number cruncher, says that as things stand it looks as if leave is heading for a 12-point lead.

02.42 We're just over halfway through the north-east declarations and the verdict is clear: leave has won comfortably in this region.

03.09 Peter Kellner, the former YouGov president who was predicting a remain win (see 10.15pm), has changed his mind.

03.24 Labour party is now working on the assumption that leave will win, according to a party source.

03.46 The pound is now down 8% at $1.36, its biggest ever one-day move (it swung by 7% in 2008). The falls have accelerated as Sheffield unexpectedly backed leave, and ITV have put an 80% chance on leave winning the vote.

04.11 In his address to supporters, Nigel Farage said he and his supporters had taken back control of the country 'without a shot being fired'.

04.14 With all but two results now declared in Scotland – with remain so far winning in 30 of 32 council areas across the country – it is painfully obvious that the constituent parts of the UK have voted in very different directions.

04.29 In Wales, 21 of 22 results have been declared – 17 for leave, four for remain. Running totals in Wales are 52.9% for leave and 47.1% for remain. Only Gwynedd to go. Wales is very much out.

04.39 ITV are calling it for leave, only Robert Peston, ITV's political editor, got his tweet wrong, declaring: 'ITV News calls Remain victory by 52% to 48%. It's done.'
(It's been a long night.)

04.41 The BBC has also called it for leave.

04.59 Asian stock markets are already being routed, as traders watch events unfold in the UK. Japan's Nikkei index has slumped by 7%, a loss of over 1,100 points. That is its worst one-day fall since March 2011, when Fukushima was hit by a devastating earthquake that triggered a tsunami and a nuclear disaster.

05.19 Northern Ireland has voted remain by a majority of 440,707 to 349,442 on an overall turnout of 62.9%.

06.01 JK Rowling has used Twitter to say that David Cameron's legacy will be 'breaking up two unions'.

06.04 Geert Wilders, a Dutch far-right politician, said on his website that Brexit has created a precedent for other European countries to exit the EU.

06.27 Marine Le Pen, the leader of France's far-right National Front party, has welcomed the result of the referendum. She says she wants a similar referendum in France.

06.37 Nigel Farage, the Ukip leader, has told ITV's *Good Morning Britain* that he thought it was a mistake for the Vote Leave campaign to say that it could save £350m a week by leaving the EU and that the money could go to the NHS.

08.10 An orchestrated move against Jeremy Corbyn appears to be under way as Labour's shadow cabinet prepares to convene this morning.

08.14 Shares plunge and the pound plummets to a 31-year low as panicked traders react to the UK's vote to leave the EU and the prospect of recession amid months of market turmoil.

08.25 Cameron announces he will resign as prime minister before the autumn.

24 June

We are living in a country so imbalanced, it has effectively fallen over

JOHN HARRIS

'If you've got money, you vote in,' she said, with a bracing certainty. 'If you haven't got money, you vote out.'

We were in Collyhurst, the hard-pressed neighbourhood on the northern edge of Manchester last Wednesday, and I had yet to find a remain voter. The woman I was talking to spoke of the lack of a local park or playground, and her sense that all the good stuff went to the regenerated wonderland of big-city Manchester, 10 minutes down the road.

An hour before, I had been there at a graduate recruitment fair, where nine out of 10 of our interviewees were supporting remain, and some spoke about leave voters with cold superiority. 'This is the 21st century,' said one 20-something. 'Get with it.' Not for the first time, the atmosphere around the referendum had the sulphurous whiff of a kind of misshapen class war.

And now here we are, with that terrifying decision to leave. Most things in the political foreground are finished, aren't they? David Cameron and George Osborne. The Labour party as we know it, a walking ghost, whose writ no longer reaches its supposed heartlands. Scotland – which voted to stay in the EU by 62 per cent to 38 per cent – will presumably soon be decisively on its way to independence. Sinn Fein is claiming that the British government 'has forfeited any mandate to represent the economic or political interests of people in Northern Ireland'. These are seismic things to happen in peacetime.

This is about so much more than the EU. It is about class, and inequality, and a politics that has left most people staring at Westminster's rituals with anger and bafflement. Add the howling political failures that compounded these problems: Iraq, the MPs' expenses scandal, the way that Cameron's flip from 'big society' niceness to hard-faced austerity summed up all the cliches about people you cannot trust.

Most of all, Brexit is the consequence of the economic bargain struck in the early 1980s, when we waved goodbye to the security of the postwar settlement, and were given an economic model that has just about served the most populous parts of the country, while leaving too much of the rest to anxiously decline. Look at those jaw-dropping vote-shares for remain in the capital – 66 per cent in Tory Kensington and Chelsea; 75 per cent in Camden; 78 per cent in Hackney – contrasted with comparable shares for leave in such places as Great Yarmouth (71 per cent), Castle Point in Essex (73 per cent), and Redcar and Cleveland (66 per cent). Here is a country so imbalanced it has effectively fallen over.

For six years, often with my colleague John Domokos, I have been travelling around the UK for our video series 'Anywhere But Westminster', ostensibly covering politics, but really trying to divine the national mood. I look back and find auguries of what has just happened. There was the temporary arrival of the British National party in electoral politics from 2006, playing on anger about immigration. A few years later, we met builders in South Shields who told us their hourly rate had come down by £3 thanks to new arrivals from eastern Europe; a mother in Stourbridge who wanted a new school for 'our kids'; a former docker in Liverpool who looked at rows of empty warehouses and simply exclaimed, 'Where's the work?'

In Peterborough in 2013, we found a town riven by cold resentments, where people claimed agencies would only hire the non-UK nationals who would work insane shifts for risible rates; in Lincolnshire, we chronicled communities divided between optimistic new arrivals and resentful locals – where Nigel Farage could pitch up for back-to-back meetings with rapturous crowds.

Even in the cities that were meant to spurn Brexit, things have been complicated. Manchester was split 60/40 in favour of remain; in Birmingham last week, I met British-Asian people who talked about leaving with a passion and frustration similar to plenty of white people on the same side.

In so many places, there has long been the same mixture of deep worry and often-seething anger. Only rarely has it tipped into outright hate (I recall women in Merthyr Tydfil town centre bellowing 'Get 'em out!').

What defines these furies is clear enough – a terrible shortage of homes, an impossibly precarious job market, a too-often overlooked sense that men (and men are particularly relevant here) feel demeaned and ignored. The attempts of mainstream politics to still the anger have probably made it worse: oily tributes to 'hard-working families', or the trope of 'social mobility' with its suggestion that all Westminster can offer working-class people is a specious chance of not being working class.

Last year, 3.8 million people voted for Ukip. The Labour party's vote is in seemingly unstoppable decline. Indeed, if politicians do know too little about their supposed 'core' voters, Jeremy Corbyn might be seen as that problem incarnate. The trade unions are nowhere to be seen, and the Thatcher-era ability of Conservatism to speak to working-class aspiration has been mislaid.

In short, England and Wales were characterised by an ever-growing vacuum, until Cameron – surely revealed as the most disastrous holder of the office in our democratic history –

made the decision that might turn out to have utterly changed our politics.

The prime minister evidently thought the whole debate could be cleanly finished in a matter of months. His Eton contemporary Boris Johnson – can you believe that the political story of the past four months has effectively been a catastrophic contest between two people who went to the same exclusive school? – opportunistically embraced the cause of Brexit. What they had not figured out was that a diffuse popular anger had not yet found a powerful enough outlet, but that the staging of a referendum and the cohering of the leave cause would deliver exactly that. Ukip had been held back by the first-past-the-post system and the polarising qualities of Farage, but the coalition for Brexit neutralised both. And so it came to pass: the cause of leaving the European Union, once the preserve of cranks and chancers, attracted a share of the popular vote for which any modern political party would give its eye teeth.

Of course, most of the media – which is largely part of the same detached London entity that the great English patriot William Cobbett called 'The Thing' – failed to see it coming. Their world is one of photo-ops, the great non-event that is PMQs, and absurd debates between figures that the public no longer cares about. Wherever I go, the press and television are the focus of as much resentment as politics. It is also time we set aside the dismal science of opinion polling, usage of which should surely be limited to product testing. Understanding of the country at large has for too long been framed in percentages and leading questions: it is time people went into the country, and simply listened.

We all know the cruel irony that sits in the midst of all this: that Britain – or what is left of it – will take a sharp turn to the right, and the problems that have fed into this moment will only get worse. If we fear how much this decision says about Britain's underlying social condition, we will have to fight. But first, we will have to think.

Orwell wrote 'The Lion and the Unicorn' when Europe was tearing itself apart, and the UK's isolation was more a matter of righteous principle than political chaos. England, he said, 'resembles a family, a rather stuffy Victorian family, with not many black sheep in it but with all its cupboards bursting with skeletons. It has rich relations who have to be kow-towed to and poor relations who are horribly sat upon, and there is a deep conspiracy of silence about the source of the family income'. With the under-25s having so obviously supported one side, and older people the other, the next line is prescient: 'It is a family in which the young are generally thwarted and most of the power is in the hands of irresponsible uncles and bedridden aunts.' And his last line: 'A family with the wrong members in control – that, perhaps, is as near as one can come to describing England in a phrase.'

With Farage crowing and Johnson and Gove exultant, those words take on a whole new power. For those of us who woke yesterday to the most awful news imaginable, they imply a question we should have asked before: how do we even begin to put England – and Wales – the right way up?

28 June

Farage is now Britain's face at the EU: petty, unlovable, essentially terrified

MARINA HYDE

In a crowded field, I think it was the flag that was the killer. The absolute state of that flag. Nigel Farage's desktop union jack, with its little sucker pad leeching obnoxiously on to the unlovely beech of the European parliament chamber. This is how we must look to those still condemned to share continent-space with us: petty, unlovable, essentially terrified, our workplace set up in a show of cod-martial defiance, which in fact only flags up our raging insecurity.

Farage has been building up to this moment his entire political life, as he tells everyone at every opportunity. In which case, how is it humanly possible that his speech to the European parliament yesterday could be so artless, so crass, a scarcely refined version of some England fans' infamous recent chant: 'Fuck off, Europe, we voted out'? This, Farage repeated once more, was a victory against 'big politics'. 'Virtually none of you,' he bellowed at the MEPs, 'have ever done a proper job in your lives.'

Watching him was like watching the live abortion of Churchill's oratorial legacy. There is soft power, and then there is politics as erectile dysfunction.

Indeed, it is becoming increasingly difficult not to speculate as to the psychological underpinnings of the Farage condition. 'When I came here 17 years ago,' he shouted, failing to hide his nervous elation, 'you all laughed at me. Well, I have to say: you're not laughing now, are you?' He made it, you losers! He got out. He's in the big leagues now. He's the guy who just turned up to his school reunion in a white limo with two dead-eyed escorts on his arm.

Above all, the performance offered a reminder that Farage makes everything in which he is involved a race to the bottom. The opposite of a Midas, he may as well be nicknamed Brown-finger. His excruciatingly aggressive display eventually drew boos from the chamber. Farage was loving it.

The victory against 'big politics', he stressed again, was for 'the little people'. Incidentally, during the general election campaign last year, I was in a Grimsby pub where Farage's supporters were waiting for him in a long-scheduled visit. He blew them out to go and have fish and chips with reality television star Joey Essex. Footsoldiers of Ukip, they were crestfallen. Yes, Farage is as elitist as the rest of them. Even the victory party for his senior referendum campaign staff was stratified, featuring a VIP snug, into which he retreated for most of the night.

And still he rises. This time the political leader who's had more farewell tours than Barbra Streisand isn't going anywhere. Whenever I touched on Farage's malevolent guiding spirit during the referendum campaign itself, I was pleased to receive all sorts of optimistic correspondence explaining that as soon as a leave vote was achieved Farage's work would be done, and he would retire triumphantly into the sunset.

How's that working out for ya? As reports of racist and xeno-phobic incidents intensify, Farage appears on Channel 4 News to warn against what he detects as 'backsliding' in the leadership of the official Vote Leave campaign. My suspicion is that these two strands of post-referendum fallout will come together in what we might call 'ever closer union'. All sides of leave know they can't deliver most of what they promised – and the coming anger will serve as Farage's greatest recruiting sergeant.

Still, don't take it from me. Let's play out with the UK's second biggest cheerleader in the European parliament, Marine Le Pen of the French National Front, and her comment to Farage after his speech: 'Look at how beautiful history is!' Don't look too hard.

1 JULY

Let the vandals know – we won't forget what they did

JONATHAN FREEDLAND

It's gripping, of course. *Game of Thrones* meets *House of Cards*, played out at the tempo of a binge-viewed box set. Who could resist watching former allies wrestling for the crown, betraying each other, lying, cheating and dissembling, each new twist coming within hours of the last? And this show matters, too. Whoever wins will determine Britain's relationship with Europe.

And yet it can feel like displacement activity, this story of Michael Gove, Boris Johnson and Theresa May – a distraction diverting us from the betrayal larger than any inflicted by one Tory bigwig on another. Now that the news cycle is measured in seconds, there's a risk that 23 June might come to feel like history, that we might move on too soon. But there can be no moving on until we have reckoned with what exactly was done to the people of these islands – and by whom.

This week's antics of Gove and Johnson are a useful reminder. For the way one has treated the other is the way both have treated the country. Some may be tempted to turn Johnson into an object of sympathy – poor Boris, knifed by his pal – but he deserves none. In seven days he has been exposed as an egomaniac whose vanity and ambition are so great he was prepared to lead his country on a path he knew led to disaster, so long as it fed his own appetite for status.

He didn't believe a word of his own rhetoric, we know that now. His face last Friday morning, ashen with the terror of victory, proved it. That hot mess of a column he served up on Monday confirmed it again: he was trying to back out of the very decision he'd persuaded the country to make. And let's not be coy: persuade it, he did. Imagine the leave campaign without him. Gove, Nigel Farage and Gisela Stuart: they couldn't have done it without the star power of Boris.

He knew it was best for Britain to remain in the EU. But it served his ambition to argue otherwise. We just weren't meant to fall for it. Once we had, he panicked, vanishing during a weekend of national crisis before hiding from parliament. He lit the spark then ran away – petrified at the blaze he started.

He has left us to look on his works and despair. The outlook for the economy is so bleak, the governor of the Bank of England talks of 'economic post-traumatic stress disorder'. The Economist Intelligence Unit projects a 6 per cent contraction by 2020, an 8 per cent decline in investment, as well as rising unemployment, falling tax revenues, and public debt to reach 100 per cent of our national output. No wonder George Osborne casually announced that the central aim of his fiscal policy since 2010 – eradicating the deficit – has now been indefinitely postponed, thereby breaking what had been the defining commitment of the Tories' manifesto at the last election, back in the Palaeolithic era known as 2015.

And what was it all for? For Johnson, it was gross ambition. Gove's motive was superficially more admirable. He, along with

Daniel Hannan and others, was driven by intellectual fervour, a burning belief in abstract nouns such as 'sovereignty' and 'freedom'. Those ideas are noble in themselves, of course they are. But not when they are peeled away from the rough texture of the real world. For when doctrine is kept distilled, pure and fervently uncontaminated by reality, it turns into zealotry.

So we have the appalling sight of Gove on Friday, proclaiming himself a proud believer in the UK even though it was obvious to anyone who cared to look that a leave vote would propel Scotland towards saying yes in a second independence referendum. The more honest leavers admit that they believe the break-up of the union is a price worth paying for the prize of sovereignty. But what kind of patriotism is this, that believes in an undiluted British sovereignty so precious it's worth the sacrifice of Britain itself?

Just look at what this act of vandalism has wrought. There has been a 500 per cent increase in the number of hate crimes reported, as migrants are taunted on the street, told to pack their bags and get out – as if 23 June were a permission slip to every racist and bigot in the land. And for what? So Boris could get a job and so Gove, Hannan and the rest could make Britain more closely resemble the pristine constitutional models of the nation state found in 17th-century tracts of political philosophy, rather than one that might fit into the interdependent, complex 21st-century world and our blood-drenched European corner of it.

They did it with lies, whether the false promise that we could both halt immigration and enjoy full access to the single market, or that deceitful £350m figure, still defended by Gove, which tricked millions into believing a leave vote would bring a cash windfall to the NHS. They did it with no plan, as clueless about post-Brexit Britain as Bush and Blair were about post-invasion Iraq. They did it with no care for the chaos they would unleash.

Senior civil servants say Brexit will consume their energies for years to come, as they seek to disentangle 40 years of agreements. It will be the central focus of our politics and our government, a massive collective effort demanding ingenuity and creativity. Just think of what could have been achieved if all those resources had been directed elsewhere. Into addressing, for instance, the desperate, decades-long needs – for jobs, for housing, for a future – of those towns that have been left behind by the last 30 years of change, those towns whose people voted leave the way a passenger on a doomed train pulls the emergency cord. Instead, all this work will be devoted to constructing a set-up with the EU that, if everything goes our way, might be only a little bit worse than what we already had in our hands on 22 June.

This week of shock will settle, eventually. Events will begin to move at a slower pace. We will realise that we have to be patient, that we need to wait till France and Germany get their elections out of the way, and we will hope that a new future can be negotiated – one that implements the democratic verdict delivered in the referendum, but which does not maim this country in the process. But even as we grow calmer, we should not let our anger cool. We should hold on to our fury, against those who, for the sake of their career or a pet dogma, were prepared to wreck everything. At a time when we mourn what horror the Europe before the European Union was capable of, we should say loud and clear of those that did this: we won't forget them.

Our country is changed utterly. Unless this summer is just a bad dream

IAN McEWAN

It's easy enough these days to wake troubled even before you remember the cause. Then you do. Everything is changed utterly. Or about to be, as soon as your new leader is chosen. The country you live in, the parliamentary democracy that ruled it, for good or bad, has been trumped by a plebiscite of dubious purpose and unacknowledged status. From our agriculture to our science and our universities, from our law to our international relations to our commerce and trade and politics, and who and what we are in the world – all is up for a curious, unequal renegotiation with our European neighbours. How did we get to this? What can you do?

By now you are putting on your shoes and running through the sequence yet one more time. The Conservative party needed to settle an old dispute within its ranks. The quarrel once wrecked the sleep of John Major. The schism needed to be healed to shore up the position and sleep of David Cameron. Certain newspaper owners and a large minority of Tory backbenchers had to be appeased. The promise to let the people decide was in the Conservative manifesto, and the country had voted for a Conservative government. It was legal and proper to have a referendum.

The campaign was conducted by and was an argument between Conservative politicians – at its simplest, Cameron-

Osborne against Johnson-Gove. The role of Ukip was merely to make everyone else seem reasonable. We watched and wondered, as Kremlinologists once did. The Jeremy Corbyn Labour party was shamefully, or shamelessly, absent until it was too late. The status of the 2015 parliamentary act that enabled the referendum was clear, but we didn't read it. Was it advisory, like some referendums are, or was it binding?

The question didn't come up. We failed to ask it. No use declaring, as you may keep declaring after it didn't go your way, that all along it was merely advisory. You should have thought of that earlier. And what was the nation's democratically tendered advice to our lawmakers? That we're almost evenly split. One third wants to leave, fractionally less than a third wants to stay, and a third doesn't know or doesn't care. Seventeen million against 16 million. Each full of contempt for the other. And on this basis we are about to redraft our constitution and much else besides.

You'll be at the coffee before you remember all over again the lies that needed to be told to gain the result. The £350m a week that would become available to the NHS; that we could halt immigration from Europe and remain in the single market; that Turkey was about to join; that we could 'take back our country' – as if any international treaty was not, in a rule-bound context, a diminution of sovereignty in exchange for a greater good.

On your second cup you might check online for the Conservative party rules for selecting a new leader, as if knowing them might empower you somehow. Or you might take another look at the far simpler Article 50 that sets out the means of our departure. Barely 400 words, remarkably easy to read, given that it was drawn up by lawyers. When we've invoked the clause we're committed to leave within two years. Our partners don't want to negotiate with us until the article is invoked. If these were the rules of a card game only a mug would sit down to play. The banker takes all. How can parliament, even assuming it has a say, vote on a deal it cannot see until it's too late?

And yet we are told, even by the defeated Tory remainer faction, that 'the people have spoken'. Perhaps this is what the party wanted all along – all of it. We hardly know. The minority of us who read newspapers know less than a tenth of what's happening. But we can be sure of the contempt each Tory caucus holds for the others, with some contempt to spare for us bystanders.

We may assume that powerful Conservative figures wanted Boris Johnson gone, for historical as well as proximal reasons. Someone lofty may have spoken smoothly into the ear of his lieutenant, Michael Gove, to persuade him he was prime minister material and that he should desert. When he did, and Johnson stepped aside, a so-called grandee – Michael Heseltine – was on hand to disembowel the corpse. Then, for his 15 minutes, Gove was before us, cross-gartered like foolish Malvolio, until another grandee, Kenneth Clarke, in concert with the *Daily Mail*, was ready to knife his guts. Two down in the summer of contempt.

Or it happened another way. We Kremlinologists can only guess at what's being turned over in the clubs of St James or the farmhouses of Oxfordshire. But we do know that what all sides are calling the greatest political crisis of our generation is a creature imagined into being by the Conservative party alone. It, not Ukip, offered the referendum; it fought it; it won as well as lost it. For such services, for the mayhem and poison that followed and are clouding the leadership contest, we should now be watching it shredded by an effective, eloquent opposition. But by their silence Corbyn and his troubled, paranoid court have delivered us, in effect – and for the time being – into a one-party state, and not the Leninist version certain courtiers dream of.

Now you watch on helplessly as your prime minister is chosen. It is, of course, constitutionally correct that you have no say in the matter. But it's hard to shake off that below-stairs feeling. We can do no more than gossip round the kitchen table. The butler has a theory, and so does the second chambermaid. Even 'boots' knows all about tactical voting. Our first-naming paradoxically measures our distance from events. Is Boris biding his time, or is he truly finished? What does it tell us about the party, post-2008, that Andrea, an ex-banker hostile to the minimum wage, could soon be prime minister? Was Theresa's reticence during the referendum campaign astute and tactical? Or merely an expression of her character? Or is she the remainers' mole? Can we believe that the chancellor isn't plotting? We hear footsteps above our head – more comings and goings. But who?

You might cling to the butler's mole theory even as you worry that your hopes are loosening your grip on reality: the powerful faction that wanted to remain, and whispered flattery and enticements in Gove's ear, has cleared the field of Johnson, and eased one of its own into place as PM. The exit negotiations begin and are inevitably protracted in a game with such stacked odds. Our European friends, watching their own backs, will not be offering kindly terms. Only a fool would want to invoke the dread article too soon.

Meanwhile, the economy is in decline, the pound is drifting towards parity with the dollar, the jobless lines are lengthening. Racists and xenophobes are gripped by an elated sense of entitlement. The cry gets louder for a second referendum. The voices come from the only quarter that matters – the party. Ex-attorney general Dominic Grieve is among the first, then some ex-ministers, then those grandees again. At last, with no loss of face, Prime Minister May reluctantly grants their wish. It's what, in her heart, she always wanted. And clearly, the public mood has shifted. On hard-pressed council estates leavers are suffering what we've learned to call buyers' remorse. Second time around, remain sweeps the board. We're back in. In fact, we never left. It was all a bad dream. The summer of contempt will be soon forgotten. Go back to bed. When you wake, Boris Johnson will be leader of the Labour party. He was, he says, always well to the left of Tony Blair. What can you do?

12 JULY

Boris? Michael? Andrea? Theresa rules the roost after manic Monday

JOHN CRACE

Just another manic Monday. Little more than a day after receiving a text from Andrea Leadsom saying 'soz I sed u wld b rubbish leedr cos u is not a mum', Theresa May walked into a meeting of the 1922 Committee in Portcullis House to be anointed as the next prime minister. Ten minutes later, she left to a standing ovation from Conservative MPs trying to outdo one another in expressions of undying devotion. Boris who? Michael who? Andrea who?

If Theresa looked a little nonplussed when she appeared with her husband and inner circle of loyal MPs outside St Stephen's Entrance, she wasn't the only one. Even by recent standards this was all a bit quick.

Only the Conservatives can combine the brutality of a Stalinist purge with the low comedy of a *Carry On* film. It had trusted the country to reach the right decision in the referendum campaign and it wasn't going to make the same mistake again by giving the untamed fringes of the Tory party a say.

'Honoured and humbled,' she mumbled. 'Brexit means Brexit.' Though not necessarily if the man by her side, Chris Grayling, were to become minister for Brexit. Grayling has yet to find a ministerial job he can't do slowly and badly. Having said the bare minimum, she scarpered off home to wonder how a day that had started off with her launching her leadership campaign in Birmingham had ended with her landing the top job. Seldom had so much been achieved in British politics by saying and doing so little.

The first sign that Westminster had accidentally overdosed on speed yet again was when the net curtains twitched at Leadsom's leadership campaign headquarters in Westminster shortly after midday. Moments later, Steve Baker, Owen Paterson, Iain Duncan Smith and Tim Loughton trooped out the front door to form a dad's army praetorian guard on the doorstep. Then came Andrea.

The wider Andrea's smile became, the more furious IDS looked. Quantity theory in action. 'I have a statement which is mine which I wish to read out,' Andrea smiled. IDS lowered his eyes. If anyone said a word out of place, the pavement was going to get it. Forget the velvet glove of compassion. There was more than one career here that was about to be shot down in flames.

'It has only just come to my attention that I have the support of just 25 per cent of Conservative MPs,' she continued, forcing the words through the fixed smile, 'and that, in these uncertain times, the country doesn't need a nine-week leadership campaign.

'I've also taken a look at the people around me and decided most of them are an electoral liability. So I have decided to withdraw my name from the contest and let Theresa May be prime minister. Sorry to have made such a nuisance of myself. I'm now going to lie down in a dark room for several years. Thank you for coming.'

Andrea declined to take any questions, so we never did get to find out how on earth it had taken her four days to work out that most of her own MPs thought she was far too hopeless to be leader when everyone else had done the sums in a matter of seconds. Percentages can't have been her strong point when she was working in the Barclays call centre.

It was left to Andrea's cracked troops to pick up the pieces. Most chose to jump ship at the earliest opportunity. 'Andrea has been absolutely brilliant but I've always secretly thought Theresa was the right man, sorry woman, for the job, party must unite blah blah and if you're recording this then I am definitely interested in any jobs that might be going.'

Only Loughton remained faithful to the Belle Dame Sans so much as a Merci. 'There have been dark forces at work,' he muttered. He meant journalists accurately reporting answers freely offered, but might just as well have been referring to the Tory party itself.

'Another Brexiteer leaves the scene of the crime,' yelled a passer-by who had just happened to catch the tail end of Leadsom's speech. He had a point. One by one, the prime architects of the Vote Leave campaign had managed to stab one another in the back, front and sides, and now the last one standing had thrown herself on the funeral pyre.

Back at No. 10, David Cameron was on the phone to his therapist trying to deal with his self-destructive issues when he heard that Theresa was going to be moving in a great deal earlier than anticipated.

'Bugger it!' he yelled. It just wasn't fair. Now he wouldn't get to fly in his brand-new Dave Force One plane to Africa. Now he'd miss his last G20. Now he'd have to find somewhere to rent as he'd given his tenants notice to leave in September. The way the day was going, George would forget to bring back a suitcase full of dollars from New York.

'I'm off on Wednesday afternoon,' he announced grumpily to the single camera parked outside the Downing Street door. 'Good luck to the lot of you.' Dave took a couple of deep breaths, trying to calm himself down as he marched back inside. It was no good. He was still furious. Perhaps humming might help. The theme to *The West Wing* somehow felt appropriate. Then for the removals. And cut.

11 JULY

Andy Murray makes his extraordinary Wimbledon feats seem everyday

OWEN GIBSON

Once more they thronged up the hill, with their hampers, their panama hats and sensible shoes. This time, though, they had come more in expectation than hope. And they were proved gloriously right. More than one newspaper had called on Andy Murray to save the country from gloom. Not for the first time, he delivered.

Having brutally closed out victory in straight sets against his big-serving Canadian opponent Milos Raonic, Murray raised his arms to the skies, dropped his racket to the floor and tried to take in his huge achievement.

Ivan Lendl – the man who has been in his corner for each of his three grand slam victories – finally got to his feet and smiled thinly. There might have even been the hint of a glaze in the eyes, his charge having defeated that of his old sparring partner John McEnroe.

As an achievement, it was towering: Murray indisputably joining the very top tier of the best of the best that Britain has produced. As an occasion, it sometimes felt oddly straightforward; history in the making. All those years, all that heartache and yet here was Murray, confidently marching to his second title.

Not that Murray cared. Pitted against three of the greatest players to ever play the game, he has kept growing and kept going. And this was his reward: finally, a final against a player who was not one of that towering triumvirate.

Yet if it had gone wrong, the consequences for his confidence could have been catastrophic. Just two men in the open era of tennis have lost more grand slam finals than Murray's eight. One of them, Lendl, was sitting in his box. The other, Roger Federer, has won far more than he has lost. Most of Murray's finals have been anguished affairs studded by tears and tantrums, weighed down heavily by the hand of history. Not so here. His rangy Canadian opponent did not freeze, but Murray's tenacious returning and inspired shotmaking were just too good. Beneath slate-grey skies that swiftly gave way to sunshine, Murray generated his own momentum, pumping his fist and roaring to his box whenever he flashed a winner cross-court or forced Raonic into an error – which was often. Only when Murray was forced to save his first break points of the match did the crowd feel the need to intervene. Suddenly, in the third set and with victory on the horizon, the volume rose.

When Murray played a one-handed backhand down the line to wrestle back control of the game, they erupted. Lendl nodded. Otherwise, the lucky few on Centre Court seemed content to sit back and watch Murray take care of business, saving their acclaim for the inevitable denouement. This was not the novel, raw experience of 2012 when, during the precursor to that golden Olympic summer, Murray went down in tearstained defeat against Federer beneath the roof.

Nor was it the manic, otherworldly, dreamlike swirl of his historic 2013 triumph over Novak Djokovic that laid to rest the ghost of Fred Perry and 77 years of men's history. Instead, this was a case study in dealing with a different kind of pressure. That of being favourite. 'I think I handled it pretty well,' Murray said with characteristic understatement as he clutched the trophy to his chest afterwards. His relieved mother, Judy, said she was able to enjoy his triumph in a way that had been impossible in 2013.

Watching approvingly were other ghosts of Centre Court past – aside from Lendl and McEnroe, Björn Borg, Boris Becker and Stefan Edberg were all in the royal box. Down in the corner, the outgoing prime minister, David Cameron, looked morose – as though taking the time to process what had happened in the past fortnight beyond SW19 – and received a mixed reception from his fellow spectators.

Raonic, too, could not help but appear bemused as Murray scurried back and forth returning whatever the Canadian could throw at him and then flashing winners past his feet. In truth, it only ever felt like there was going to be one winner. If Irn-Bru is made in Scotland from girders, Murray must have been minted in Dunblane in granite. As the crowd toasted his success with champagne, he created his own internal pressure to see him home – ranting at his box at the end of the second set.

Off court, Murray remains as unaffected as a wildly driven elite sportsperson with $50m in the bank can be. He negotiates the inanity of the Wimbledon press room with aplomb. Asked last week whether he was bothered that the Henman Hill tag still persisted, he laughed. 'He's welcome to it.'

Up on that hill, though, they celebrated his victory with fervour. When Raonic described Murray as a 'workaholic' before the final, it sounded like faint praise. But it was in many ways the ultimate compliment to a player who has relentlessly made the most of his natural talent. His consistency threatens to inure us to the scale of his achievement. Perhaps it will only be fully appreciated when his success is no longer a fixture here, year after extraordinary year.

11 JULY

Why the Euro 2016 final was overrun by moths

PATRICK BARKHAM

It will forever be remembered as the mothballs final: a rather drab climax to Euro 2016 enlivened by a swarm of moths. As soon as pictures were broadcast of dozens of moths flapping around the stadium during the warm-up, out fluttered the moth memes. It became a meme swarm for many British critics of the Portuguese captain, after Ronaldo fell – injured – to the turf at the Stade de France, and a moth tended to his arched eyebrow.

Dozens of 'Ronaldo's Moth' Twitter accounts were created within seconds. 'The diving bell and the butterfly,' joked one wag. 'Just put £20 on #Ronaldo swallowing a moth, choking and rolling around on the floor for 20 minutes,' said another.

Ronaldo's moth was one of thousands of Silver Y moths, a migratory species that moves north through Europe each summer in search of new breeding grounds, returning south in the autumn.

'It's an obligate migrant species – a proper migratory species,' says Richard Fox of Butterfly Conservation. 'Individuals must migrate and choose the right winds to fly at different altitudes to maximise the efficiency of their migration. There's very clever stuff going on.'

On a warm summer's evening, the lights of the stadium act like an enormous moth trap, drawing down a migrating front of thousands of these moths.

Pictures show the moths rising from the turf in clouds as the referee, Mark Clattenburg, and officials first stepped on to the pitch. The moths had arrived in the stadium before the footballers – almost certainly drawn down on the previous night when the floodlights were reportedly left on.

'When you've got all these big mammals tramping around on the grass, the moths quite sensibly flew up and away,' said Fox.

With winds blowing from the south and south-west over the past few days, Fox said the footballing Silver Ys could end up in Britain. After a miserable wet summer, their presence will at least give people something to spot in the Big Butterfly Count, the world's biggest insect-recording scheme, which is launched by Butterfly Conservation this Friday.

Ronaldo's moth-anxiety followed by injury heartbreak turned to joy when Portugal won the tournament. Given that the swarm of Silver Ys proved a lucky omen, perhaps Ronaldo's crowning glory could be to become their champion: how about honorary president of Butterfly Conservation?

How technology disrupted the truth (extract)

KATHARINE VINER

One Monday morning last September, Britain woke to a depraved news story. The prime minister, David Cameron, had committed an 'obscene act with a dead pig's head', according to the *Daily Mail*. 'A distinguished Oxford contemporary claims Cameron once took part in an outrageous initiation ceremony at a Piers Gaveston event, involving a dead pig,' the paper reported. Piers Gaveston is the name of a riotous Oxford University dining society; the authors of the story claimed their source was an MP who said he had seen photographic evidence: 'His extraordinary suggestion is that the future PM inserted a private part of his anatomy into the animal's mouth.'

The story, extracted from a new biography of Cameron, sparked an immediate furore. It was gross, it was a great opportunity to humiliate an elitist prime minister, and many felt it rang true for a former member of the notorious Bullingdon Club. Within minutes, #Piggate and #Hameron were trending on Twitter, and even senior politicians joined the fun: Nicola Sturgeon said the allegations had 'entertained the whole country', while Paddy Ashdown joked that Cameron was 'hogging the headlines'. At first, the BBC refused to mention the allegations, and 10 Downing Street said it would not 'dignify' the story with a response – but soon it was forced to issue a denial. And so a powerful man was sexually shamed, in a way that had nothing to do with his divisive politics, and in a way he could never really respond to. But who cares? He could take it.

Then, after a full day of online merriment, something shocking happened. Isabel Oakeshott, the *Daily Mail* journalist who had co-written the biography with Lord Ashcroft, a billionaire businessman, went on TV and admitted that she did not know whether her huge, scandalous scoop was even true. Pressed to provide evidence for the sensational claim, Oakeshott admitted she had none.

'We couldn't get to the bottom of that source's allegations,' she said on Channel 4 News, 'so we merely reported the account that the source gave us ... We don't say whether we believe it to be true.' In other words, there was no evidence that the prime minister of the United Kingdom had once 'inserted a private part of his anatomy' into the mouth of a dead pig – a story reported in dozens of newspapers and repeated in millions of tweets and Facebook updates, which many people today presumably still believe to be true.

Oakeshott went even further to absolve herself of any journalistic responsibility: 'It's up to other people to decide whether they give it any credibility or not,' she concluded. This was not, of course, the first time that outlandish claims were published on the basis of flimsy evidence, but this was an unusually brazen defence. It seemed that journalists were no longer required to believe their own stories to be true; nor, apparently, did they need to provide evidence. Instead it was up to the reader – who does not even know the identity of the source – to make up their own mind. But based on what? Gut instinct, intuition, mood?

When a fact begins to resemble whatever you feel is true, it becomes very difficult for anyone to tell the difference between facts that are true and 'facts' that are not. Twenty-five years after the first website went online, it is clear that we are living through a period of dizzying transition. For 500 years after Gutenberg, the dominant form of information was the printed page: knowledge was primarily delivered in a fixed format, one that encouraged readers to believe in stable and settled truths.

Now, we are caught in a series of confusing battles between opposing forces: between truth and falsehood, fact and rumour, kindness and cruelty; between the few and the many, the connected and the alienated; between the open platform of the web as its architects envisioned it and the gated enclosures of Facebook and other social networks; between an informed public and a misguided mob.

What is common to these struggles – and what makes their resolution an urgent matter – is that they all involve the diminishing status of truth. This does not mean that there are no truths. It simply means, as this year has made very clear, that we cannot agree on what those truths are, and when there is no consensus about the truth and no way to achieve it, chaos soon follows.

Increasingly, what counts as a fact is merely a view that someone feels to be true – and technology has made it very easy for these 'facts' to circulate with a speed and reach that was unimaginable in the Gutenberg era (or even a decade ago). A dubious story about Cameron and a pig appears in a tabloid one morning, and by noon, it has flown around the world on social media and turned up in trusted news sources everywhere. This may seem like a small matter, but its consequences are enormous.

'The Truth', as Peter Chippindale and Chris Horrie wrote in *Stick It Up Your Punter!*, their history of the *Sun* newspaper, is a 'bald statement which every newspaper prints at its peril'. There are usually several conflicting truths on any given subject, but in the era of the printing press, words on a page nailed things down, whether they turned out to be true or not. The information felt like the truth – at least until the next day brought another update or a correction – and we all shared a common set of facts.

This settled 'truth' was usually handed down from above: an established truth, often fixed in place by an establishment. This arrangement was not without flaws: too much of the press often exhibited a bias towards the status quo and a deference to authority, and it was prohibitively difficult for ordinary people to challenge the power of the press. Now people distrust much of what is presented as fact – particularly if the facts in question are uncomfortable, or out of sync with their own views – and while some of that distrust is misplaced, some of it is not.

In the digital age, it is easier than ever to publish false information, which is quickly shared and taken to be true – as we often see in emergency situations, when news is breaking in real time. To pick one example among many, during the November 2015 Paris terror attacks, rumours quickly spread on social media that the Louvre and Pompidou Centre had been hit, and that François Hollande had suffered a stroke. Trusted news organisations are needed to debunk such tall tales.

Sometimes rumours like these spread out of panic, sometimes out of malice, and sometimes deliberate manipulation, in which a corporation or regime pays people to convey their message. Whatever the motive, falsehoods and facts now spread the same way, through what academics call an 'information cascade'. As the legal scholar and online-harassment expert Danielle Citron describes it, 'people forward on what others think, even if the information is false, misleading or incomplete, because they think they have learned something valuable'. This cycle repeats itself, and before you know it, the cascade has unstoppable momentum. You share a friend's post on Facebook, perhaps to show kinship or agreement or that you're 'in the know', and thus you increase the visibility of their post to others.

Algorithms such as the one that powers Facebook's newsfeed are designed to give us more of what they think we want – which means that the version of the world we encounter every day in our own personal stream has been invisibly curated to reinforce our pre-existing beliefs. When Eli Pariser, the co-founder of Upworthy, coined the term 'filter bubble' in 2011, he was talking about how the personalised web – and in particular Google's personalised search function, which means that no two people's Google searches are the same – means that we are less likely to be exposed to information that challenges us or broadens our worldview, and less likely to encounter facts that disprove false information that others have shared.

Pariser's plea, at the time, was that those running social media platforms should ensure that 'their algorithms prioritise countervailing views and news that's important, not just the stuff that's most popular or most self-validating'. But in less than five years, thanks to the incredible power of a few social platforms, the filter bubble that Pariser described has become much more extreme.

On the day after the EU referendum, in a Facebook post, the British internet activist and mySociety founder, Tom Steinberg, provided a vivid illustration of the power of the filter bubble – and the serious civic consequences for a world where information flows largely through social networks:

I am actively searching through Facebook for people celebrating the Brexit leave victory, but the filter bubble is SO strong, and extends SO far into things like Facebook's custom search that I can't find anyone who is happy *despite the fact that over half the country is clearly jubilant today* and despite the fact that I'm *actively* looking to hear what they are saying.

This echo-chamber problem is now SO severe and SO chronic that I can only beg any friends I have who actually work for Facebook and other major social media and technology to urgently tell their leaders that to not act on this problem now is tantamount to actively supporting and funding the tearing apart of the fabric of our societies ... We're getting countries where one half just doesn't know anything at all about the other.

But asking technology companies to 'do something' about the filter bubble presumes that this is a problem that can be easily fixed – rather than one baked into the very idea of social networks that are designed to give you what you and your friends want to see.

Facebook, which launched only in 2004, now has 1.6 billion users worldwide. It has become the dominant way for people to find news on the internet – and in fact it is dominant in ways that would have been impossible to imagine in the newspaper era. As Emily Bell has written: 'Social media hasn't just swallowed journalism, it has swallowed everything. It has swallowed political campaigns, banking systems, personal histories, the leisure industry, retail, even government and security.'

Bell, the director of the Tow Center for Digital Journalism at Columbia University – and a board member of the Scott Trust, which owns the *Guardian* – has outlined the seismic impact of social media for journalism. 'Our news ecosystem has changed more dramatically in the past five years,' she wrote in March, 'than perhaps at any time in the past 500.' The future of publishing is being put into the 'hands of the few, who now control the destiny of the many'. News publishers have lost control over the distribution of their journalism, which for many readers is now 'filtered through algorithms and platforms which are opaque and unpredictable'. This means that social media companies have become overwhelmingly powerful in determining what we read – and enormously profitable from the monetisation of other people's work. As Bell notes: 'There is a far greater concentration of power in this respect than there has ever been in the past.'

Publications curated by editors have in many cases been replaced by a stream of information chosen by friends, contacts and family, processed by secret algorithms. The old idea of a wide-open web – where hyperlinks from site to site created a non-hierarchical and decentralised network of information – has been largely supplanted by platforms designed to maximise your time within their walls, some of which (such as Instagram and Snapchat) do not allow outward links at all.

Of course, Facebook does not decide what you read – at least not in the traditional sense of making decisions – and nor does it dictate what news organisations produce. But when one platform becomes the dominant source for accessing information, news organisations will often tailor their own work to the demands of this new medium. (The most visible evidence of Facebook's influence on journalism is the panic that accompanies any change in the newsfeed algorithm that threatens to reduce the page views sent to publishers.)

In the last few years, many news organisations have steered themselves away from public-interest journalism and toward junk-food news, chasing page views in the vain hope of attracting clicks and advertising (or investment) – but like junk food, you hate yourself when you've gorged on it. The most extreme manifestation of this phenomenon has been the creation of fake news farms, which attract traffic with false reports that are designed to look like real news, and are therefore widely shared on social networks. But the same principle applies to news that is misleading or sensationally dishonest, even if it wasn't created to deceive: the new measure of value for too many news organisations is virality rather than truth or quality.

Of course, journalists have got things wrong in the past – either by mistake or prejudice or sometimes by intent. (Freddie Starr probably didn't eat a hamster.) So it would be a mistake to think this is a new phenomenon of the digital age. But what is new and significant is that today, rumours and lies are read just as widely as copper-bottomed facts – and often more widely, because they are wilder than reality and more exciting to share. The cynicism of this approach was expressed most nakedly by Neetzan Zimmerman, formerly employed by Gawker as a specialist in high-traffic viral stories. 'Nowadays it's not important if a story's real,' he said in 2014. 'The only thing that really matters is whether people click on it.' Facts, he suggested, are over; they are a relic from the age of the printing press, when readers had no choice. He continued: 'If a person is not sharing a news story, it is, at its core, not news.'

The increasing prevalence of this approach suggests that we are in the midst of a fundamental change in the values of journalism – a consumerist shift. Instead of strengthening social bonds, or creating an informed public, or the idea of news as a civic good, a democratic necessity, it creates gangs, which spread instant falsehoods that fit their views, reinforcing each other's beliefs and driving each other deeper into shared opinions, rather than established facts.

But the trouble is that the business model of most digital news organisations is based around clicks. News media around the world has reached a fever pitch of frenzied binge-publishing, in order to scrape up digital advertising's pennies and cents. (And there's not much advertising to be got: in the first quarter of 2016, 85 cents of every new dollar spent in the US on online advertising went to Google and Facebook. That used to go to news publishers.)

In the newsfeed on your phone, all stories look the same – whether they come from a credible source or not. And, increasingly, otherwise-credible sources are also publishing false, misleading or deliberately outrageous stories. 'Clickbait is king, so newsrooms will uncritically print some of the worst stuff out there, which lends legitimacy to bullshit,' said Brooke Binkowski, an editor at the debunking website Snopes, in an interview with the *Guardian* in April. 'Not all newsrooms are like this, but a lot of them are.'

We should be careful not to dismiss anything with an appealing digital headline as clickbait – appealing headlines are a good thing, if they lead the reader to quality journalism, both serious and not. My belief is that what distinguishes good journalism from poor journalism is labour: the journalism that people value the most is that for which they can tell someone has put in a lot of work – where they can feel the effort that has been expended on their behalf, over tasks big or small, important or entertaining. It is the reverse of so-called churnalism, the endless recycling of other people's stories for clicks.

A news-publishing industry desperately chasing down every cheap click doesn't sound like an industry in a position of strength, and indeed, news publishing as a business is in trouble. The shift to digital publishing has been a thrilling development for journalism. It has meant we have found new ways to get stories – from our audience, from data, from social media. It has given us new ways to tell stories – with interactive technologies and now with virtual reality. It has given us new ways to distribute our journalism, to find new readers in surprising places; and it has given us new ways to engage with our audience, opening ourselves up to challenge and debate.

But while the possibilities for journalism have been strength-ened by the digital developments of the last few years, the business model is under grave threat, because no matter how many clicks you get, it will never be enough. And if you charge readers to access your journalism, you have a big challenge to persuade the digital consumer who is used to getting information for free to part with their cash.

News publishers everywhere are seeing profits and revenue drop dramatically. If you want a stark illustration of the new realities of digital media, consider the first-quarter financial results of the *New York Times* and Facebook, declared within a week of one another earlier this year. The *New York Times* announced that its operating profits had fallen by 13 per cent, to $51.5m – healthier than most of the rest of the publishing industry, but quite a drop. Facebook, meanwhile, revealed that its net income had tripled in the same period – to a quite staggering $1.51bn.

Many journalists have lost their jobs in the past decade. The number of journalists in the UK shrank by up to one-third between 2001 and 2010; US newsrooms declined by a similar amount between 2006 and 2013. In Australia, there was a 20 per cent cut in the journalistic workforce between 2012 and 2014 alone. Not because of a problem with journalism, but because of a problem with funding it.

But journalists losing their jobs is not simply a problem for journalists; it has a damaging impact on the entire culture. As the German philosopher Jürgen Habermas warned, back in 2007: 'When reorganisation and cost-cutting in this core area jeopardise accustomed journalistic standards, it hits at the very heart of the political public sphere. Because, without the flow of information gained through extensive research, and without the stimulation of arguments based on an expertise that doesn't come cheap, public communication loses its discursive vitality. The public media would then cease to resist populist tendencies, and could no longer fulfil the function it should in the context of a democratic constitutional state.'

Perhaps, then, the focus of the news industry needs to turn to commercial innovation: how to rescue the funding of journalism, which is what is under threat. Journalism has seen dramatic innovation in the last two digital decades, but business models have not. In the words of my colleague Mary Hamilton, the *Guardian*'s executive editor for audience: 'We've transformed everything about our journalism and not enough about our businesses.'

The impact on journalism of the crisis in the business model is that, in chasing down cheap clicks at the expense of accuracy and veracity, news organisations undermine the very reason they exist: to find things out and tell readers the truth – to report, report, report.

Many newsrooms are in danger of losing what matters most about journalism: the civic, pounding-the-streets, sifting-the-database, asking-challenging-questions hard graft of uncovering things that someone doesn't want you to know. Serious, public-interest journalism is demanding, and there is more of a need for it than ever. Facts and reliable information are essential for the functioning of democracy – and the digital era has made that even more obvious.

But we must not allow the chaos of the present to cast the past in a rosy light – as can be seen from the recent resolution to a tragedy that became one of the darkest moments in the history of British journalism. At the end of April, a two-year-long inquest ruled that the 96 people who died in the Hillsborough disaster in 1989 had been unlawfully killed and had not contributed to the dangerous situation at the football ground. The verdict was the culmination of an indefatigable 27-year campaign by the victims' families to uncover the real truth about what happened at Hillsborough, and the subsequent cover-up by the police, abetted by the *Sun* newspaper, whose aggressive rightwing editor, Kelvin MacKenzie – according to Horrie and Chippindale's history of the *Sun* – overruled his own reporter to blame the fans for the disaster, under a front-page headline 'THE TRUTH'.

It is hard to imagine that Hillsborough could happen now: if 96 people were crushed to death in front of 53,000 smartphones, with photographs and eyewitness accounts all posted to social media, would it have taken so long for the truth to come out? Today, the police – or Kelvin MacKenzie – would not have been able to lie so blatantly and for so long.

The truth is a struggle. It takes hard graft. But the struggle is worth it: traditional news values are important and they are worth defending.

The digital revolution has meant that journalists – rightly, in my view – are more accountable to their audience. And as the Hillsborough story shows, the old media were certainly capable of perpetrating appalling falsehoods that could take years to unravel. Some of the old hierarchies have been decisively undermined, which has led to a more open debate and a more substantial challenge to the old elites whose interests often dominated the media. But the age of relentless and instant information – and uncertain truths – can be overwhelming. We careen from outrage to outrage, but forget each one very quickly: it's doomsday every afternoon.

At the same time, the levelling of the information landscape has unleashed new torrents of racism and sexism, and new means of shaming and harassment, suggesting a world in which the loudest and crudest arguments will prevail. It is an atmosphere that has proved particularly hostile to women and people of colour, revealing that the inequalities of the physical world are reproduced all too easily in online spaces. The *Guardian* is not immune – which is why one of my first initiatives as editor-in-chief was to launch the 'Web We Want' project, in order to combat a general culture of online abuse and ask how we as an institution can foster better and more civil conversations on the web.

Above all, the challenge for journalism today is not simply technological innovation or the creation of new business models. It is to establish what role journalistic organisations still play in a public discourse that has become impossibly fragmented and radically destabilised. The stunning political developments of the past year – including the vote for Brexit and the nomination of Donald Trump as the Republican candidate for the US presidency – are not simply the by-products of a resurgent populism or the revolt of those left behind by global capitalism.

As the academic Zeynep Tufekci argued in an essay earlier this year, the rise of Trump 'is actually a symptom of the mass media's growing weakness, especially in controlling the limits of what it is acceptable to say'. (A similar case could be made for the Brexit campaign.) 'For decades, journalists at major media organisations acted as gatekeepers who passed judgment on what ideas could be publicly discussed, and what was considered too radical,' Tufekci wrote. The weakening of these gatekeepers is both positive and negative; there are opportunities and there are dangers.

As we can see from the past, the old gatekeepers were also capable of great harm, and they were often imperious in refusing space to arguments they deemed outside the mainstream political consensus. But without some form of consensus, it is hard for any truth to take hold. The decline of the gatekeepers has given Trump space to raise formerly taboo subjects, such as the cost of a global free-trade regime that benefits corporations rather than workers, an issue that American elites and much of the media had long dismissed – as well as, more obviously, allowing his outrageous lies to flourish.

When the prevailing mood is anti-elite and anti-authority, trust in big institutions, including the media, begins to crumble.

I believe that a strong journalistic culture is worth fighting for. So is a business model that serves and rewards media organisations that put the search for truth at the heart of everything – building an informed, active public that scrutinises the powerful, rather than an ill-informed, reactionary gang that attacks the vulnerable. Traditional news values must be embraced and celebrated: reporting, verifying, gathering together eyewitness statements, making a serious attempt to discover what really happened.

We are privileged to live in an era where we can use many new technologies – and the help of our audience – to do that. But we must grapple with the issues underpinning digital culture, and realise that the shift from print to digital media was never just about technology. We must also address the new power dynamics that these changes have created. Technology and media do not exist in isolation – they help shape society, just as they are shaped by it in turn. That means engaging with people as civic actors, citizens, equals. It is about holding power to account, fighting for a public space, and taking responsibility for creating the kind of world we want to live in.

22 JULY

Why Pokémon Go really is a national health service

GABY HINSLIFF

If parenting is one long process of discovering that it doesn't really happen like they say in the books, then school holidays are proof positive that *Swallows and Amazons* was fiction. Every July starts, at least in this house, with starry-eyed delusions about a summer spent messing about on rivers, climbing trees and having wholesome adventures. Or, failing that, perhaps a summer of cheery educational play as per the more optimistic newspaper supplements, where the kids thrill to your kitchen science experiments and treasure hunts round National Trust properties.

And every July ends with the realisation that actually it's not going to be like that. We will not spend summer picnicking and playing beach cricket, because it is going to rain all August. We won't be that family in the museum whose kids just beg to hear more about the ancient Egyptians, because we will be that family whose kids roll their eyes sarcastically at the very idea of filling in the museum's lovely quiz. There will be afternoons where nobody looks up from Minecraft. And yet a tiny flicker of hope remains, for this is the summer of the Pokémon Go app.

The craze for this remarkably silly mobile phone game – which involves chasing cartoony little virtual monsters around the surrounding real world, as they pop into shot on your phone's camera – is currently outstripped only by the craze for stories about stupid things people do while playing it. A Holocaust museum in Washington was forced to remind visitors that it's crassly inappropriate to catch imaginary gonks on your phone while wandering round a memorial to victims of genocide. Tragically, a teenager in Guatemala was shot while playing the game – although whether the game had anything to do with the death remains unclear. There are reports of drivers crashing cars while surreptitiously playing on their phones, and a woman stuck up a tree while chasing Pokémon.

Yet what makes Pokémon Go irresistible is that it's basically a good old-fashioned treasure hunt crossed with a fairytale, adding up to that parenting holy grail: an excuse to go out in the fresh air and move.

Friends with boys in the awkward tweens – too old and self-conscious for running round the garden; too young to hunker moodily in bedrooms – report a sudden revival of 'playing out' in the park under the guise of Pokémon hunting. It's as if the app gives them an excuse to be kids again.

And those dry police reports about increased 'foot traffic' in cities thanks to overgrown kidults playing the game? That's code for what public health campaigns have struggled for decades to achieve, namely getting people out of the house and walking. If I were the NHS, I'd be pleading with Nintendo to cluster Pokémon characters along hiking routes and bike trails, up mountains and in woods. For every nine players who move through, not lifting their eyes from their phones, there will be one who looks up and sees something they might not otherwise have.

Yet all new technology must seemingly pass through three stages before we can reach such acceptance, and Pokémon Go is no exception. First comes the fear that it's somehow going to kill us (tick); second, the inevitable articles about how single women in New York are using it to meet men (tick); and finally, a moral panic over what it supposedly reveals about human nature that actually we already knew (getting there). Yes, people have done dumb and risky things while playing Pokémon Go. But replace the words 'playing Pokémon Go' with almost any activity and that sentence remains true. Why, it's almost as if the fault lies with people, not with the tools we ingeniously devise to satisfy that most endearingly human of instincts: play.

Talk of British creative industries, and people think of theatre, music or film. But gaming is a multibillion-pound player now – the point where arts meets tech – and as embedded in British culture as telly, without being quite so generously acknowledged. Having never got the bug myself, the sight of anyone hunched over a screen will never make my heart sing, but watching my son and his friends play dispels the fear that there's something inherently antisocial about it. They don't want to play alone, or with faceless strangers over the internet. What they crave is to be all in the same room, hooking up their individual devices to one Wi-Fi, building a sprawling Minecraft empire in which they share virtual adventures while chatting away in real life.

They're deep in an imaginary world, just as I was as a little girl playing shops, but it's interleaved with the physical world around them, and they move quite naturally between the two. No wonder, then, that this summer's hit isn't some overhyped virtual reality game but an augmented reality; one that takes game elements and overlays them on our shared real world.

As all games do, it has the potential to get messy. There's always someone who gets carried away, tips the Monopoly board over and ruins it for everyone. But humans will always want to play, and there's something oddly moving about the lengths to which we will go to invent new games for each other. How touching that, after all this time, we still so badly want to play together.

30 JULY

Harry Potter and the Cursed Child: the script will be a slog – but it's still our Harry

SIAN CAIN

I literally grew up with Harry Potter. When the final book came out almost a decade ago, we were both 17. With more than 450 million books sold since *Harry Potter and the Philosopher's Stone* was published in 1997, JK Rowling's series transformed reading into something genuinely cool during my lifetime. By my late teens, I was such a big fan I donned a Sirius Black costume before queueing for the final instalment.

But when it was announced in 2015 that Harry would return in a new story, the play *Harry Potter and the Cursed Child*, and that he'd be 37, an overworked civil servant struggling with parenting, I was dismayed. How had he gained 12 years on me? With every subsequent announcement, I got more cynical: it's five hours long? Split into two parts? The final nail in the coffin: a midnight release for the play script in book form. It was marketed as a benevolent gesture to those who could not see the play in London, but even as someone who queued for at least four Harry Potter books, it was hard to imagine kids lining up for screeds of stage directions.

Should plays be read? Many would say no – plays are written to be performed. Many actors argue that Shakespeare's plays shouldn't be studied in schools, as he is only truly appreciated through performance. But then what of *The Iliad* or *Beowulf*, composed for recitation but plonked on the page for posterity – would we not consider those literature?

When *The Cursed Child* box office opened, 175,000 tickets sold out in 24 hours – more than half of them to under-35s. At the performance I attend, the audience is mainly 20-somethings taking selfies; two guys behind me discuss the representational politics of Dumbledore's homosexuality. I'm sitting next to one of the youngest people I can see – Maddie, 16, who tells me things like: 'Did you know there are 142 staircases in Hogwarts?' – and I am filled with a profound sense of pride in the kids these books produced.

Minutes into the play, I begin to feel sorry for all the fans worldwide whose experience will be restricted to reading *The Cursed Child*'s script. As a book, it will be a slog: it is the equivalent of three *Harry Potter* novels squeezed into one, running on a Groundhog Day grasp of time travel and a *Star Wars*-esque handling of oedipal myth. But as a live experience, it is unique and incredible. An obsessive audience gasps at each of the reveals, cheers for the illusions, claps at the showdowns. For me, a lot of the joy comes from sitting next to Maddie, hearing her laugh, shout, cry. I can imagine that struggling through the script might be a lonely experience: something communal rendered solitary.

But during the break between plays (I'm seeing both on the same day) I head to the nearby Foyles bookshop, the site of a *Potter* pilgrimage for 25- to 30-year-olds, and any cynicism I have for the script's midnight release evaporates in the face of the genuine excitement all around me. Many of those who have already seen the play intend to join the queue. There are wide-eyed kids who had been too young for the last *Potter* launch. Students who make faces at the suggestion of dressing up, but mention they have swapped Sunday shifts to spend the day reading. Grey-haired adults who proudly announce they have kept their costumes for a decade – Kingsley Shacklebolt, Luna Lovegood, a female Harry.

Like me, these fans see no distinction between the characters in their heads, on Rowling's pages and the actors on stage. This new, older Harry is still my Harry. Watching the play, I feel an irrational desire to pull him off the stage and ask where he's been for the last decade. The whole theatre is united by a longing for something too complex to define: nostalgia for afternoons spent reading, a reminder of childhoods gone by.

So at midnight, no one will be lining up simply to buy a script, just as no one was in that theatre simply to see a play: they're there for Harry, in any form they can get him. *The Cursed Child*, either as a performance or a script, is going to make a lot of people really happy. Should you read a play? If it features Harry Potter, I'm going to.

6 August

Modern tribes:
the holiday organiser

CATHERINE BENNETT

Welcome! Here's your room, afraid it's on the main road, the rest of us are such light sleepers, you can't see the sea from your side, but it's handy for the loo, just don't put anything down it, no, including paper, it's all in the instructions, we're taking it in turns to empty the bin. Don't drink the water, we looked in the visitors' book, someone had to be flown home last year.

House rules, breakfast at eight, so it's still cool for sightseeing, lunch at one, drinks at seven, that leaves plenty of time for bridge after dinner, not to worry, you'll soon learn. We're taking it in turns to cook, here's the rota, oh look, you're doing tonight, so you'd better get cracking, you'll want time for the fish market and the bakery, don't worry, I'll draw a map, shouldn't take you more than two hours for the round trip.

So, money, four rooms, seven adults, we're dividing by four with half-rates for me, I'm on the 5:2, and counting a child as a person who doesn't drink, if you want to put £100 in the kitty that should be good for a day or so, you wouldn't believe the price of fish. Plus would you mind getting some stuff from the pharmacist for jellyfish stings, and a mezzaluna, the knives here are awful.

Just anything simple would be lovely, yesterday Robert did a few quails' eggs with the drinks, that Nigella cauliflower thing to start, then fish stew and a basic fruit salad, I've no idea how it took him all afternoon, could you bear to drop off the rubbish on the way? No, somebody already did roast chicken. We'll be poolside, so don't try ringing, the only signal is in your room, if you don't mind people popping in now and again, and don't be surprised, we've agreed no swimsuits by the pool, and it's hardly worth dressing to go indoors.

I don't want to nag, but the supermarket closes at two, here's the list, did I mention you'll need a vegan option and I'm gluten intolerant?

8 AUGUST

So long, Marianne

SUZANNE MOORE

A short goodbye. A few sentences. But words of such clarity, simplicity and beauty. Many of us have by now read Leonard Cohen's letter to a woman he once loved, on her deathbed, and those who didn't know it already have seen that Cohen is a class act, a man you don't meet every day.

Informed that Marianne Ihlen was dying, two hours later he wrote to her saying that he too was old and his body failing. He had, of course, written for her many years before, with the lyrics of 'So Long, Marianne' and 'Bird on the Wire'. This time he told her: 'Know that I am so close behind you, that if you stretch out your hand, I think you can reach mine … Goodbye old friend. Endless love, see you down the road.'

Cohen has never shied away from talking of ageing: 'My friends are gone and my hair is grey. I ache in the places where I used to play', he sang in 'Tower of Song'. A few years ago in Manchester, he reminisced about how he had last stood on that stage as a young blade of 60. There wasn't a woman there not won over by him. The fedora tipped in gratitude. The incantation of a thousand kisses deep.

When Marianne was slipping into unconsciousness, her friend said that she did reach out her hand. She heard what Cohen said. His letter also stated that he didn't need to talk about her beauty and her wisdom, 'because you know all about that'. The 10 years they were together on and off, their intimacies, their passions, their endings, those – despite the songs – are all a part of their own personal story.

Now he wishes her love on her journey – to death. It is, of course, everyone else's journey too, but few speak so directly of it, not even while whispering in the waiting rooms.

Was she Cohen's greatest muse? What does it matter? Here they are on Hydra, the Greek island where they met in the 1960s. She, a barefoot goddess, feet on the earth, light streaming on to her strong face. In those times on Hydra women loved, we are told, to look after creative men, even though Marianne already had a child.

Every account of her, even in her 70s, is of a woman with a lightness of touch, who made others feel good. She was a model, yet seemed entirely detached from her own beauty. Cohen loved her for a good while. He loved his four bottles of wine a day before he took himself off to the Buddhist monastery where he was given the dharma name of Jikan, which means 'silence'. But he knows about silence as he also knows about the tower of song.

Death is so often met with silence or with sentiments that are an inane babble to fill a void. The mawkish inscriptions and epitaphs seek to cauterise the grief, to fix it for a while. For how to write of loss? How do you write to a person you will never see again? I have done it – clumsily, inelegantly, with false jauntiness and then a wish for them to rest. Whatever that means.

So Cohen's economy of words, the syntax of love, his ability to go straight to the only matter that matters – her death, his mortality, their love – is a thing of beauty and wisdom in itself. His ever-deepening voice, the self-mockery, to see him now deadpan and dapper is still quite something. But once she held him like a crucifix and he let her go: 'I'm cold as a new razor blade' he sang in 'So Long, Marianne'. He jokes about death, apologising for not dying yet, but then his Zen master lived to be 107. And in his 2014 work, 'Almost Like the Blues', Cohen plays with death again, teases it even: 'I have to die a little between each murderous thought. And when I'm finished thinking, I have to die a lot.'

Some think of him as a doom-monger but he is profoundly funny, still worrying about war, torture and bad reviews. About the silence that will come when even the crickets hesitate.

Humour and faith were always there. 'I think I was touched as a child by the music and the kind of charged speech I heard in the synagogue, where everything is important,' he said in his eighth decade, adding ironically that he was singing 'a lot of Jew-sounding songs in different keys'.

That his words are charged is the reason they touch us. In my local park, there is an inscription on a bench for a friend who died, and the words are taken from 'So Long, Marianne': 'It's time that we began to laugh and cry and cry and laugh about it all again.'

Cohen once said: 'Poetry is just the evidence of your life. If your life is burning well, poetry is just the ash.' What ash though? Warm, sacred, dancing us to the end of love; young passions, old bodies, a rare and gracious farewell. So long, Marianne. Thank you, Mr Cohen.

15 AUGUST

An inspiring night in Rio

BARNEY RONAY

Faster, higher, stronger, Farah. Never mind the dead hand of London 2012. Bundle those memories of Super Saturday back in the sock drawer.

There were so many obvious symmetries on Rio 2016's first bravura night of track and field. Perhaps the more parochial will cast this middle Saturday as glorious but still a notch down from the rush of London four years ago, but in the event this was an occasion that stood without the need for comparison. Three hours of utterly absorbing Olympic athletics on a chilly, slightly wild night in Rio.

It was always a wonderful piece of theatre that the Stratford three – Mo Farah, Jessica Ennis-Hill and Greg Rutherford – should compete again simultaneously. In the event only Farah held on to his gold, producing the most thrilling medal race of his collection, a performance of tactical clarity and real matadorial edge.

Rutherford snaffled the long jump bronze in a tight, claustrophobic competition that went right to the last trailed hand in the sand. Jarrion Lawson's final jump of the Games would have nudged Rutherford off the podium, but it was marked down for the tiniest imprint of a stray wrist. The heptathlon also went to the wire, with a supreme emergent performance from Nafissatou Thiam edging Ennis into silver in what might just have been her own competitive farewell.

At times there was even something oddly poignant in the sight, once again, of a miserably empty Olympic stadium. Four years ago in London the bleachers were in a state of uproar as Ennis crossed the line to take gold. In one corner an entire row of nurses could be seen embracing a squadron of sailors in old-school white suits, plonked next to one another as part of a spare-ticket giveaway, producing an impossibly cinematic scene of unbound celebration.

Rio, not so much. The dive pool has turned green, and by the end here the Olympic stadium had turned the colour of empty blue plastic.

The consensus seems to be that this is a shameful state of affairs. But shameful for whom? Tickets here are expensive relative to income. The most obvious culprits are the wonks and politicians of Rio 2016's organising committee, who bid for the Games with wild abandon and then simply failed to pull the people into the show. Unmonitored by the International Olympic Committee, they created over seven years a crushingly costly spectacle drenched in indifference.

You can't kill the spirit though. As the heptathletes strolled their lap of honour, hugging and smiling and waving at a minuscule crowd, it was tempting to glory simply in the pared-back spectacle. Athletics remains a beautifully simple sport surrounded by confusion. In the end this is all you need: a track, someone to compete against, and someone, anyone, to cheer.

As the night kicked into gear, Rutherford sat once again at the edge of the running track as Ennis threw the javelin – a swirl of Olympic deja vu flickering beneath the tension. Rutherford put in a solid start, going further with his first jump than he had to win gold in London. But then he has never really been about pure distance, more a kind of warrior of the sandpit, a hard-edged and ornery competitor. His third jump hit the mark, nudging him out in front.

By now Farah had appeared on the near side of the stadium, swaggering to the 10,000m line like a man prepared for a fight.

For the first three laps he prowled along, three yards off the back marker. It is a showy, predatory kind of tactic, but a sensible one when the rest of the race fears you. Back there, Farah can see everyone. Steadily he crept up the field. For a while he hit the front. Then he abruptly fell over, ankle tapped by his training partner Galen Rupp. Farah rolled and scrabbled and sprinted back.

At first, three red Kenyan shirts boxed him out of the front, refusing to budge as the race unwound with an increasingly helter-skelter whirl of bluff and feint and bump. But again Farah was coiled right where he needed to be with a lap to go.

Paul Tanui made his move just after the bell. The gap opened briefly, but Farah stamped his way back and at the final bend made his move, skipping out from the slipstream and powering away. He had it won in that moment, the stadium rising as he collapsed across the line, holding his head and writhing in joy on the blue track. Briefly there was a tearful Mobot, then a sombre, exhausted walk towards the fans at the perimeter to drape himself in the union jack.

It was a perfect race in many ways. The entire field bent to Farah's racing will, allowing him to bunch them in, then finding themselves burned away by his finishing speed.

Meanwhile, Rutherford had been hauled back. Jeff Henderson of the US pushed the gold mark up to 8.38m, a distance Rutherford, fourth now, had barely jumped in his career. The talk with Rutherford is always of his competitive will. Well, here it was. One leap to crash the podium. Pit or bust.

Rutherford slapped his thighs and made some gurning faces at the end of his run. He nailed it too, edging into bronze position, then hanging in there as Lawson's huge final jump was dragged back to 7.78m, his coach leaping up in fury and calling fruitlessly for a do-over.

So it came down to the final knockings. Ennis-Hill needed to win her last event, the 800m, by an improbable margin to haul in a Belgian who set five personal bests here. She went out like a hare, leading from start to finish and pushing herself to the limits of whatever two days of competition had left. Thiam hung on to become a truly worthy gold medallist, the champ who beat the champ.

At the end, Ennis-Hill seemed to be half saying goodbye – beaming and sobbing, cuddling into her flag like somebody sealing in the moment. Either way, the chintz of London 2012's grand middle Saturday can now be safely packed away for good, never again to be disturbed. For Rio this was something more, a night of thrilling competition and another reminder in among the sludge and the noises off that sport can still provide not just moments of victory, but shades of something more profoundly uplifting.

18 AUGUST

To shed tears for the injured children of Syria is not enough

ZAHER SAHLOUL

The pictures of the injured five-year-old Omran Daqneesh have shocked the world, but doctors in Aleppo see dozens of desperate children like him every week, often with worse injuries, many entirely beyond help.

Perhaps his tragedy will have a small silver lining if it reminds people far beyond Syria of the tragedy that has been unfolding for years. Every time I work there I treat children who are often so terribly wounded and traumatised that I wonder if the ones who survived were unluckier than the ones who died.

I keep a picture drawn by a seven-year-old in Aleppo, of helicopters bombing the city, blood and destruction below, but what is really shocking for me is that the dead children in the drawing are smiling while the living ones are crying.

I also keep photos of my first-ever patient in Aleppo, a toddler called Hamzeh, who had been shot by a government sniper and brought to the hospital's intensive care unit with a bullet in his brain. I had to tell his family he was brain-dead, and then turn off the ventilator, which can be particularly hard in Syria because if the heart is beating many people cannot accept their child has no hope of survival.

Then there was Abdullah, who was 12, injured by shrapnel from a barrel bomb. He asked me, screaming in pain but somehow still polite, to stop trying to insert a tube into his chest without anaesthetic. 'I kiss your hand, uncle. Please stop,' he begged me, but we had no painkillers and he would die if I did not drain the blood pooling around his lungs, so I carried on. I also think often of the two young sisters who were brought to another emergency room hugging each other, but already dead.

Omran survived without losing a limb or an eye, but he will be traumatised for ever. There are bombings every day, so who knows what will happen in the coming days or weeks; he could be hit again. We say this is a powerful picture, but will it translate into meaningful action to protect these children? They are not dolls to cry over and then move on.

Last time I entered the outskirts of Aleppo, the air thick with the stench of death from decaying bodies, gunfire and explosions in the distance, our driver warned us to 'say your final prayers now', in case we didn't make it.

I could never have imagined I would take such risks with my life when I went to medical school, when the main thing we expected to worry about was lawsuits. And, after each medical mission to Syria, people ask me how I can leave my loving family and comfortable home in Chicago, knowing I may not come back.

I ask this question myself sometimes, sipping morning coffee in my suburban backyard, watching birds and butterflies. But then a message arrives from Syria, asking for help treating a gruesome injury shown in an iPhone photo, informing me of the death of another colleague or sharing images of a devastating new attack.

I go there so I can come back and bear testimony to the tragedy unfolding, to show solidarity to the few remaining brave doctors and nurses in rebel-held east Aleppo, but also because our help is needed in these areas.

After years of bombing by Russian and regime aircraft, hundreds of doctors have been killed or have fled. Only 35 remain in the east of the city to serve more than 300,000 civilians, and there is not a single critical-care doctor – my own speciality – even though there is an abundance of critically ill patients.

During my dozen medical missions to Syria, I have had to trust smugglers and brave Aleppo's sniper alley, crawl under border fences, jump walls, walk over mountain passes, wait in basements for jets to pass overhead. But the memories that haunt me are not of personal danger but from the hospitals where I have worked, of those I did not have the time, the staff or the equipment to save.

What would you do if you had a child with head injuries from a barrel bomb but no CT scanner to figure out if she has bleeding on the brain or not? What would you do if your hospital was bombed but it was the only place in town providing healthcare to a helpless population? Would you leave or stay?

These are real dilemmas that doctors there have to face, and as they work to keep others alive, it is always at huge risk to themselves. I think often of doctors like Hassan al-Araj, a cardiologist from the western Syrian city of Hama, whose last operating theatre was inside the 'central cave hospital', dug into the heart of a mountain for protection. He was killed anyway by an airstrike, when his car was hit on his way to work.

What is going on in Syria is a medical emergency that has been unfolding in slow motion for five years. We can't wait for politicians to fix the crisis. We can't wait for a no-fly zone to stop the bombing. Doctors can save many lives by doing what we do best: using our stethoscopes, skills and compassion. Aid groups and the people who fund them can save many more by delivering medical supplies and ambulances across the border, training local doctors and nurses, setting up mobile clinics to reach displaced populations.

Inside Aleppo, fortified or underground hospitals protected from bombs, portable technology that can be hidden or moved after bombing raids, and telemedicine connecting overworked doctors to experts overseas all save lives.

And all of us can help by advocating on behalf of the doctors and their patients, refusing to accept their suffering is normal, even if the world can sometimes seem inured to Syria's pain. Every life is precious. Omran has reminded us all of the terrible suffering of the children caught up in this war. Let us not forget them again.

25 AUGUST

I created the burkini
to set women free

AHEDA ZANETTI

When I invented the burkini, in early 2004, it was to give women freedom, not to take it away. My niece wanted to play netball but she couldn't get on to the team because she was wearing a hijab. My sister had to fight for her daughter to play, had to debate the issue and ask: why is this girl prevented from playing netball because of her modesty?

When she was finally allowed to play, we all went to support her, and what she was wearing was totally inappropriate for a sports uniform: a 'skivvy' – a long-sleeved, tight-fitting shirt – tracksuit bottoms and her hijab. It was totally unsuitable for any sport. She looked like a tomato, she was so red and hot!

So I went home and began to look for something that might be better for her to wear – sportswear for Muslim girls – and I couldn't find anything. I knew there was nothing in Australia. It got me thinking, because when I was a girl I missed out on sport. We didn't participate in anything because we chose to be modest. But for my niece I wanted to find something that would adapt to the Australian lifestyle and western clothing, but at the same time fulfil the needs of a Muslim girl.

So I sat down on my lounge floor and designed something. I looked at the veil and took away a lot of the excess fabric, which made me nervous – would my Islamic community accept this? The veil is supposed to cover your hair and your shape; you just don't shape a garment around your body. But my design was shaped around the neck. I thought, it's only the shape of a neck – it doesn't really matter.

Before I launched it, I produced a sample with a questionnaire to find out what people would think: Would you wear this? Would this encourage you to be more active, play more sport, swim?

A lot of people in my community didn't know how to react to my design, but I developed it commercially. It was about integration and acceptance and being equal, and about not being judged. Sport is so important, and we are Australian! I wanted to do something positive – and anyone can wear this: Christians, Jews, Hindus. It's just a garment to suit a modest person, or someone who has skin cancer, or a new mother who doesn't want to wear a bikini. It's not a symbol of Islam.

When I named it the burkini, I didn't really think it was a burqa for the beach. Burqa is not in any Islamic text. I had to look the word up, and it was described as a kind of coat and coverall. And at the other end, you had the bikini. So I combined the two.

What is happening now in France – the burkini is banned on beaches – makes me so sad. I hope it's not because of racism. I think they have misunderstood a garment that is so positive – it symbolises leisure and happiness and fun and fitness and health, and now they are demanding women get off the beach and back into their kitchens.

This garment has given women freedom, and they want to take that freedom away. So who is better, the Taliban or French politicians? They are as bad as each other.

I don't think any man should worry about how women are dressing. No one is forcing us. It's a woman's choice.

I would love to be in France to say this: you have misunderstood. And there are enough problems in the world to worry about; why create more? You've taken a product that symbolised happiness and joyfulness and fitness, and turned it into a product of hatred.

What are 'French values'? When you say that the burkini is incompatible with French values, what does that mean? Liberty? You telling us what to wear, telling us what not to do, will drive women back into their homes. And what do you want us to do then? There will be a backlash. If you are dividing the nation and not listening and not working towards something, you are naturally going to have someone who will get angry. Pushing people away and isolating them is definitely not a good thing for any politician to do, in any country.

I remember when I first tested the burkini in my bath. I had to make sure it worked. Then I had to test it by diving in it, so I went to the local pool to test that the headband would stay put, and I remember everyone staring at me: what was I wearing?

I went right to the end of the pool and got on the diving board and dived in. The headband stayed in place, and I thought: Beauty! Perfect.

It was my first time swimming in public, and it was absolutely beautiful. I remember the feeling so clearly. I felt freedom. I felt empowerment. I felt like I owned the pool. I walked to the end of that pool with my shoulders back.

Diving into water is one of the best feelings in the world.

25 September

Now Labour's two sides can start to bridge the great divide

GARY YOUNGE

In 1987 the left activist and academic Hilary Wainwright wrote a book called *Labour: A Tale of Two Parties*, in which she outlined its two competing strands. On one side was the Labour establishment that thrived on a top-down leadership model with an almost exclusive interest in electoral success, as though government were an end in itself. On the other was a grassroots contingent with one foot in the party and one in broader social movements, more interested in the kind of fundamental societal transformation that parliament alone cannot deliver.

The former prides itself on its pragmatism – the capacity to engage with the world as it is rather than as it would like it to be, so it can get into power in Westminster and produce incremental improvements that might make a difference to large numbers of people. The latter is guided by its activism – mobilising communities to challenge the distribution of power itself, so that it can effect change that is more thorough-going but may also be less immediate.

Now Jeremy Corbyn has romped home to an even more emphatic win than he did last year, these two traditions need to return to their respective founding principles if they are to coexist productively. Both are failing on their own terms. And that failure is costing the party and the country dear.

Both sides are not equally to blame. Unable to either accept Corbyn's mandate – which was resounding the first time round

– or present a credible alternative candidate or programme to replace him, the parliamentary party has mistaken petulance for politics. They have now ended up handing a leader they loathe an even greater mandate than he had before. They used to blame the hard left for spending more energy fighting its own side than the Tories; curiously they do not notice that same trait in themselves.

Nonetheless, serious questions remain about Corbyn's capacity to fulfil his parliamentary role, both managerially and in how he is performing. Some were prepared to work with him and became disillusioned – goodwill, already a rare commodity in Westminster, was squandered. We have yet to see what his leadership would look like if he wasn't taking fire from his own side. He has won the right to be accepted as leader, although serious doubts remain about his ability to do the job, and he will have the benefit of none of them.

But while the two wings do not share equal blame for past mistakes, they are equally responsible for the future. This sometimes fragile and perennially fractious coalition has held for as long as it has because the relationship has been symbiotic – and it has the potential to remain so, even as the balance between the two sides has reversed this last year.

Principle and pragmatism are not mutually exclusive, and neither side owns a monopoly on either. Political parties do need to win elections, but they are more likely to do so if they stand for something more than just power. There are genuine political disagreements here that cannot be ignored. But there are also real strategic opportunities if both sides are able to raise their game.

The Labour right has always claimed its core impulse was 'realism'. There are a number of things we'd like in an ideal world, they'd argue. But the world is not ideal. It is no good simply blaming the electorate for not voting for us, we must meet the people where they are and bring them with us. They now need to apply this same logic to the Labour party. The reality is that Corbyn is overwhelmingly the party's choice. That choice represents something beyond him personally. It suggests a disaffection with business as usual in Westminster, a desire for a more ambitious policy platform, a sense of ownership over a party that has taken their loyalty for granted. A year has been wasted refusing to accept that reality in the hope that reality itself would change. It hasn't. The party's right have thrown everything they've got at Corbyn. Not only is he still standing, he's now standing taller than he was before.

Often, as they explained why he had to go, Corbyn's opponents would invoke their love of the party as their guiding motivation. That is touching. But they run the risk of loving it to death. The Labour party is not an artefact. It has people in it, and as such, is a living organism that is constantly evolving. They don't have to agree with Corbyn's supporters, but if that love means anything they'll take the trouble to listen to them.

They need to find out why the party is evolving in the way that it is, and how they need to evolve to engage with it. They need to find out where people are, and work out how they can reach them, not stand in their comfort zone and blame everybody else for being in the wrong place. The party they love loves someone – and more importantly – something else. Few suitors win back a lost love by sulking.

But if the party's right should cease whining the left should not start crowing. Corbyn has won again, but he has yet to do much with the first victory. The Labour left has always insisted that the party establishment too readily caved to the Tory orthodoxy on economic and social issues, rather than creating a more compelling narrative that benefitted the many rather than the few. Supported by the social movements it sought to galvanise outside parliament, it claimed it could create a more progressive consensus for a less alienated electorate.

The left must now live up to its promise. Last year Corbyn stood to shift the debate and make a point. The debate has shifted, the point has been made. Having enthused huge crowds around the country the left must now do something with that energy beyond rallying them for his election. Having dismissed austerity and militarism, it must evoke some new viable future that has popular appeal. If everything the left has long said about the vested interests in the media, Westminster and the City is true, then it must come up with a strategy to circumvent or challenge them. In short, it must take itself more seriously.

It is true that elections are often won in the centre – but the centre is not a fixed point. It shifts, buffeted by the prevailing political winds. The Tories are vulnerable. The Brexit referendum revealed their base is also in revolt, and their U-turns on disability payments and tax credits show they have a tin ear for the public mood. Currently they are more vulnerable to their own hubris than to the opposition. But that could change. They can be beaten.

Whether Labour can beat them under Corbyn remains to be seen. Anyone who predicted four years ago that Britain would be heading out of Europe, Corbyn would be leading Labour, or that the party would have just one MP in Scotland deserves a deferential hearing about how the 2020 general election will play out. Everyone else should approach the current volatility in British electoral politics with more humility.

One thing that is certain is that Labour can't win if they carry on as they have for the past 12 months. On Saturday the party confirmed the decision it made last year. Respecting that decision is not just a matter of good faith, it is also good politics.

Index